ENGLISH PRACTICE GRAMMAR

Michael Macfarlane

Arabic consultant:
Dr Abdel Halim A. Abo Jalalah

Garnet
EDUCATION

Published by Garnet Publishing Ltd
8 Southern Court, South Street, Reading,
Berkshire RG1 4QS, UK

First edition

British Library Cataloguing-in-Publication Data
A catalogue record for this book is available from the British Library.
ISBN 1 85964 064 8

Editor: **Jane Hobbs**
Arabic consultant: **Dr Abdel Halim A. Abo Jalalah**
Design: **David Rose and Mark Slader**
Illustration: **Mark Stock**
Typesetting: **Samantha Abley and Vicky Henriksen**

Printed in Lebanon

Contents

Adjectives and adverbs

Prepositions

The sentence and its parts

Appendices

Index

Introduction to the student

Is *English Practice Grammar* the right level for me?

- Yes, if you are no longer a beginner.
- Yes, if you are not yet an advanced user of English.
- Yes, if you feel that you still need further explanation in your own language.

How can this book help me?

Study *English Practice Grammar* when you have a problem with a particular point. It will help you to understand it and practise it.

Do not try to read the book from the beginning to the end. It is not a course book!

What does the book contain and why?

The Contents on pages 3 to 5 and the Index on pages 217 to 224 help you to find the grammar point you want.

The 88 Units on pages 8 to 205 explain the essential grammar of English and provide practice exercises for each point. Most of the Units have two pages – a page of grammar on the left and a page of practice exercises on the right. Some important grammar points have two pages of explanation and two pages of exercises.

The Appendix sections on pages 206 to 216 give you information about irregular verbs, spelling rules, punctuation, numbers, days, dates and times.

What's in a Unit?

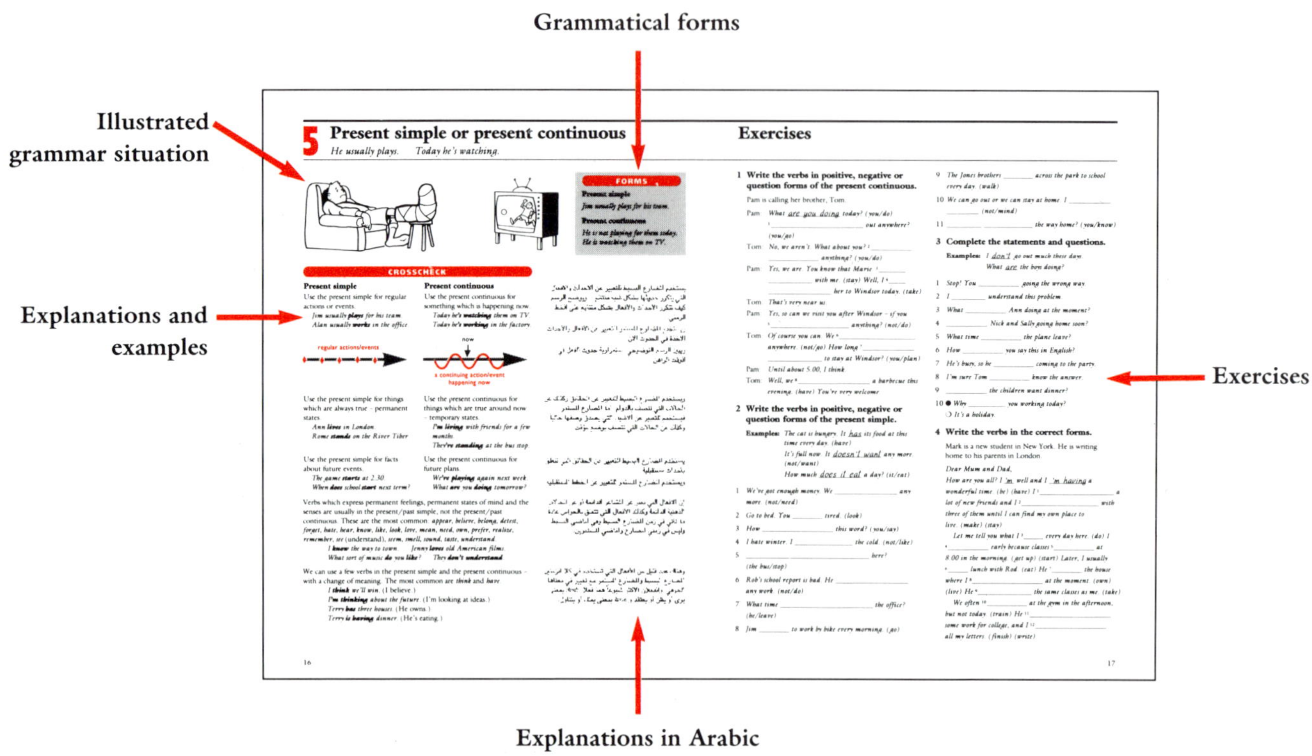

How do I use the book?

1 Find the grammar point you want to study in the Contents or the Index.
2 Turn to the correct Unit. Study the illustrated grammar situation, the grammatical forms, explanations and examples. Study the explanations in Arabic to make sure that you have understood everything.
3 Do the exercises.
4 Check your answers.
5 If you have made any mistakes, read the grammar explanation again to understand what you did wrong.
6 Study the Appendix sections if you want information about irregular verbs, spelling rules, punctuation, numbers, days, dates and times.

Introduction to the teacher

English Practice Grammar is designed mainly for self-study by students who may be learning at secondary school, college or adult levels. You may want to recommend that students study particular Units to supplement, reinforce or revise work that has been done in class. The exercise material can of course also be used in class, the reference materials then being used as a reminder and summary of your own language presentations.

Acknowledgements

To my many students who have helped me find ways of explaining that thing that is so difficult to explain – English grammar.

To my Editor, **Jane Hobbs**, and **Tony Hobbs** for all their help and encouragement over a very long period.

To **Dr Abdel Halim A. Abo Jalalah** for his advice and Arabic explanations.

To **David Rose** and **Mark Slader** for the design.

To **Mark Stock** for the illustrations.

To **Samantha Abley** and **Vicky Henriksen** for preparing the typescript.

Dedication

This book is dedicated to Ishitaro Niioka who, more than most, understood the need for language and the power of communication.

1 Imperatives

Light the firework.

Light the firework ... and stand back!

FORMS

Positive

Light the firework.
Be careful!

Negative

Do not hold the firework.
Don't be stupid!

The basic imperative is the infinitive, or dictionary form of a verb. Use a main verb infinitive for an action.

__Light__ the firework ... and __stand back__!

تتكون الصيغة الأساسية للأمر من مصدر الفعل الرئيسي المستخدم.

Make a formal or written negative imperative with *Do not.*

***Do not hold** the firework.*

اما الصيغة الرسمية التي تستخدم عند الكتابة فتتكون من *Do not*.

Make an informal spoken negative with *Don't.*

***Don't hold** the firework.*

وتأتي صيغة الأمر التي تستخدم في الحوار العادي مختصرة مع *Don't*.

Use *be* + adjective.

***Be careful**! **Don't be stupid**!*

ويستخدم مصدر فعل الكينونة *be* + صفة.

Use imperatives to give orders.

***Be** quiet! **Don't talk**!*

وتستخدم صيغة الأمر لتصدير الأمر.

Use imperatives to give instructions, eg for operating machines and in cookery books.

***Turn** the handle to the left and **press** the red button.*
***Chop** an onion and **fry** it in oil until it is brown.*

وتستخدم صيغة الأمر لإعطاء التعليمات كما هو الحال عند تشغيل آلة ما وكذلك في كتب الطبخ.

Use imperatives for polite instructions.

*Please **turn** to page 15.*

وتستخدم صيغة الأمر لإعطاء أوامر بصيغة مهذبة.

Use imperatives for warnings.

***Look out**! It's going to fall! **Be** careful not to hurt yourself.*
***Don't play** with that knife or you'll hurt yourself.*

كما أنها تستخدم عند التحذير.

Use imperatives for friendly advice.

***Relax**! **Don't worry**! Everything will be all right.*

وكذلك عند إسداء النصح.

Use imperatives for invitations.

***Come** and **have** dinner on Saturday.*
*Hello! **Come in** and **sit down**. **Make** yourself at home.*

وكذلك تستخدم صيغة الأمر لتوجيه الدعوات.

Use imperatives for directions.

***Go** straight on, **take** the first turning on the left, **cross** the bridge, and the bank is on the right.*

كما أنها تستخدم عند إرشاد شخص ما كي يصل إلى مكان بعينه.

Use *Let's* + imperative to suggest doing something together.

***Let's buy** some fireworks.*

وتستخدم صيغة الأمر مسبوقة بـ *Let's* عند اقتراح القيام بعمل ما معاً.

Form the negative with *Let's not.*

***Let's not go out** today.*

وتتشكل صيغة النفي لهذا النوع من الأمر باستخدام *Let's not ...*.

Exercises

1 Complete the imperative sentences.

١ـ اكمل تركيب الجمل التالية بصيغة الامر:

Example: *The bus leaves at exactly 4.00, so* don't be *late.*

1 ________ *quiet, everyone. You're too noisy.*

2 ● *Is the plane going to crash?*
❍ *Oh,* ________ *silly. Of course it isn't.*

3 ________ *careful with that knife. It's sharp.*

4 ________ *mean, Joe. Give Sam the toys.*

5 ________ *quick, Larry. There isn't much time.*

6 *Drive carefully.* ________ *such an idiot!*

7 ________ *helpful to your mother. She's very busy.*

8 *Why are you crying?* ________ *so sad.*

2 Complete the imperative sentences with these verbs.

٢ـ اكمل الجمل التالية بصيغة الأمر مع هذه الافعال:

drive, forget, go, play, press, take, talk, turn off, write

Example: Go *home now. It's late.*

1 ________ *with matches. They're dangerous.*

2 ________ *this money to the bank, please.*

3 *It's time to sleep now.* ________ *the lights.*

4 ________ *to your sister like that. It's rude.*

5 ________ *to collect the air tickets on your way to the airport.*

6 *To open the machine,* ________ *this button.*

7 ________ *so fast. You'll have an accident.*

8 ________ *your name, age and address here, please, madam.*

3 Complete the instructions with these verbs.

٣ـ اكمل التعليمات مع هذه الافعال:

choose, enjoy, place, press, pull down, push, put, put in, take

Ben: *How do I work this drinks machine, Sam? I'd really like some coffee.*

Sam: *It's easy. Do you want milk and sugar?*

Ben: *Sugar, please, but no milk.*

Sam: *OK, first* pull down *a plastic cup from this hole on the right. Then* [1]________ *your money. Now* [2]________ *the cup under here and* [3]________ *the sugar button. Now* [4]________ *your drink – black coffee.* [5]________ *your cup under here,* [6]________ *the button and the coffee comes out. And now just* [7]________ *your coffee and* [8]________ *it!*

Ben: *Thanks, Sam.*

4 Study the map and complete the directions to May's Garage. Use these verbs.

cross, drive, follow, go, pass, take, turn

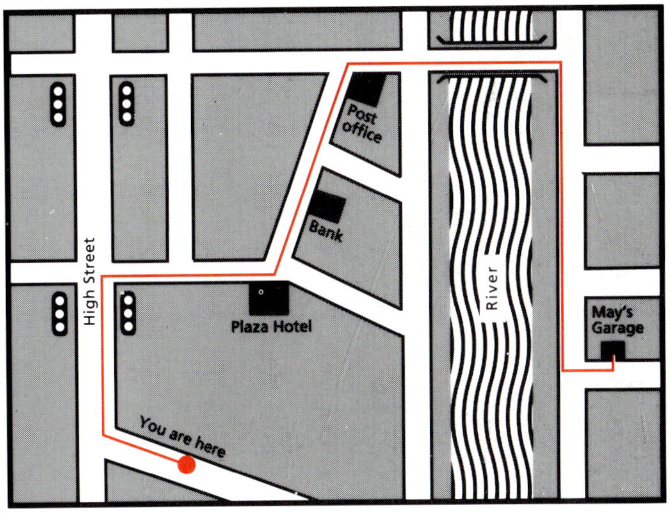

1 *To get to May's Garage,* go *to the end of this road.*

2 ________ *right into the High Street.*

3 ________ *right again at the first traffic lights.*

4 ________ *the second left opposite the Plaza Hotel.*

5 ________ *the bank on the right.*

6 ________ *the road to the end and* ________ *right at the post office.*

7 ________ *the bridge and* ________ *right.*

8 ________ *along the side of the river and* ________ *the third left. May's Garage is near the corner, on the left.*

2 Present simple

Ann works at A.B.C.

Ann works from 8.00 to 4.30 every day.

FORMS

Statements

I / *You* / *We* / *They*	*work.* / *do not work.*
He / *She* / *It*	*works.* / *does not work.*

***Yes/No* questions**

Do	*I* / *you* / *we* / *they*	*work?*
Does	*he* / *she* / *it*	*work?*

***Wh* questions**

Where do you work?
When does Ann start work?

Full answers

I work at A.B.C.
She starts work at 8.00.

Short forms: *do not = don't* *does not = doesn't*

In positive statements a verb usually has no ending.
*I **work**. You **talk**. We **write**. They **go**.*

The 3rd person singular is different. The verb usually ends in *s*.
*He **works**. It **moves**.*

If the verb ends in *y*, change the *y* to *ies*.
cry → cries, fly → flies, try → tries

If the verb ends in *o, ch, sh, ss* or *x*, add *es*.
go → goes, watch → watches, wish → wishes, miss → misses, box → boxes

Verbs in negative statements and most questions have no ending. They all need the auxiliary verb *do/does*. (See Unit 21 for information about *do/does* as a main verb and auxiliary verb.)
*I **don't like** this music. She **doesn't talk**.*
***Do** you **know** him? **Does** it **work**?*
*When **do** they **start**? Where **does** he **live**?*

Use the present simple for permanent states and situations.
*I **live** in London. I **have** two sisters.*

Use the present simple for things which always happen.
*The sun **rises** in the east. Water **boils** at 100° C.*

Use the present simple for repeated actions and events.
*I **get up** at 7.00 most days. Ann often **has** coffee at 11.00.*

Use the present simple for facts about future events.
*Flight 765 **leaves** at 10.30.*
*The President **arrives** at midday tomorrow.*

Some verbs usually take the present simple and not the present continuous. (See Unit 5 for a list of these.)
*I **know** what to do next. Susan **doesn't like** cold weather.*
*Do they **understand** English?*

عند تكوين الجمل الخبرية المثبتة، لا يضاف للفعل عادة أيّ نهايات.

وينتهي الفعل بـ S عادة مع ضمائر الغائب المفردة.

وعند استخدام فعل ينتهي بالحرف y يجري استبداله بـies.

وعند استخدام افعال تنتهي بـo , ch, sh, ss, او x نضيف للفعل es.

عند استخدام الجمل الخبرية في حالة النفي، وكذلك في معظم الجمل الاستفهامية، لا تضاف اي نهايات للفعل، بل يستخدم الفعل المساعد do أو does (انظر unit 21 للمزيد من المعلومات حول do/does كفعل رئيسي وكفعل مساعد).

يستخدم المضارع البسيط للتعبير عن الحالات والمواقف التي تتصف بالديمومة.

ويستخدم المضارع البسيط للتعبير عن الاحداث التي تحدث دائماً.

ويستخدم المضارع البسيط للتعبير عن احداث وافعال تتكرر.

ويستخدم المضارع البسيط للتعبير عن الحقائق التي تتعلق باحداث مستقبلية.

وهناك مجموعة من الافعال التي تأتي عادةً في المضارع البسيط وليس في المضارع المستمر. (انظر اللائحة بهذه الافعال في unit 5)

Exercises

1 Write the verbs in the correct forms.

Example: *Rob often* watches *TV. (watch)*

1 *We ___________ in London. (live)*
2 *I really ___________ this picture of you. (like)*
3 *That baby ___________ every night! (cry)*
4 *Ann and Mary ___________ work at 8.30. (start)*
5 *Ann ___________ home at 4.30. (go)*
6 *Mary's husband ___________ her from work at 5.00. (fetch)*
7 *Our cat ___________ fish for lunch every day. (have)*

2 Write the verbs in positive or negative forms.

Examples: *We* need *to explain again. (need) She* doesn't understand. *(not/understand)*

1 *I ___________ to visit Rome again. (want) I really ___________ the city. (love)*
2 *We sometimes ___________ the stereo, but it ___________________ very well. (use) (not/work)*
3 *Charlie's fat! He ___________________ any exercise, and he ___________ too much! (not/get) (eat)*
4 *They aren't interested in sport. They ___________________ football, and they ___________________ volleyball either. (not/like) (not/enjoy)*
5 *Roy ___________________ very often, but Andy ___________ swimming every day. (not/swim) (go)*
6 *I ___________________ coffee before bed time because it ___________ me awake. (not/drink) (keep)*
7 *Sally ___________________, so she always ___________ to work. (not/drive) (walk)*

3 Write the questions for the answers.

Example: *(come/from Britain)*

● Do you come from Britain?
❍ *Yes, I do. I'm from London.*

1 *(Tom/drive)*

● ___________________________________
❍ *Yes, he does. He's got a blue Nissan.*

2 *(you/know/Ann Smith)*

● ___________________________________
❍ *Yes, I do. She's an old friend.*

3 *(the TV/work)*

● ___________________________________
❍ *No, it doesn't. It's broken.*

4 *(you/go out/much)*

● ___________________________________
❍ *No, we don't. We usually stay at home.*

5 *(Marie/speak/French)*

● ___________________________________
❍ *Yes, she does. She's fluent.*

6 *(Fred and Mary/live/near here)*

● ___________________________________
❍ *Yes, they do. They live in the next road.*

4 Change the statements into questions.

Example: *I go swimming. (How often)*
How often do you go swimming?

1 *Tom goes to work. (How)*
____

2 *Sally visits her parents. (When)*
____

3 *They go on holiday every year. (Where)*
____

4 *I get home in the evening. (What time)*
____

5 *We always make mistakes. (Why)*
____

6 *The children watch TV after school. (How long)*
____

7 *The cat has lunch at 1.00. (What)*
____

3 Present simple: *be*

Jim is a really good player.

FORMS

Statements			**Yes/No questions**		
I	*am* *am not*	*Jim.*	*Am*	*I*	*Jim?*
He *She* *It*	*is* *is not*	*fast.*	*Is*	*he* *she* *it*	*fast?*
We *You* *They*	*are* *are not*	*players.*	*Are*	*we* *you* *they*	*players?*

Wh questions	**Full answers**
How old is Jim?	*He is 22.*
Where are you from?	*I am from England.*

Short forms: *I am = I'm* *he/she/it is = he's, she's, it's*
we/you/they are = we're, you're, they're *I am not = I'm not*
he is not = he isn't, he's not *we are not = we aren't, we're not*

Use the present simple of *be* for any state.

يستخدم فعل الكينونة be في زمن المضارع البسيط للتعبير عن اي من الحالات المبينة.

Age: *I'm 22. Carol **isn't** 10. She's 11.*
Description: *Jim **is** tall and dark. How tall **is** Ann?*
Height: *She's 1 metre 70. **Is** he as tall as me?*
Weight: *Jim **is** 78 kilos.* *How heavy **is** the parcel?*
Feelings: *We're tired, hungry and angry!*
Distance: *The town **is** about five kilometres away.*
Size: *The room **is** five metres by six.*
Price: *How much **are** these shoes, please?*
Time: *What time **is** it?* *What's the time?*

Use the present simple of *be* in *there is/there are.*

ويستخدم فعل be في زمن المضارع البسيط للتعبير عن معنى «يوجد» there is/ there are.

● ***Is there** a post office near here?*
❍ *Yes, **there's** one in the next street.*

Use *Yes/No* questions to check information. Form them like this.

يستخدم نوع الاسئلة التي يجاب عنها بـ «نعم» او «لا» للاستفسار عن معلومة معينة.. وتتكون كما هو موضح...

*She **is** clever. → **Is** she clever?*
*The students **are** in Room 1. → **Are** the students in Room 1?*

You can answer *Yes/No* questions with short answers.

ويمكن الاجابة عن هذا النوع من الاسئلة بشكل مختصر.

● ***Is** she clever?* ❍ *Yes, she **is**.*
● ***Are** the students in Room 1?* ❍ *No, they **aren't**.*

We always use full forms in *Yes* answers, when the verb is the last word.

ولا يستخدم الاختصار عند الإجابة بِـ«بنعم» عندما يكون الفعل آخر كلمة في الجملة.

*Yes, I **am**.* *Yes, he **is**.* *Yes, they **are**.*

We usually use short forms in *No* answers.

تستخدم عادة الصيغ المختصرة عند الاجابة بـ«لا».

*No, she **isn't**.* *No, we **aren't**.* (But *No, **I'm not**.*)

Use *Wh* questions to get more information.

تستخدم الاسئلة التي تبدأ بأداة استفهام للحصول على المزيد من المعلومات.

● *Who **is** she?* ❍ *Her name **is** Pam Woods.*
● *Where **is** she now?* ❍ *She's in Room 1.*

Exercises

1 Complete the statements and questions.

Examples: *This* is *my book.*
Are *these your books?*

1 *Those* ______ *your shoes.*

2 ______ *that your teacher?*

3 *The time* ______ *10.30.*

4 ______ *I late for the bus? Oh, no!*

5 ______ *they the new students?*

6 *Ann* ______ *Rosie's best friend.*

7 ______ *you from Japan?*

8 *Dear Sir,*
My brother and I are writing in reply to your advertisement today in the Daily Times. I ______ *20 years old, and he* ______ *19. We* ______ *both experienced drivers.*

2 Write the short forms.

Examples: *she is* she's
we are not we aren't/we're not

1 *I am* ______	5 *I am not* ______
2 *he is* ______	6 *he is not* ______
3 *they are* ______	7 *they are not* ______
4 *you are* ______	8 *you are not* ______

3 Correct the statements.

Example: *Sue is a nurse. (doctor)*
Sue isn't a nurse. She's a doctor.

1 *I'm 80 kilos. (85)*
I ______

2 *Alan is in Berlin. (Paris)*
Alan ______

3 *You're 1 metre 75. (1 metre 80)*
You ______

4 *They're at home. (school)*
They ______

4 Answer the questions. Use short forms.

Examples: ● *Are you from Britain? (Yes)*
❍ Yes, I am.
● *Is Sam from LA? (No) (Miami)*
❍ No, he isn't. He's from Miami.

1 ● *Is Sally from London? (Yes)*
❍ ______

2 ● *Are we on time? (No) (very late)*
❍ ______

3 ● *Is it 1st May today? (No) (30th April)*
❍ ______

4 ● *Are there any people on the beach? (Yes)*
❍ ______

5 ● *Are you 30? (No) (only 28)*
❍ ______

5 Read. Then write questions and answer them.

Example: *(What/name)*
● What's his name?
❍ Nick.

Nick is 25. He is a designer at A.B.C. His office is on the second floor. There are six other people in the same room. Nick's desk is the one by the window.

1 *(How old)*
● ______
❍ ______

2 *(What/job)*
● ______
❍ ______

3 *(Where/office)*
● ______
❍ ______

4 *(How many people)*
● ______
❍ ______

5 *(Which/desk)*
● ______
❍ ______

4 Present continuous

I'm flying!

FORMS

Statements

I	*am* *am not*	*flying.*
He *She* *It*	*is* *is not*	*moving.*
We *You* *They*	*are* *are not*	*stopping.*

Yes/No questions

Am	*I*	*flying?*
Is	*he* *she* *it*	*moving?*
Are	*we* *you* *they*	*stopping?*

Wh questions

What is he doing?
Why are we stopping?

Full answers

He is swimming.
We are stopping for lunch.

Short forms: *I am = I'm* *he/she/it is = he's, she's, it's* *we/you/they are = we're, you're, they're* *I am not = I'm not* *he is not = he isn't, he's not* *we are not = we aren't, we're not*

Form the present continuous with *am, is, are* + main verb + *ing*. (See Unit 21 for information about *be* as a main verb and auxiliary verb.)

*Peter **is flying** to New York now.*
***Are** the boys **stopping** for a rest?*

If the main verb ends in *e*, leave it out.

move → moving, come → coming, drive → driving

If the main verb ends in a single consonant after a short vowel, double the consonant.

stop → stopping, run → running, swim → swimming

If the main verb ends in *ie*, change *ie* to *y*.

die → dying, lie → lying

Use the present continuous for things which are happening now.

*Look! **I'm flying**!*
*Listen! Something **is moving** over there.*

Use the present continuous for temporary states and activities.

***I'm staying** with friends for a month.*
*Paul **is painting** his house this week.*

Use the present continuous for future plans.

*Sam **is playing** football tomorrow.*
***Are** you **doing** anything on Saturday?*

Some verbs usually take the present simple and not the present continuous. (See Unit 5 for a list of these.)

*I **know** what to do next.* *Susan **doesn't like** cold weather.*
***Do** they **understand** English?*

يتكون المضارع المستمر من am أو is أو are + الفعل مضافاً له ing. (انظر unit 21 للمزيد من المعلومات حول be كفعل رئيسي وكفعل مساعد.

يحذف حرف e عند استخدام فعل اساسي ينتهي به.

عند استخدام فعل اساسي ينتهي بحرف ثابت مسبوق بحرف متحرك قصير، يكتب الحرف الثابت مرتين.

اذا كان الفعل الاساسي ينتهي بـ ie يجري ابدالهما بالحرف y.

يستخدم المضارع المستمر للتعبير عن الاحداث التي تجري في الوقت الحاضر.

ويستخدم المضارع المستمر للتعبير عن الحالات والمناشط العارضة.

ويستخدم المضارع المستمر للتعبير عن الخطط المستقبلية.

هناك افعال تستخدم عادة، في زمن المضارع البسيط عوضاً عن المضارع المستمر (انظر لائحة بهذه الافعال في unit 5)

Exercises

1 Write the short forms.

Examples: *She is going.* She's going.
We are not going. we aren't/we're not going.

1 *I am going.* ________
2 *You are not going.* ________
3 *He is not going.* ________
4 *They are going.* ________
5 *It is not going.* ________

2 Write the verbs in positive or negative forms.

Examples: *You* 're talking *too much. (talk)*
Let's go out. It isn't raining *now. (not/rain)*

1 *Stop the car. I* ________ *well. (not/feel)*
2 *Be careful! You* ________ *too fast. (go)*
3 *It's dark! The lights* ________ *(not/work)*
4 *The phone* ________ *, but Cathy* ________ *it. (ring) (not/answer)*
5 ● *I* ________ *Tim. Is he here? (look for)*
❍ *I'm sorry. He* ________ *here this week. (not/work) He* ________ *our Paris office. (visit)*
6 ● *Hello. Can I speak to Alice, please?*
❍ *I'm afraid not. She* ________ *a bath at the moment. (have)*
7 *Paul and Pat* ________ *television. (not/watch). They* ________ *to some of their favourite music. (listen)*

3 Complete the questions and answers.

Examples: ● *What* are you doing? *(you/do)*
❍ *I* 'm mending *the door. (mend)*

1 ● *What* ________ *(the children/do)*
❍ ________ *in the garden. (they/play)*
2 ● ________ *the film? (you/enjoy)*
❍ *Yes, I* ________ *It's really good.*
3 ● *Why* ________ *so much? (Bill/train)*
❍ ________ *to get into the team. (he/try)*
4 ● ________ *to the party? (Sally/go)*
❍ *No, she* ________ *She's very tired.*
5 ● *How fast* ________ *(we/fly)*
❍ ________ *700 kph. (we/do)*
6 ● ________ *the car? (the boys/wash)*
❍ *No, they* ________ . ________ *the grass. (they/cut)*
7 ● *What* ________ *(the cat/eat)*
❍ ________ *fish. (it/eat)*

4 Write these verbs in the correct forms.

choose, cut, get, have, leave, make, plan, write

Example: *She* 's having *a cup of tea.*

1 *He* ________ *his tools from the garage.*
2 *The boys* ________ *a library book.*
3 ________ *a new book, Professor?*
4 *I* ________ *to visit Canada next year.*
5 *We* ________ *in a minute. Give me your case.*
6 *Why* ________ *the wood into pieces, Dad?*
7 *Sarah* ________ *a cake. (make)*

5 Write these verbs in the correct forms.

build, do, go, start, study, train, work

Two old college friends meet by chance.

Nina: *Hello, Alan! What* are *you* doing *here?*

Alan: *Oh, hi! I* [1]________ *for my uncle's construction company. We* [2]________ *some offices here in London. Tell me,* [3]________ *you still* [4]________ *at college?*

Nina: *No, I* [5]________ . *I* [6]________ *to be a banker.*

Alan: *And* [7]________ *your brother still* [8]________ *to school?*

Nina: *No, he's left school now. He* [9]________ *at college next month.*

5 Present simple or present continuous

He usually plays. *Today he's watching.*

FORMS

Present simple

Jim usually plays for his team.

Present continuous

He is not playing for them today.
He is watching them on TV.

CROSSCHECK

Present simple

Use the present simple for regular actions or events.

Jim usually ***plays*** *for his team.*
Alan usually ***works*** *in the office.*

Present continuous

Use the present continuous for something which is happening now.

Today he ***'s watching*** *them on TV.*
Today he ***'s working*** *in the factory.*

Use the present simple for things which are always true – permanent states.

Ann ***lives*** *in London.*
Rome ***stands*** *on the River Tiber.*

Use the present continuous for things which are true around now – temporary states.

I'm living *with friends for a few months.*
They ***'re standing*** *at the bus stop.*

Use the present simple for facts about future events.

The game ***starts*** *at 2.30.*
When ***does*** *school* ***start*** *next term?*

Use the present continuous for future plans.

We ***'re playing*** *again next week.*
What ***are*** *you* ***doing*** *tomorrow?*

Verbs which express permanent feelings, permanent states of mind and the senses are usually in the present/past simple, not the present/past continuous. These are the most common: *appear, believe, belong, detest, forget, hate, hear, know, like, look, love, mean, need, own, prefer, realize, remember, see* (understand), *seem, smell, sound, taste, understand.*

I ***know*** *the way to town.* *Jenny* ***loves*** *old American films.*
What sort of music ***do*** *you* ***like****?* *They* ***don't understand****.*

We can use a few verbs in the present simple and the present continuous – with a change of meaning. The most common are *think* and *have.*

I ***think*** *we'll win.* (I believe.)
I'm thinking *about the future.* (I'm looking at ideas.)
Terry ***has*** *three houses.* (He owns.)
Terry ***is having*** *dinner.* (He's eating.)

يستخدم المضارع البسيط للتعبير عن الأحداث او الأفعال التي يتكرر حدوثها بشكل شبه منتظم؛ ويوضح الرسم كيف تتكرر الاحداث والافعال بشكل متتابع على الخط الزمني.

ويستخدم المضارع المستمر للتعبير عن الافعال والاحداث الآخذة في الحدوث الآن.

ويبين الرسم التوضيحي استمرارية حدوث الفعل في الوقت الراهن.

ويستخدم المضارع البسيط للتعبير عن الحقائق وكذلك عن الحالات التي تتصف بالدوام. اما المضارع المستمر، فيستخدم للتعبير عن الأشياء التي يَصْدُق وصفها حالياً وكذلك عن الحالات المؤقتة.

يستخدم المضارع البسيط للتعبير عن الحقائق التي تتعلق باحداث مستقبلية.

ويستخدم المضارع المستمر للتعبير عن الخطط المستقبلية.

ان الأفعال التي تعبر عن المشاعر الدائمة او الحالات الذهنية الدائمة، وكذلك الأفعال التي تتعلق بالحواس تأتي عادةً في زمن المضارع البسيط وفي زمن الماضي البسيط، وليس في زمني المضارع والماضي المستمرين. واكثر هذه الافعال شيوعاً هي التالية:

وهناك عدد قليل من الافعال التي تستخدم في كلا الزمنين، المضارع البسيط والمضارع المستمر مع تغيير في معناها الحرفي. والفعلان الاكثر شيوعاً هما فعل think بمعنى يرى او يظن او يعتقد وفعل have بمعنى يملك او يتناول.

Exercises

1 Write the verbs in positive, negative or question forms of the present continuous.

Pam is calling her brother, Tom.

Pam: *What* are you doing *today? (you/do)* 1________________ *out anywhere? (you/go)*

Tom: *No, we aren't. What about you?* 2__________ __________ *anything? (you/do)*

Pam: *Yes, we are. You know that Marie* 3_______ __________ *with me. (stay) Well, I* 4______ ____________ *her to Windsor today. (take)*

Tom: *That's very near us.*

Pam: *Yes, so can we visit you after Windsor – if you* 5________________ *anything? (not/do)*

Tom: *Of course you can. We* 6________________ *anywhere. (not/go) How long* 7____________ ____________ *to stay at Windsor? (you/plan)*

Pam: *Until about 5.00, I think.*

Tom: *Well, we* 8________________ *a barbecue this evening. (have) You're very welcome.*

2 Write the verbs in positive, negative or question forms of the present simple.

Examples: *The cat is hungry. It* has *its food at this time every day. (have)*
It's full now. It doesn't want *any more. (not/want)*
How much does it eat *a day? (it/eat)*

1 *We've got enough money. We* ________________ *any more. (not/need)*

2 *Go to bed. You* ________ *tired. (look)*

3 *How* ________________ *this word? (you/say)*

4 *I hate winter. I* ______________ *the cold. (not/like)*

5 ______________________________ *here? (the bus/stop)*

6 *Rob's school report is bad. He* __________________ *any work. (not/do)*

7 *What time* _______________________ *the office? (he/leave)*

8 *Jim* ________ *to work by bike every morning. (go)*

9 *The Jones brothers* ________ *across the park to school every day. (walk)*

10 *We can go out or we can stay at home. I* __________ ________ *(not/mind)*

11 ______________________ *the way home? (you/know)*

3 Complete the statements and questions.

Examples: *I* don't *go out much these days.*
What are *the boys doing?*

1 *Stop! You* __________ *going the wrong way.*

2 *I* ________ *understand this problem.*

3 *What* __________ *Ann doing at the moment?*

4 __________ *Nick and Sally going home soon?*

5 *What time* __________ *the plane leave?*

6 *How* __________ *you say this in English?*

7 *He's busy, so he* __________ *coming to the party.*

8 *I'm sure Tom* __________ *know the answer.*

9 __________ *the children want dinner?*

10 ● *Why* _________ *you working today?*
❍ *It's a holiday.*

4 Write the verbs in the correct forms.

Mark is a new student in New York. He is writing home to his parents in London.

Dear Mum and Dad,

How are you all? I 'm *well and I* 'm having *a wonderful time. (be) (have) I* 1________________ *a lot of new friends and I* 2________________ *with three of them until I can find my own place to live. (make) (stay)*

Let me tell you what I 3_____ *every day here. (do) I* 4__________ *early because classes* 5__________ *at 8.00 in the morning. (get up) (start) Later, I usually* 6_____ *lunch with Rod. (eat) He* 7________ *the house where I* 8______________ *at the moment. (own) (live) He* 9____________ *the same classes as me. (take)*

We often 10__________ *at the gym in the afternoon, but not today. (train) He* 11________________ *some work for college, and I* 12________________ *all my letters. (finish) (write)*

6 Past simple

I washed them yesterday.

FORMS

Statements

I	*washed it.*
You	
He	*did not wash it.*
She	
It	
We	
They	

***Yes/No* questions**

Did	*I*	*wash it?*
	you	
	he	
	she	
	it	
	we	
	they	

***Wh* questions**	**Full answers**
When did she do it?	*She did it yesterday.*
What did she do?	*She washed his jeans.*

Short form: *did not = didn't*

Use the past simple for actions which started and finished in the past. Look for past time markers such as *yesterday*.

*Ann **phoned** us yesterday.* *Leo **arrived** home last night.*

In past simple statements the verb usually ends with *ed*.

*She **washed** his jeans.* *He **played** with his friends all morning.*

If the verb ends in *e*, add *d*.

*We **moved** to our new house a month ago.*

If the verb ends in a *y*, we usually cut *y* and add *ied*. (But not in *say, pay* and *lay*. See Appendix 1 for the past forms of these verbs.)

*I **hurried** to catch the bus.* *She **carried** her baby to bed.*

If the verb ends in a single consonant after a short vowel, double the consonant.

*We **stopped** work for lunch.* *They **fitted** the pieces together.*

A lot of important verbs are irregular, and their past forms do not end in *ed*. You have to learn these one by one. (See Appendix 1 for a list of these.)

come → came, go → went, drink → drank, eat → ate

Positive statements need only a main verb.

*I **went** to the cinema last night. I **enjoyed** the film.*

Most questions and negatives need the auxiliary verb *did*. (See Unit 21 for information about *do* as a main verb and auxiliary verb.)

● *What **did** you **see**? **Did** you **enjoy** it?*
❍ *I **saw** Robocop 4. I **didn't enjoy** it much.*

Some verbs usually take the past simple and not the past continuous. (See Unit 5 for a list of these.)

*I **knew** what to do next.* *Susan **didn't like** cold weather.*

We can use the form *used to* + verb for something that often happened in the past, but does not happen now.

*I **used to go** training every day.* *I **didn't use to smoke**.*
*How often **did** Alan **use to go** abroad?*

يستخدم الماضي البسيط للتعبير عن الأَفعال التي بدأت وانتهت في الماضي... وتحوي الجمل كلمات تدل على الماضي مثل yesterday.

عادةً ينتهي الفعل في الجمل الخبرية في الماضي البسيط بـ ed.

إذا كان الفعل ينتهي بـ e يضاف اليه حرف d فقط.

إذا كان الفعل ينتهي بـ y يحذف هذا الحرف ويضاف، عوضاً عنه، ied ولكن الحال يختلف مع الافعال lay و pay و say (انظر الملحق 1 الخاص بتصريف الافعال).

إذا كان الفعل ينتهي بحرف ثابت مفرد مسبوق بحرف متحرك قصير، يكتب الحرف الثابت مرتين.

العديد من الافعال المهمة غير قياسية، ولا تنتهي صيغ الماضي الخاصة بها بـed.. وهذه الافعال يجب تعلمها كل على حدة. (انظر لائحة بهذه الافعال في الملحق 1.)

تحتاج الجمل الخبرية المثبتة إلى فعل أساسي واحد فقط. وتحتاج غالبية الجمل الاستفهامية وكذلك الجمل المنفية الى الفعل المساعد did (انظر unit 21 لمزيد من المعلومات حول do كفعل رئيسي و كفعل مساعد).

وهناك من الافعال ما يأتي عادة، في زمن الماضي البسيط وليس في زمن الماضي المستمر (انظر لائحة بها في unit 5).

وتستخدم صيغة used to + فعل للتعبير عن فعل معتاد الحدوث في الماضي ولا يحدث في الوقت الحاضر.

Exercises

1 Write the past forms.

Examples: *clean* cleaned *sell* sold

1 *ask* ________
2 *be* ________
3 *break* ________
4 *call* ________
5 *do* ________
6 *drive* ________
7 *eat* ________
8 *find* ________
9 *go* ________
10 *have* ________
11 *invite* ________
12 *jump* ________
13 *keep* ________
14 *leave* ________
15 *meet* ________
16 *need* ________
17 *open* ________
18 *run* ________
19 *see* ________
20 *wake up* ________

Which verbs are irregular?
Which verbs can be main verbs and auxiliary verbs?

2 Complete the paragraph with verbs from Exercise 1.

This morning, I woke up *late. When I* [1]________ *the time, I* [2]________ *out of bed, and I* [3]________ *downstairs. I* [4]________ *a piece of bread, and I* [5]________ *a glass of orange juice. I* [6]________ *the house at 8.00, and I* [7]________ *at 100 kph all the way to work!*

3 Write statements with positive and negative forms.

Example: *(see/his parents ✓) (see/his sister ✗)*
Sam saw his parents *last night, but he* didn't see his sister.

1 *(find/my old suit ✓) (find/my new one ✗)*
I ________________ *yesterday, but I* ________________

2 *(clean/her red shoes ✓) (clean/her black ones ✗)*
Tina ________________ *this morning, but she* ________________

3 *(call/their mother ✓) (call/their sister ✗)*
They ________________ *the other day, but they* ________________

4 Write questions and short answers.

Example: *I went to the beach. (Ben) (Yes)*
● Did Ben go to the beach too?
❍ Yes, he did.

1 *Andy visited Paris last year. (Tim and Fred) (No)*
● ________________
❍ ________________

2 *Sue ran well in the race. (Ann) (Yes)*
● ________________
❍ ________________

3 *They had a Maths test. (French) (No)*
● ________________
❍ ________________

4 *Peter practised the violin. (piano) (Yes)*
● ________________
❍ ________________

5 Read. Then write questions for the answers. Use these question words.

How, What time, When, Where, Who, Why

Example: ● Where did Susan Hill go?
❍ *She went to London.*

Susan Hill went to London last Thursday because she wanted to buy a wedding present for her sister. She went by train and she got there at 10.30. She met an old school friend at the station and they went shopping together.

1 ● ________________
❍ *She went there last Thursday.*

2 ● ________________
❍ *She went by train.*

3 ● ________________
❍ *Because she wanted to buy a wedding present.*

4 ● ________________
❍ *She got there at 10.30.*

5 ● ________________
❍ *She met an old school friend.*

6 ● ________________
❍ *They met at the station.*

7 Past simple: *be*

They were by my bed.

FORMS

Statements

I	*was*	*there.*
He		
She	*was not*	
It		
We	*were*	*at home.*
You		
They	*were not*	

***Yes/No* questions**

Was	*I*	*there?*
	he	
	she	
	it	
Were	*we*	*at home?*
	you	
	they	

***Wh* questions**	**Full answers**
What was that noise?	*It was an animal.*
Where were they?	*They were at home.*

Short forms: *was not = wasn't* *were not = weren't*

Use the past simple of *be* for any state.

تستخدم صيغ الماضي من فعل be للتعبير عن اي من الحالات المبينة في الامثلة.

Age: *The boys **weren't** 15. They **were** 16.*
Description: *She **was** beautiful with fair hair.*
Height: *He **was** only 1 metre 50 when he was 13.*
Weight: *I **was** 80 kilos last week. How heavy **was** the parcel?*
Feelings: ***Were** you sad at the end of the holiday?*
Distance: *How far **were** they from the sea?*
Size: *The house **was** about 2,000 square metres.*
Price: ***Was** that watch expensive?*
Time: *What time **was** your lesson yesterday?*

Use the past simple of *be* in *there was/there were*.

ويستخدم الماضي من فعل be في صيغتي there was وthere were.

- ***Was there** a big match on Saturday?*
- ❍ *Yes, and **there were** thousands of fans at the match.*

Use *Yes/No* questions to check information. Form them like this.

وتستخدم الاسئلة التي يجاب عنها بِـ«نعم» او «لا» للتأكد من المعلومات، وتتكون كما هو وارد في الامثلة.

*She **was** clever. → **Was** she clever?*
*The students **were** in Room 1. → **Were** the students in Room 1?*

You can answer *Yes/No* questions with short answers.

ويمكن الاجابة بطريقة مختصرة عن الاسئلة التي يجاب عنها بِـ«نعم» او «لا».

- ***Was** she clever?* ❍ *Yes she **was**.*
- ***Were** the students in Room 1?* ❍ *No, they **weren't**.*

We always use full forms in *Yes* answers, when the verb is the last word.

وتستخدم الصيغ الكاملة دائماً، عند الاجابة بِـ«نعم»، عندما يكون الفعل آخر كلمة في الجملة.

*Yes, I **was**.* *Yes, he **was**.* *Yes, they **were**.*

We usually use short forms in *No* answers.

تستخدم عادة الصيغ المختصرة عند الاجابة بِـ«لا».

*No, she **wasn't**.* *No, we **weren't**.*

Use *Wh* questions to get more information.

وتستخدم أدوات الاستفهام التي تبدأ بحرفي (wh) للحصول على مزيد من المعلومات.

- *Who **was** she?* ❍ *Her name **was** Pam Woods.*
- *Where **was** she?* ❍ *She **was** in Room 1.*

Exercises

1 Complete the statements and questions.

Example: ● *How old* were *you in 1989?*
❍ *I* was *13.*

1 *It* ________ *late, and the children* ________ *tired.*

2 *The Johnson brothers* ________ *at the same college. Rod* ________ *a medical student, and Harry and Tony* ________ *law students.*

3 *We* ________ *30 minutes early for the party and there* ________ *nobody there. The room* ________ *empty!*

4 ● *How long* ________ *you and your wife in Cairo?*
❍ *I* ________ *there for three years, but she* ________ *there for only two.*

2 Complete the conversation.

Two friends meet after a party.

Jenny: *We* were *sad that you* weren't *at the party.*

Robin: *I* [1]________ *sorry to miss it too.* [2]________ *it a good one?*

Jenny: *Yes, it* [3]________ *There* [4]________ *a lot of old friends there. Where* [5]________ *you and the family?*

Robin: *Dad* [6]________ *away on business, and Mum* [7]________ *very well. And my brothers* [8]________ *back from holiday. They* [9]________ *still away.*

3 Read. Then write questions and answer them.

Example: *(When/they/at the house)*
● When were they at the house?
❍ Last night.

We saw a lovely house yesterday. We were there last night. It was about 100 years old, and we wanted to buy it immediately. There were four bedrooms upstairs. Downstairs, there was a beautiful dining-room, and the living-room was very big – 12 x 5 metres. The kitchen at the back of the house was large too, and very modern. Outside there was a beautiful garden with a stream. We loved the house! The only problem was the price. It was £200,000!

1 *(How old/the house)*
● ________________________
❍ ________________________

2 *(How many bedrooms)*
● ________________________
❍ ________________________

3 *(How big/the living-room)*
● ________________________
❍ ________________________

4 *(Where/the kitchen)*
● ________________________
❍ ________________________

5 *(What/outside)*
● ________________________
❍ ________________________

6 *(What/the only problem)*
● ________________________
❍ ________________________

7 *(How much/the house)*
● ________________________
❍ ________________________

4 Complete the statements.

Example: *Maria* wasn't *good at English at school, but she* 's *excellent now.*

1 *Go and see the old city. There* ________ *thousands of old buildings there. Some of them* ________ *over 500 years old.*

2 *Simon* ________ *at home yesterday, but he* ________ *there now.*

3 *We* ________ *wrong to leave the main road. Now we* ________ *lost!*

4 *The children* ________ *tired after the party, but I* ________ *nearly asleep.*

5 *Alan* ________ *at work yesterday, but he* ______ *at home today. Here* ______ *his phone number. You can call him.*

8 Past continuous

It was raining again.

They looked out of the window. It was raining again.

FORMS

Statements

I	*was*	*looking.*
He		
She	*was not*	
It		
We	*were*	*running.*
You		
They	*were not*	

***Yes/No* questions**

Was	*I*	*looking?*
	he	
	she	
	it	
Were	*we*	*running?*
	you	
	they	

***Wh* questions**

What was she doing?
Where were they sitting?

Full answers

She was reading.
They were sitting in the garden.

Short forms: *was not = wasn't* *were not = weren't*

Form the past continuous with *was, were* + main verb + *ing*. (See Unit 21 for information about *be* as a main verb and auxiliary verb.)

*I **was reading** all last night.* *What **were** you **doing** at 2.00?*

Remember the spelling rules with *ing*. (See Unit 4.)

move → moving, stop → stopping, die → dying

Use the past continuous for things which were continuing at a certain moment in the past.

● *What **were** you **doing** at 12.00?* ❍ *I **was going** home for lunch.*

Use the past continuous for emphasizing that something was continuing for a long time – often something unwanted.

*The baby **was crying** all night.*

Use the past continuous for things which were continuing (a continuing action) when something else suddenly happened (a short action).

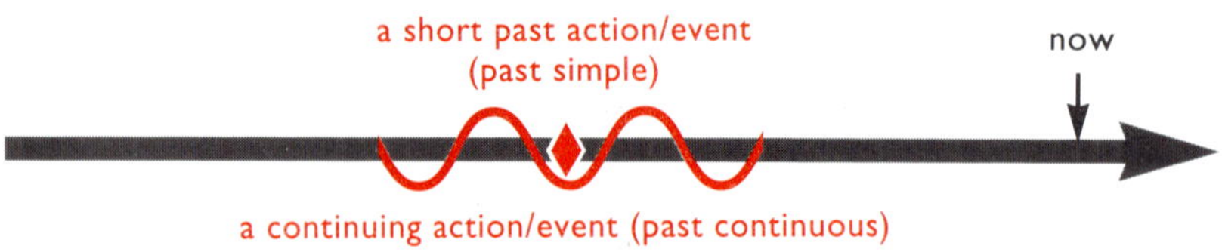

When the two actions are in one sentence, use the connectors *when, as* or *while* to join the two sentence parts.

*Jenny **was reading when** Ann **phoned**.*
*The truck **hit** my car **as** I **was turning**.*
*The policeman **arrived while** we **were having** dinner.*

Do not confuse these two different ideas.

*When Tom **arrived**, we **were having** tea.* (Tea was continuing.)
*When Tom **arrived,** we **had** tea.* (Tom arrived. Then tea started.)

Some verbs usually take the past simple and not the past continuous. (See Unit 5 for a list of these.)

*I **knew** what to do next.* *Susan **didn't like** cold weather.*

يتكون الماضي المستمر من was او were + الفعل مضافاً له ing.

يجب مراعاة قواعد الاملاء عند اضافة ing لبعض الافعال (انظر unit 4).

يستخدم الماضي المستمر للتعبير عن الاحداث التي استمر حدوثها في وقت محدد في الماضي.

يستخدم الماضي المستمر للتأكيد على ان حدثاً ما قد استمر حدوثه طويلاً في الماضي... وغالباً ما يكون حدثاً غير مرغوب فيه.

يستخدم الماضي المستمر للتعبير عن حدث استمر حدوثه في الماضي (فعل مستمر) عندما تخلل حدوثه فعلٌ آخر بشكل مفاجئ (فعل مقتضب). ويوضح الرسم استمرارية الحدث من خلال الخط المتعرج، وكيف قاطع استمراريتَه حدثٌ آخر قصير تمثله العلامة السوداء في المنتصف.

عندما تحوي الجملة فعلين تستخدم كلمات الربط when او as او while لربط جزءي الجملة.

وعلينا ان نفرق بعناية بين الفكرتين المختلفتين اللتين تمثلهما الجملتان التاليتان.

وهناك مجموعة من الافعال التي تأتي عادة، في زمن الماضي البسيط وليس في الماضي المستمر. (انظر لائحة بهذه الافعال في unit 5).

Exercises

1 Write the verbs in the correct forms.

The Carter family all remember what they were doing when the last Californian earthquake happened.

Example: Sally: *I* was cooking *lunch for John. (cook)*

1 John: *I* ____________ *my boss in New York. (call)*

2 Ron and Sue: *We* ____________ *at the lake with Paul. (swim)*

3 Tom: *I* ____________ *a football game on TV. (watch)*

4 Ann and Carol: *We* ____________ *a Pepsi at the Corner Café. (have)*

5 Flo: *I* ____________ *ready to go out with some friends. (get)*

6 Tim and Bill: *We* ____________ *our bikes in the park. (ride)*

2 Complete the questions and answers.

Examples: ● Was *Sally* cooking *dinner? (cook)*

❍ *No, she* wasn't. *She* was cooking *lunch.*

● *What* were *Ann and Carol* doing? *(do)*

❍ *They* were having *a Pepsi at the Corner Café. (have)*

1 ● *Who* ________ *Ron and Sue* ____________ *with? (swim)*

❍ *They* ____________ *with Paul.*

● ____________ *at the swimming pool?*

❍ *No, they* ________ *They* ________ ____________ *at the lake.*

2 ● ________ *Tom* ____________ *to the radio? (listen)*

❍ *No, he* ________ *He* ____________ *TV. (watch)*

● *What* ____________

❍ *He* ____________ *a football game.*

3 ● *Where* ________ *Tim and Bill* ________ *their bikes? (ride)*

❍ *They* ____________ *their bikes in the park.*

4 ● *Who* ________ *John* ____________ *(call)*

❍ *He* ____________ *his boss.*

3 Write the verbs in the correct forms.

Examples: *I* was making *lunch when the earthquake* happened. *(make) (happen)*

What were the children doing *at this time last week? (the children/do)*

1 *What* ____________ *at this time yesterday? (you/do)*

2 *Why* ____________ *along the street at 10.00 last night? (he/run)*

3 *She* ____________ *home when her new car* ____________ *(drive) (break down)*

4 *I* ________ *the window. (open) The sun* ____________ *(shine)*

5 *They* ____________ *in the garden when the phone* ________ *(work) (ring)*

6 *The storm* ______ *the boat as it* ____________ *to reach the harbour. (hit) (try)*

7 *The plane* ____________ *to land when it* ________ *(try) (crash)*

4 Write the verbs in the correct forms.

When I went *out at 9.00 the sun* was shining. *(go) (shine) It* [1]________ *a beautiful spring day and the birds in the park* [2]____________ *(be) (sing) I* [3]____________ *along the road beside the park when suddenly I* [4]____________ *my old friend, John. (walk) (notice) He* [5]____________ *football with his son in the park. (play) I* [6]________ *to him and he* [7]________ *round in surprise. (call) (look) Then he* [8]________ *back and* [9]________ *me to join them. (shout) (invite) Soon all of us* [10]________ ________ *football together. (play) Then we* [11]________ *to get some ice-creams. (stop) While we* [12]____________ *them, we* [13]________ *to go to the lake and hire a boat. (eat) (decide) Then something terrible* [14]________ *(happen) Just as I* [15]____________ *into the boat, it* [16]________ *to move away, and I* [17]________ *straight into the water between the boat and the shore. (get) (start) (fall) Hundreds of people* [18]____________ *, and they all* [19]________ *(watch) (laugh) I* [20]________ *really embarrassed! (feel)*

9 Present perfect 1

I've washed the car.

FORMS

Statements

I	*have*	*washed it.*
You		
We	*have not*	
They		
He	*has*	*finished.*
She		
It	*has not*	

***Yes/No* questions**

Have	*I*	*washed it?*
	you	
	we	
	they	
Has	*he*	*finished?*
	she	
	it	

***Wh* questions**

What have you done?
How long has the job taken?

Full answers

I have washed the car.
It has taken an hour.

Short forms: *I/you/we/they have = I've, you've, we've, they've*
he/she/it has = he's, she's, it's *have not = haven't*
has not = hasn't

Form the present perfect with *have, has* + past participle. With regular verbs the past participle is the same as the past simple form – main verb + *ed*.

*I've **washed** the car. I've just **finished**.*

● ***Has** she **finished** dinner?* ❍ *No, she **hasn't**.*

If the verb ends in *e*, add *d*.

*The train **has arrived**. There it is! Let's run.*

If the verb ends in *y*, change the *y* to *ied*.

*Mary **has carried** the case for an hour. She's tired.*

These are different.

say → said, pay → paid, lay → laid

If the verb ends in a single consonant after a short vowel, double the consonant.

*The bus **has stopped**. We can get off now.*

A lot of important verbs are irregular, and their past forms do not end in *ed*. The verbs *be, do* and *have* are all irregular. (See Unit 21 for information about *have* as a main verb and auxiliary verb.)

Infinitive	Past form	Past participle
be	*was/were*	*been*
do	*did*	*done*
have	*had*	*had*

Many common main verbs are irregular too. You have to learn these one by one. (See Appendix 1 for a list of these.)

Infinitive	Past form	Past participle
hit	*hit*	*hit*
make	*made*	*made*
speak	*spoke*	*spoken*
give	*gave*	*given*

يتكون المضارع التام من have أو has + التصريف الثالث للفعل. والتصريف الثالث للافعال القياسية هو نفس صيغة الماضي البسيط. وهو يتكون بإضافة ed إلى أصل الفعل.

واذا كان الفعل ينتهي بـ e يضاف إليه d فقط.

كذلك يبدل الحرف y اذا جاء في نهاية الفعل بـ ied.

والحال يختلف بالنسبة للافعال التالية:

اذا كانت نهاية الفعل حرفاً ثابتاً مسبوقاً بحرف متحرك قصير، يكتب الحرف الثابت مرتين.

هناك العديد من الافعال الهامة من النوع اللاقياسي التي لا تنتهي صيغة الماضي منها بـ ed، منها فعل be و do وhave، وكلها لا قياسية. (انظر unit 21 للمزيد من المعلومات حول فعل have كفعل رئيسي وكفعل مساعد).

وهناك العديد من الافعال الاساسية الشائعة من النوع اللاقياسي ايضاً والتي يجب تعلمها كل على حدة. (انظر لائحة بهذه الافعال في الملحق 1).

Use the present perfect when something happened in the past, and affects us now.

Tom ***has cleaned*** *the car.* (So now it's really clean.)
Ann ***has broken*** *her arm.* (So now she can't write.)

يستخدم المضارع التام للتعبير عن حدث وقع في الماضي وله أثر واضح في الحاضر.

Use the present perfect when something started in the past and continues to the present. Look out for the words *yet* and *just*.

yet means 'up to now'.

● ***Have*** *they* ***repaired*** *the car* ***yet****?*
❍ *No, they* ***haven't had*** *time* ***yet****. They're going to do it tomorrow.*

يستخدم المضارع التام للتعبير عن حدث بدأ في الماضي واستمر حدوثه حتى الوقت الحاضر... وتستخدم في هذه الجمل كلمة *yet* (وتعني حتى الآن) وكلمة *just*.

just means 'only a very short time ago'.

The water ***has just boiled****. Would you like a cup of tea?*
Our new car ***has just arrived****. Come and look.*

وتعني كلمة *just* منذ برهة قصيرة فقط.

We sometimes use *yet* and *just* together.

● ***Have*** *you* ***finished*** *your homework* ***yet****?*
❍ *Not* ***yet****.* ***I've just finished*** *question 1, but* ***I haven't finished*** *question 2.* (I'm doing it now.)

وتستخدم كلمتا *yet* و *just* معاً أحيانا في جملة واحدة.

Use *still ... not* for something that happens late.

I started this last week and I ***still haven't finished.***

ويستخدم التعبير اللغوي *not ... still* للتدليل على حدث تأخر الانتهاء منه.

Use *already* for something that happens early.

*It's only 8.00 in the morning and they****'ve already done*** *three hours work.*

وتستخدم كلمة *already* لتفيد معنى الانتهاء من عمل ما في وقت سابق.

We sometimes use *still ... not* and *already* together.

● *I suppose Joe* ***still hasn't started*** *work!*
❍ *You're wrong. He****'s already finished****!*

وأحياناً تستخدم *not ... still* و *already* معاً في جملة واحدة.

The *'s* short form can mean *is* or *has*, so check the main part of the verb. Study the different meanings.

*She****'s come*** *home.* (***'s come*** = *has come*)
*She****'s coming*** *home.* (***'s coming*** = *is coming*)

قد تعني الصيغة المختصرة *'s* إما *is* أو *has*، الأمر الذي يتطلب التأكد من الجزء الخاص بالفعل الأساسي في الجملة. لاحظ فروق المعاني في الأمثلة التالية.

Exercises

1 Write the past participles.

Example: *buy* bought *happen* happened
meet met

1 *ask* ______
2 *be* ______
3 *choose* ______
4 *do* ______
5 *eat* ______
6 *find* ______
7 *give* ______
8 *have* ______
9 *invite* ______
10 *join* ______
11 *keep* ______
12 *leave* ______
13 *make* ______
14 *need* ______
15 *open* ______
16 *put* ______
17 *run* ______
18 *start* ______
19 *take* ______
20 *wake up* ______

Which verbs are irregular?
Which verbs can be main verbs and auxiliary verbs?

2 Complete the paragraph with verbs from Exercise 1 (including the examples).

Dear Mum,
Well, a lot of things have happened *since our move to Australia. Larry has* [1] ______ *a good job at a bank, and we have* [2] ______ *a small house outside town for $70,000. Peter and Sally have* [3] ______ *at their new school, and they're very happy there. Peter has* [4] ______ *the football team and Sally has* [5] ______ *a lot of good friends in her class. I have* [6] ______ *all the neighbours now, and they have* [7] ______ *very kind. In fact, our next-door neighbour has* [8] ______ *all of us to a barbecue lunch on Sunday.*

3 Write these verbs in the correct forms.

arrive, break, catch, get, paint, win

Example: *Tom* has cleaned *the car. Now it looks like new.*

1 *They* ______ *the TV. It doesn't work.*
2 *The police* ______ *the bank robbers. They're at the police station now.*
3 *Ann* ______ *the room. It's pink now.*
4 *My parents* ______ *Their car is outside.*
5 *Mark* ______ *the race. He's the new champion.*
6 *Dad* ______ *the tickets, so we can go in.*

4 Write statements with positive and negative forms.

Example: *(find/a job ✓) (find/a house ✗)*
Alan has found a job, *but he* hasn't found a house.

1 *(join/the school drama group ✓) (join/the tennis club ✗)*
Tony ______
______ *but he* ______
______

2 *(make/a cake ✓) (make/any sandwiches ✗)*
Julie ______ *but she*
______

3 *(bring/their books ✓) (bring/their pens ✗)*
The boys ______ *but*
they ______

4 *(choose/the carpets for their new house ✓) (choose/any furniture ✗)*
Ian and Sue ______
______ *but they*
______
______

5 *(wash/the car ✓) (wash/the children's bikes ✗)*
I ______ *but I*
______
______

6 *(invite/Alan to the party ✓) (invite Joe ✗)*
We ______
but we ______

5 Write questions and and short answers.

Examples: *Lisa has cleaned her shoes. (boots) (Yes)*
● Has she cleaned her boots too?
❍ Yes, she has.

Peter has eaten his lunch. (Bill) (No)
● Has Bill eaten his lunch too?
❍ No, he hasn't.

1 *The boys have done their Maths homework. (French homework) (No)*
● ______
______
❍ ______

2 *Vicky has been busy all day. (Mark) (Yes)*

● ___

___

❍ ___

3 *Barry has learnt to fly. (you) (Yes)*

● ___

___

❍ ___

4 *Petra and I have brought our books. (Sally) (No)*

● ___

___

❍ ___

6 Re-order the words to make questions.

Example: *(gone/where/girls/have/the)*
Where have the girls gone?

1 *(lived/Emma/how long/London/has/in)*

___

___

2 *(late/come/you/why/so/have/home)*

___

___

3 *(my/what/you/have/with/shirt/done)*

___

___

4 *(the/has/Andy/where/put/bike)*

___

___

5 *(kilometres/you/how many/today/driven)*

___

___

7 Write the answers. Use *just* or *yet*.

Examples: ● *Is the TV working? (Yes) (mend/it)*
❍ *Yes, I've just mended it.*

● *Have you seen your picture in today's newspaper? (No) (buy/one)*
❍ *No, I haven't bought one yet.*

1 ● *Has Ruth moved? (Yes) (go to/Rome)*
❍ ___

2 ● *Do you know the Smiths? (No) (not/meet/them)*
❍ ___

3 ● *Does Bob like sweet things? (Yes) (buy/some chocolate)*
❍ ___

___

4 ● *Are we going home now? (No) (not/finish/work)*
❍ ___

___

5 ● *Have the boys had lunch? (No) (not/come/home)*
❍ ___

6 ● *Have you got enough petrol?(Yes)(buy/some)*
❍ ___

7 ● *Have you moved my books? (Yes) (put/them/in your case)*
❍ ___

8 Write statements. Use *already* or *But . . . still . . . not.*

Examples: *Tom's boots are dirty. (clean/them ✗)*
But he still hasn't cleaned them.

Ann works very fast. (do/her Maths ✓)
She's already done her Maths.

1 *I asked you to talk to Bill yesterday. (call/him ✗)*

___

___

2 *We're planning to go to Spain. (buy/the tickets ✓)*

___

___

3 *I asked you to get ready. (pack/your bag ✗)*

___

___

4 *She's saving for a CD player. (get/£50 ✓)*

___

5 *Number 33 is moving fast now. (do/300 kph ✓)*

___

___

6 *I write three weeks ago. (have/a reply ✗)*

___

___

10 Present perfect 2

I've lived here for 35 years. *Have you ever visited Scotland?*

FORMS

Present perfect + *for/since*

I have lived here	*for 35 years.* *for a long time.* *for ages.*
I haven't lived here	*since I was young.* *since 1960.* *since yesterday.*

Present perfect + number of times

● *Have you ever been back to Sydney?*
❍ *Yes, I have been back three times.*

She has visited Spain	*once or twice.* *four times this year.* *every year since 1985.*

Present perfect + *for/since*

Use the present perfect when something started in the past and it continues to the present. We often use *for* and *since*. *for* shows how long something has continued. *since* shows when something started.

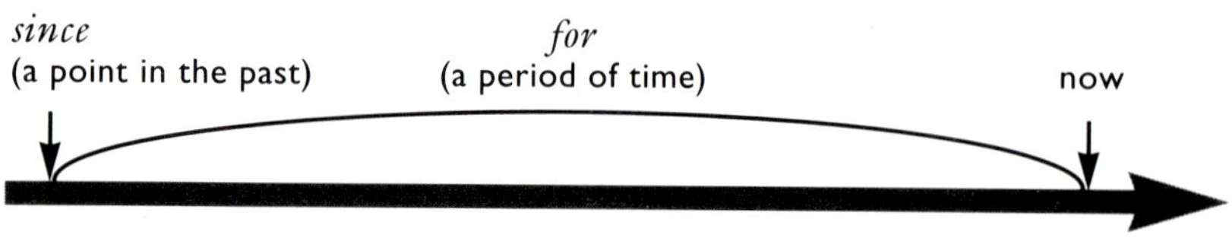

*Karen **has been** a nurse **for 15 years**.* OR ***since 1980**.*

يستخدم المضارع التام عندما نعبر عن فعل بدأ في الماضي واستمر حدوثه حتى الوقت الحاضر. وغالباً ما نستخدم في هذه الحالة كلمتي for و since. وتبين كلمة for الفترة الزمنية التي استغرقها الحدث، في حين تبين كلمة since نقطة بداية حدوث الفعل.

ويوضح الرسم عند السهم الاول نقطة البداية since، في حين تبين for الفترة الزمنية التي استغرقها حتى الوقت الحاضر (السهم الثاني).

Present perfect + number of times

Use the present perfect when things have happened in a period of time that started in the past and continue to the present. We often use *ever* and *never* and time expressions such as *this year, this week, today, since 1960.*

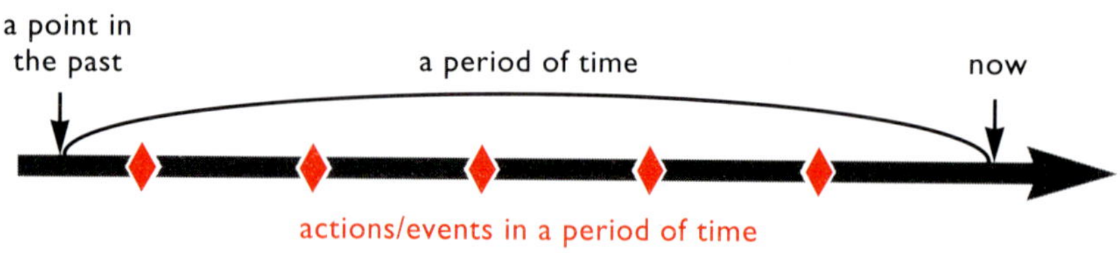

● ***Have** you **ever been** back to Sydney?* (In the 35-year period.)
❍ *Three times.*
● ***Have** you **ever visited** Scotland?*
❍ *Yes, **I've been** there many times.* OR *No, **I've never been** there.*

ويستخدم المضارع التام للتعبير عن احداث حصلت خلال فترة زمنية بدأت في الماضي وتستمر حتى الوقت الحاضر. وغالباً ما نستخدم كلمتي ever و never اضافة إلى عبارات الدلالة الزمنية مثل this year..الخ.

ويوضح الرسم تعدد تكرار الحدث خلال فترة زمنية بدأت في الماضي كما يشير إلى ذلك السهم الأول، والى استمرارها حتى الوقت الحاضر كما يشير إلى ذلك السهم الثاني.

Study the different meanings of *been* and *gone*.

*He's **been** to India. He went there last year.* (And now he's home again.)

*He's **gone** to India. He's working in Calcutta.* (He's there now.)

يجب التعرف من خلال الامثلة على اختلاف المعنى عند استخدام been و gone.

Exercises

1 Write statements.

Examples: *(Charlie/live/there/35 years)*
Charlie has lived there for 35 years.
(he/be/there/20 years old)
He's been there since he was 20 years old.

1 *(this land/belong to/Mr Hill/1950)*
____
____

2 *(Sally/have/the same car/five years)*
____
____

3 *(we/live/in this house/I was 25)*
____
____

2 Complete the questions and answers.

Example: ● *I live in London.*
❍ *How long* have you lived *there?*
● Since *1985.* OR For *ten years.*

1 ● *Nick and Sue have a Mercedes.*
❍ *How long* ________________ *it?*
● ________ *last month.*

2 ● *My brother works for IBM.*
❍ *How long* ________________ *for them?*
● ________ *three years.*

3 ● *The Carter family want to move house.*
❍ *How long* ________________ *to do that?*
● ________ *Mr Carter got a job in London.*

4 ● *Nick Ellis lives on a small island.*
❍ *How long* ________________ *there?*
● ________ *most of his life.*

3 Write negative answers for the questions.

Example: ● *When was the last time you had an ice-cream? (ages)* OR *(last week)*
❍ I haven't had an ice-cream for ages. OR since last week.

1 ● *When did Tim last see Susan? (three weeks)*
❍ ____________________________________
____

2 ● *When did the whole family last meet? (Claire's wedding)*
❍ ____________________________________
____

3 ● *When was the last time we had fish for dinner? (months)*
❍ ____________________________________
____

4 Write questions. Use *ever* where possible. Then answer the questions.

Examples: *(you/stay/in Miami) (three times)*
● Have you ever stayed in Miami?
❍ Yes, I've stayed there three times.
(How often/he/stay/there) (once)
● How often has he stayed there?
❍ He's stayed there once.

1 *(you/study/English/before) (once)*
● ____________________________________
____
❍ ____________________________________

2 *(How many times/he/see/Superman) (seven times)*
● ____________________________________
____
❍ ____________________________________

3 *(they/try/Indian food) (a few times)*
● ____________________________________
____
❍ ____________________________________

4 *(How often/it/rain/today) (twice)*
● ____________________________________
❍ ____________________________________

5 Complete the questions and answers.

Example: ● *Does Susan like sailing?*
❍ *She loves it! She* 's been *sailing every weekend this year. She* 's gone *again this weekend.*

1 ● ________ *you ever* ________ *to Rome?*
❍ *No, but my brother* ________ *just* ________ *there this week. He's there now.*

2 ● *Where's Alan?*
❍ *He* ________ *to the bank to get some money.*

3 *Sue* ________ *never* ________ *to China.*

11 Present perfect or past simple

It has opened. *It opened last week.*

CROSSCHECK

Present perfect

Use the present perfect when something happened in the past, but you do not know when.

*The new sports shop **has opened**.*

Use the present perfect when something happened in the past, but it affects us now.

*He's **broken** his leg.* (The leg is still broken.)

Use the present perfect when something started in the past and it continues to the present.

*Mary **has lived** in London for seven years.* (And she still lives there now.)

Use the present perfect when something has happened in a period of time up to the present, eg *today, this year.*

*She's **written** three letters today.*

***Have** you **had** exams this year?*

Use the present perfect to find out if something has happened, not when.

***Has** Peter **gone** home yet?*

We often start to talk about an event at an unstated time in the past.

● ***Have** you ever **visited** Japan?*

❍ *Yes, I've **been** there three times.*

Past simple

Use the past simple when something happened completely in the past.

*It **opened** last week.*

Use the past simple when something started and finished in the past and you know when.

*He **broke** his leg last year.* (His leg is OK now.)

Use the past simple when something started and finished in the past.

*Mary **lived** in London for seven years.* (But she doesn't live there now.)

Use the past simple when something happened in a period of past time, eg *yesterday, last year.*

*She **wrote** five letters yesterday.*

***Did** you **have** exams last year?*

Use the past simple to find out when something happened.

*When **did** Peter **go** home?*

We then fix the details of the event in the past with the past simple.

● *When **were** you last there?*

❍ *I **stayed** there last summer.*

يستخدم المضارع التام للتعبير عن فعل حدث في وقت غير محدد في الماضي.

ويستخدم الماضي البسيط للتعبير عن فعل وقع وانتهى في الماضي.

يستخدم المضارع التام للتعبير عن فعل وقع في الماضي وما زالت آثاره حتى الوقت الحاضر.

ويستخدم الماضي البسيط للتعبير عن فعل بدأ وانتهى في وقت محدد في الماضي.

يستخدم المضارع التام للتعبير عن فعل بدأ في الماضي ويستمر حدوثه حتى الوقت الحاضر.

ويستخدم الماضي البسيط للتعبير عن فعل بدأ وانتهى في الماضي.

يستخدم المضارع التام للتعبير عن فعل حدث خلال فترة زمنية امتدت حتى الوقت الحاضر (اليوم أو هذا العام).

ويستخدم الماضي البسيط للتعبير عن فعل حدث في فترة زمنية انتهت في الماضي (أمس أو العام الماضي).

يستخدم المضارع التام للاستدلال عن وقوع فعل ما وليس عن زمن وقوعه بشكل محدد.

ويستخدم الماضي البسيط للاستدلال عن وقت حدوث فعل ما بشكل محدد.

غالباً ما نتحدث عن وقوع حدث ما في وقت غير محدد في الماضي.

ثم نعمل على تحديد تفاصيل هذا الحدث الماضي باستخدام الماضي البسيط.

Exercises

1 Write the verbs in positive, negative or question forms of the past simple.

Rob: *You know, last night* was *terrible. (be) I* locked *myself out of the house. (lock)*

Lyn: *Oh, no! What* [1] ________________ *(you/do)*

Rob: *I* [2] ________ *round the house and I* [3] ________ *for an open window. (go) (look)*

Lyn: [4] ________________ *one? (you/find)*

Rob: *There* [5] ________ *any on the ground floor, but there* [6] ________ *one upstairs. (not/be) (be)*

Lyn: *It's a pity you* [7] ________________ *us. (not/call) You're always welcome to stay here.*

Rob: *Thanks, but I* [8] ________________ *to give you any trouble. (not/want)*

Lyn: *So what* [9] ________________ *after that? (you/do)*

Rob: *I* [10] ________ *the police. (phone)*

2 Write the verbs in positive, negative or question forms of the present perfect.

Tina and Bill are getting ready for school.

Example: Mum: Have you had *enough to eat? (you/have)*
Tina: *Thanks, Mum. I* 've eaten *lots. (eat)*
Bill: *Well, I* haven't *. I'm still hungry.*

1 Tina: *Bill, where* ________________ *my coat? (you/put)*
Bill: *I* ________________ *your coat since last week. (not/see)*

2 Mum: ________________ *your bag for school, Tina? (you/pack)*
Tina: *Yes, but I* ________ *my pencil case upstairs. (leave)*

3 Mum: ________________ *you your lunch money, Bill? (Dad/give)*
Bill: *No, he* ________ *Can you give me some?*

4 Dad: *I* ________________ *the car to the front door. (bring) Are you ready to go?*
Bill: *I am, but Tina* ________ *upstairs for her pencil case. (go)*

3 Write the past forms and past participles.

Examples: *write* wrote written

1 *ask* ________ ________
2 *be* ________ ________
3 *cut* ________ ________
4 *do* ________ ________
5 *find* ________ ________
6 *go* ________ ________
7 *have* ________ ________
8 *invite* ________ ________
9 *join* ________ ________
10 *keep* ________ ________

Which verbs are irregular?
Which verbs can be main verbs and auxiliary verbs?

4 Complete the statements and questions.

Examples: *Helen* has *never been to Canada.*
Did *you spend much money yesterday?*

1 *How long* ________ *Ann been at home?*
2 *I'm sure Peter* ________ *make a mistake.*
3 *Tom* ________ *finished work yet.*
4 ________ *anybody see the news at 1.00?*
5 *We* ________ *found the way, but we're trying.*
6 ________ *anybody seen my sweater?*
7 *When* ________ *the accident happen?*
8 *How many times* ________ *you seen that film?*

5 Write the verbs in the correct forms.

Mark is writing home to his parents in London.

6th November

Dear Mum and Dad,

Well, I arrived *here in New York on 6th September, so I* 've been *here for two months. (arrive) (be) I'm sorry I* [1] ________________ *to you since last month, but life* [2] ________ *very busy. (not/write) (be) Classes* [3] ________ *and I* [4] ________ *a lot of things to do. (begin) (have) I* [5] ________ *you about Rod in my last letter. (tell) He* [6] ________ *me stay at his place since I first* [7] ________ *here. (let) (get) But, at last I* [8] ________________ *a place of my own. (find) I* [9] ________ *the agreement with the owner last night, and he* [10] ________ *me a key. (sign) (give)*

12 Present perfect continuous

I've been waiting for an hour.

FORMS

Statements

I / *You* / *We* / *They*	*have* / *have not*	*been waiting.*
He / *She* / *It*	*has* / *has not*	*been playing.*

***Yes/No* questions**

Have	*I* / *you* / *we* / *they*	*been waiting?*
Has	*he* / *she* / *it*	*been playing?*

***Wh* questions**

What have you been doing?
How long has he been waiting?

Full answers

I have been watching TV.
He has been waiting for an hour.

Short forms: *I/you/we/they have = I've, you've, we've, they've*
he/she/it has = he's, she's, it's *have not = haven't* *has not = hasn't*

We often use the present perfect continuous instead of the present perfect. We use it to emphasize that something has continued for a long time.

*I've **been waiting** for an hour!*
*Tom **has been building** that boat since 1985. Will he ever finish?*
*How long **have** you **been learning** English?*

غالباً ما يستخدم المضارع التام المستمر عوضاً عن المضارع التام، وذلك للتأكيد على أن الحدث قد استمر لفترة طويلة من الزمن.

ويوضح الرسم بداية الفعل من نقطة في الماضي عند السهم الاول، واستمرار حدوثه طوال الفترة الزمنية حتى الوقت الحاضر (عند السهم الاخير).

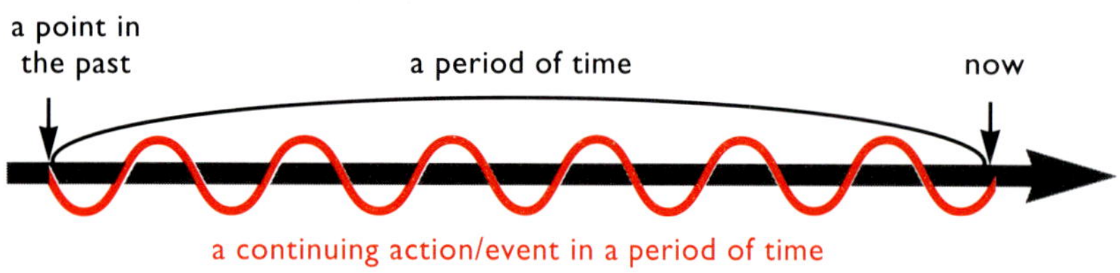

We can use the present perfect continuous when something stops just before the present, but it affects us now.

*Look, the road is wet. It**'s been raining**.*
*Bob **has been travelling** on business, but he's home now.*

ويمكن استخدام المضارع التام المستمر للتعبير عن حدث توقف قبل اللحظة الحاضرة ولكنه يؤثر فينا الآن.

We can use the present perfect continuous when things have happened many times from the past to the present.

*We**'ve been going** to France for our holidays for ten years.*
*How long **have** you **been going** to work by bicycle?*

ويمكن استخدام المضارع التام المستمر للتعبير عن الاحداث التي تكرر حدوثها من الماضي وحتى الوقت الحاضر.

ويوضح الرسم استمرار تكرار حدوث الفعل بين نقطة بدء حدوثه في الماضي، التي يشير اليها السهم الاول، طوال الفترة الزمنية حتى الوقت الحاضر، والتي يشير اليها السهم الاخير.

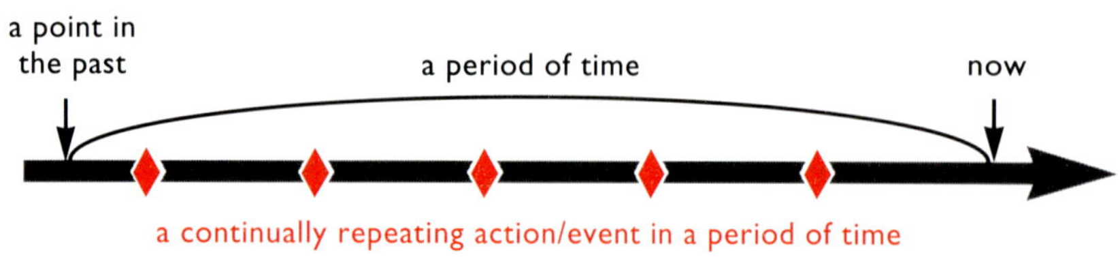

We use many adverbs and other expressions of time to help emphasize 'how long', eg *for, since, lately, recently, all morning/day/week, the whole morning/day/week*. (See Unit 10 for the difference between *for* and *since*.)

*We**'ve been waiting for an hour**.* *I**'ve been feeling** ill **lately**.*
*We**'ve been working since 6.00 this morning**.*

ويستخدم العديد من الظروف والتعبيرات الزمنية الاخرى للمساعدة في تأكيد طول الفترة الزمنية... مثل for و since و lately... الخ.

Exercises

1 Complete the answers.

Example: ● *Why are you so tired?*
❍ *I* 've been studying *all night. (study)*

1 ● *Hello! Where have you been recently?*
❍ *I* ______________ *in London. (work)*

2 ● *Why are the children so dirty?*
❍ *They* ______________ *in the garden. (play)*

3 ● *I can't find my Walkman. Where is it?*
❍ *John* ______________ *it upstairs. (use)*

4 ● *Why haven't you washed the car yet?*
❍ *I* ______________ *jobs for Mum. (do)*

5 ● *Maria speaks very good English.*
❍ *Yes. She* ______________ *very hard. (study)*

2 Complete the answers.

Example: ● *Have the children been helping Mum?*
❍ *No, they* haven't been helping *her. They* 've been watching *TV. (watch)*

1 ● *Has Tony been spending all his money?*
❍ *No, he* ______________ *it. He* ______________ *it. (save)*

2 ● *Have we been going the wrong way?*
❍ *No, we* ______________ *the wrong way. We* ______________ *the right way. (go)*

3 ● *Has Ann been doing her homework?*
❍ *No, she* ______________ *that. She* ______________ *to her new CD. (listen)*

3 Complete the questions.

Examples: You meet an old friend who is now at college.
● *How* have you been getting on *at college? (you/get on)*

You ask about your friend's brother. He's recently started at a new school.
● Has your brother been enjoying *his new school? (your brother/enjoy)*

1 You meet a friend. You haven't seen her for a month.
● *What* ______________ *recently? (you/do)*

2 You ask Tom's sister about him. He's been studying Spanish in Spain.
● *How* ______________ *in Spain? (he/get on)*

3 You want to know about Tom's studies.
● ______________ *a lot of Spanish? (he/learn)*

4 Your small brother's hands and mouth are dirty.
● ______________ *chocolate? (you/eat)*

5 Someone tells you about some friends. They're working in London.
● *How long* ______________ *there? (they/work)*

4 Write questions and answer them.

Examples: Joe is travelling round the world. He left at the end of last year OR six months ago.
● *What* has Joe been doing *recently?*
❍ He's been travelling round the world.
● *How long* has he been doing *that?*
❍ Since the end of last year. OR For six months.

1 Pam is looking for a new job. She started last month
● *What* ______________ *recently?*
❍ ______________
● *How long* ______________ *that?*
❍ ______________

2 Nick and Andy are training for the London Marathon. They began three months ago.
● *What* ______________ *recently?*
❍ ______________
● *How long* ______________ *that?*
❍ ______________

13 Past perfect and past simple

When they arrived the film had started.

When they arrived the film had started.

FORMS

Statements

I	*had*	*started.*
You		
He	*had not*	
She		
It		
We		
They		

***Yes/No* questions**

Had	*I*	*started?*
	you	
	he	
	she	
	it	
	we	
	they	

***Wh* questions**

What film had they gone to see?

What time had it started?

Full answers

They had gone to see Superman 6.

It had started at 7.00.

Short forms: *I/you/he/she/we/they had = I'd, you'd, he'd, she'd, we'd, they'd* *had not = hadn't*

Form the past perfect with *had* + past participle.

*The film **had started** before we arrived.*
***Had** it **begun** before you arrived?*

يتكون الماضي التام من had + التصريف الثالث للفعل.

Use the past perfect for a past event before another past event. Use it to show the time connection between two events.

يستخدم الماضي التام للتعبير عن فعل سبق في حدوثه فعلاً آخر في الماضي... وهو بالتالي يبين العلاقة الزمنية بين الحدثين.

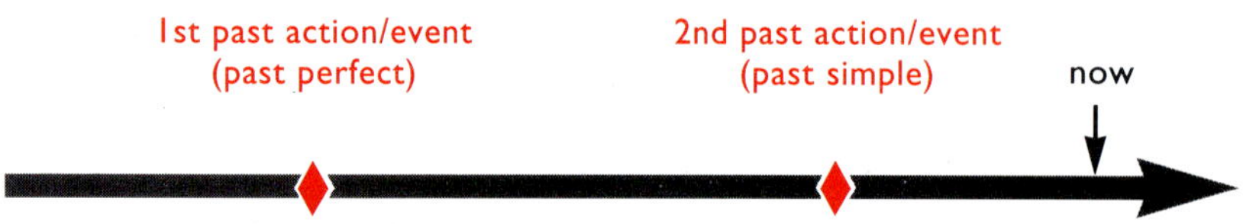

*At the airport I couldn't find my passport. **I'd left** it at home.*
*The rain **had** just **stopped**, so we decided to go out for a walk.*
*I got to the party at 8.00. My friends **had** already **gone**.*

ويوضح الرسم الوقت الذي حدث فيه الفعل في الماضي وهو الماضي التام، ثم وقت وقوع الفعل الآخر الذي يأتي في الماضي البسيط.

The past perfect shows the end of one past event before the start of another past event. We can talk about these two events in one sentence. Use these words to connect the two sentence parts: *when, after, before, once, until, as soon as.*

*When the last person **had** finally **come**, the meeting started.*
*Susan cried for ages **after** her brother **had gone**.*
*We went out **as soon as** the rain **had stopped**.*

ويبين الماضي التام نهاية فعلٍ ما في الماضي قبل بدء حدثٍ آخر في الماضي ايضاً. ويمكن جمع هذين الحدثين في جملة واحدة.

ويستدعي ذلك استخدام الكلمات التالية لربط جُزْءَي الجملة.

Do not over-use the past perfect. Use the past simple for two events that happen quickly after one another.

*I **saw** Peter and I **said** hello.*
*When I **got** home, I **sat** down and **turned on** the TV.*

ويجدر التنويه بأهمية عدم التمادي في استخدام الماضي التام حيث يمكن استخدام الماضي البسيط للتعبير عن حدثين وقعا متتابعين بشكل سريع.

Note the difference in meaning between the following.

*When the Director **arrived**, the meeting **started**.* (First the Director arrived and then the meeting started.)
*When the Director **arrived**, the meeting **had started**.* (First the meeting started and then the Director arrived.)

كذلك يجب ملاحظة الفارق في المعنى بين هذين المثالين.

Exercises

1 Write the verbs in the correct forms.

Example: *It was a strange house. Nobody* had lived *there for years. (live)*

1 *The town was empty. Everyone* ________________ *(go)*
2 *The car wasn't there. A thief* ________________ *it. (take)*
3 *The biscuit tin was empty. Tim* ________________ *them all. (eat)*
4 *I didn't recognize old Mr Jarvis. He* ________________ *a lot. (change)*
5 *We decided to buy a sofa which we* ____________ *the weekend before. (see)*
6 *We went back to the shop to get the sofa, but somebody else* ________________ *it. (buy)*
7 *I wanted to speak to Mr Jones, so I phoned his office. Unfortunately he* ____________ *five minutes before. (leave)*
8 *Bob was late for football practice and they* ________________ *without him. (start)*

2 Write the verbs in the correct forms.

Example: *We* 'd only been *at home for a few minutes when the phone rang. (only/be)*

1 *I invited Pat, but she* ________________ *to go out. (already/arrange)*
2 *They were amazed. They* ________________ *such a beautiful place. (never/see)*
3 *Celia* ________________ *dinner when the police called. (just/start)*
4 *Mrs Spear was worried. She* ________________ ________________ *her son's accident. (recently/hear about)*
5 *I phoned the garage, but they* ________________ ________________ *my car. (still/not/repair)*
6 *Tony wanted to buy a bike with the money, but Tina* ________________ *it. (already/spent)*
7 *The Grant family* ________________ *their house for a year when it burned down. (only/have)*

3 Write the verbs in the correct forms.

Example: *Alan* had lost *his key, so he* broke *a window to get in. (lose) (break)*

1 *I* __________ *at the party at 8.00, but my friends* ____________ *(arrive) (go)*
2 *The horses* ________________ *before we* __________ *the gate. (get away) (close)*
3 *Once we* ____________ *the river, we* __________ *to move faster. (cross) (be able)*
4 *The manager* ________ *us all there until we* ____________ *everything possible. (leave) (do)*
5 *They* ____________ *because they* ________________ *food and water. (turn back) (run out of)*

4 Join each pair of statements to make one statement. Use *when*.

Example: *We went out. We had breakfast.*
We went out when *we* 'd had *breakfast.*

1 *We drove out of town. We loaded the jeep.*

____

2 *We stopped for a rest. We drove into the hills.*

____

3 *We started again. We had a good rest.*

____

4 *We stopped for the night. We were on the road for ten hours.*

____

5 *We started to cook dinner. We unpacked the jeep.*

____

6 *We went to sleep. We finished dinner.*

____

14 Future with *going to*

We're going to drive.

FORMS

Statements

I	*am* *am not*	*going to drive.*
He *She* *It*	*is* *is not*	*going to go.*
We *You* *They*	*are* *are not*	*going to travel.*

***Yes/No* questions**

Am	*I*	*going to drive?*
Is	*he* *she* *it*	*going to go?*
Are	*we* *you* *they*	*going to travel?*

***Wh* questions**

Where are they going to drive?
How long is the trip going to take?

Full answers

They are going to drive to Perth.
It is going to take a month.

Short forms: *I am = I'm* *he/she/it is = he's, she's, it's*
we/you/they are = we're, you're, they're *I am not = I'm not*
he is not = he isn't, he's not *we are not = we aren't, we're not*

Use *going to* to explain future plans.

- ● *What **are** you **going to do** on Saturday?*
- ❍ ***I'm going to visit** my grandparents.*

تستخدم صيغة going to لشرح الخطط المستقبلية.

Use *going to* to talk about a decision to do something in the very near future.

*I'm just **going to make** some salad. Then we can have dinner.*

- ● *Dad, can you help me with my homework?*
- ❍ *Sure, **I'm** just **going to watch** the news. I'll help you when it's finished.*

وتستخدم صيغة going to للحديث عن قرار القيام بعملٍ ما في المستقبل القريب جداً.

Use *going to* when it is clear that something must happen soon.

*Look at the clouds. **It's going to rain**.*
*Listen to the car! **It's going to break down**!*

تستخدم صيغة going to عند وجود علامات واضحة تدل على قرب حدوث شيء ما.

Use *going to* with *go*, just like any other verb.

***We're going to go** to the cinema.*

تستخدم صيغة going to مع فعل go مثلما تستخدم مع اي فعل آخر.

CROSSCHECK

Present continuous

We often use the present continuous to talk about future arrangements.

- ● ***Are** you **doing** anything tomorrow?*
- ❍ *Yes, **I'm seeing** Sally. **We're meeting** at 3.00.*

غالباً ما يستخدم المضارع المستمر للتعبير عن خطط مستقبلية.

going to

When we use *going to*, the arrangements sound more carefully planned.

- ● *What **are** you **going to do**?*
- ❍ *First **we're going to take** a trip on the river. Then **we're going to see** a film.*

وعند استخدام going to فإن ذلك يوحي بان الخطط المستقبلية معدة بمزيد من الدقة.

Exercises

1 Complete the answers.

Example: ● *Have you had dinner yet? (later)*
❍ *No, not yet. I* 'm going to have it later.

1 ● *Have you washed the car yet? (after lunch)*
❍ *No, not yet. I* ______________________

2 ● *Has Tessa cleaned her shoes yet? (now)*
❍ *No, not yet. She* ______________________

3 ● *Have the boys mended their bikes yet? (this evening)*
❍ *No, not yet. They* ______________________

4 ● *Has the cat had its food yet? (in a minute)*
❍ *No, not yet. It* ______________________

2 Write the verbs in positive or negative forms.

Example: Your local football team are in the cup final, but they're playing badly.
● *They* 're going to lose. *(lose)*
❍ *They* aren't going to win. *(not/win)*

1 You're in the hills. There are black clouds.
● *It* ______________ *(rain)*
❍ *We* ______________ *very wet. (get)*

2 Alan should be on his way to the airport to catch a plane, but he's still in bed.
● *He* ______________ *there in time. (not/get)*
❍ *He* ______________ *his plane. (miss)*

3 Your car is very low on petrol, and you're still a long way from the petrol station.
● *We* ______________ *petrol. (run out of)*
❍ *We* ______________ *the petrol station in time. (not/reach)*

4 Your friend is in a marathon race. He's very tired, but he's very near the end of the race.
● *He* ______________ *now. (not/give up)*
❍ *He* ______________ *for sure. (finish)*

3 Write questions and short answers.

Example: *(we/be/late) (No)*
● Are we going to be late?
❍ No, we aren't.

1 *(Sam/pass/his exams) (Yes)*
● ______________
❍ ______________

2 *(your parents/take/you out) (No)*
● ______________
❍ ______________

3 *(you/watch/TV this evening) (Yes)*
● ______________
❍ ______________

4 *(Sally/buy/a newspaper) (No)*
● ______________
❍ ______________

4 Write questions.

Example: ● *I'm planning to go on holiday.*
❍ *(Where/you/go)*
Where are you going to go?

1 ● *Ann has bought some lovely flowers.*
❍ *(Where/she/put them)*
____

2 ● *The Smith family have sold their house.*
❍ *(When/they/move out)*
____

3 ● *I'm making some cakes for the party.*
❍ *(How many/you/do)*
____

4 ● *Bill is planning to go to the cinema.*
❍ *(What/he/see)*
____

15 Future with *will*

People will live in space.

FORMS

Statements

I	*will*	*start.*
You		
He	*will not*	
She		
It		
We		
They		

***Yes/No* questions**

Will	*I*	*start?*
	you	
	he	
	she	
	it	
	we	
	they	

***Wh* questions**

When will they build the space station?
Where will the station be?

Full answers

They will start soon.
It will be between the Earth and the Moon.

Short forms: *I/you/he/she/it/we/they will = I'll, you'll, he'll, she'll, it'll, we'll, they'll* *will not = won't*

Use *will* to express future facts.

*Sam **will be** 20 next month.* *The new road **will be** eight lanes wide.*

Use *will* to predict something in the future – something that you know or believe will happen.

*One day soon people **will live** in space.*
*Don't worry! I'm sure **you'll pass** your exams.*

Use *will* to say what you decide to do at the time of speaking.

*I've left the window open. **I'll go back** and **close** it.*

Use *will* to offer, promise or threaten to do something.

*That looks heavy. **I'll help** you.* *I promise I **won't be** late.*

Use *will* to ask somebody to do something and to agree or refuse to do it.

● ***Will** you **post** this card for me?* ❍ *Yes, **I'll post** it on my way home.*

We use *will* to predict the future, so we often use it with words such as *sure, certain, probably, definitely* and *certainly*. Note that the *ly* words change position in *will* and *won't* sentences.

*He**'ll definitely love** Rome. He **probably won't want** to come home.*

Do not use *will* to express plans and arrangements.

*I can't see you tomorrow as **I'm visiting/going to visit** my parents.* (not *will visit*)

will often goes with verbs like *expect, think* and *know*.

*I **expect I'll be** late home tonight.*
*I **don't think** he**'ll agree** to the idea.*

We sometimes use *shall/shall not (shan't)* instead of *will/will not*, but only with *I* or *we*. We usually use it for suggestions, offers and asking for instructions or suggestions.

*You look terrible! **Shall** we **call** a doctor?*
*I've finished this job. What **shall** I **do** next?*

تستخدم will للتعبير عن الحقائق المستقبلية.

وتستخدم will للتنبؤ بحدوث شيء في المستقبل. هنا يكون الشخص عارفاً او معتقداً بان هذا الشيء سوف يحدث.

وتستخدم will عند تقرير القيام بعمل ما في لحظة التكلم.

وتستخدم will عند التطوع بالقيام بعمل ما، وعند الوعد او التهديد بعمل ما.

وتستخدم will عند طلب عمل ما من شخص معين وعند الموافقة او رفض القيام بهذا العمل.

تستخدم will للتنبؤ بالمستقبل، لذلك فهي غالباً ما تستخدم مع كلمات مثل sure.... الخ. ويلاحظ ان الكلمات التي تنتهي بـ ly تغير موقعها في الجمل التي تستخدم فيها will او won't.

يجدر عدم استخدام will للتعبير عن الخطط والترتيبات.

تستخدم will عادةً مع الافعال expect وthink وknow.

تستخدم shall او shall not (shan't) احياناً عوضاً عن will وwill not وذلك مع الضميرين I وwe فقط. وهي تستخدم للتعبير عن الاقتراحات وعن التطوع بعمل ما، او عند طلب تعليمات او اقتراحات.

Exercises

1 Write the verbs in positive or negative forms.

Examples: *The film* will start *at 8.00. (start)*
It won't finish *until 11.00. (not/finish)*

1 *I've hidden the presents, so the children ______________ them. (not/find)*

2 *The bridge ______________ the river here. (cross)*

3 *The road ______________ until next year. (not/open)*

4 *Ask the boys. They ______________ the job for you. (do)*

5 *Paul ______________ 20 until next year. (not/be)*

2 Complete the offers and promises with positive or negative forms of these verbs.

be, buy, close, forget, look after, lose, make, wash

Example: ● *Please look after my jewellery.*
❍ *Don't worry. I* 'll look after *it.* OR
❍ *Don't worry. I* won't lose *it.*

1 ● *We haven't got any milk.*
❍ *All right. I ______________ some at the shop.*

2 ● *Be sure to get there on time.*
❍ *Don't worry. I ______________ late.*

3 ● *The car is very dirty.*
❍ *OK. I ______________ it.*

4 ● *Look, the windows are open.*
❍ *All right. I ______________ them.*

5 ● *Try to get everything right this time.*
❍ *No problem. I ______________ any mistakes.*

6 ● *Remember to take this letter and post it.*
❍ *Don't worry. I ______________ it.*

3 Complete the answers with these verbs. Use the correct pronouns.

be, carry, cut, get, give, phone

Example: ● *Please give your parents a call.*
❍ *Yes,* I'll phone *them now.*

1 ● *Is Simon at work now?*
❍ *No, not yet. ______________ to the office at 9.00.*

2 ● *I'm thirsty.*
❍ *Ask Sue. ______________ you a Pepsi.*

3 ● *This case is very heavy.*
❍ *Give it to me. ______________ it for you.*

4 ● *Dad's very late.*
❍ *Don't worry. ______________ home soon.*

5 ● *We need some wood for the fire.*
❍ *OK. ______________ some pieces now.*

4 Write questions and short answers.

Example: *(Joe/win/the competition) (No)*
● Will Joe win the competition?
❍ No, he won't.

1 *(Ann/be/ten next week) (Yes)*
● ______________
❍ ______________

2 *(the boys/like/their new school) (No)*
● ______________
❍ ______________

3 *(Mr Hall/arrive/tonight) (Yes)*
● ______________
❍ ______________

4 *(next term/start/on 15th April) (No)*
● ______________
❍ ______________

5 Write the verbs in the correct forms.

Luke and his friends are planning a class river trip.

Luke: *Here's my idea. We* 'll take *some boats and go up the river. (take)*

Andy: *OK, but how much* will it cost? *(it/cost)*

Luke: *I don't know. I* [1]______________ *the boat company and ask. (phone) But I'm sure it* [2]______________ *too expensive. (not/be)*

Andy: [3]______________ *to go? (everybody/want)*

Luke: *Yes, I'm sure they* [4]______________

Tony: *What* [5]______________ *to take? (we/need)*

Luke: *We* [6]______________ *take a picnic. (have to)*

Andy: [7]______________ *raincoats? (we/need)*

Luke: *No, we* [8]______________ *Don't worry. The TV weatherman says we* [9]______________ *a lovely day tomorrow, and he promises it* [10]______________ *(have) (not/rain)*

16 Future continuous

I'll be swimming.

FORMS

Statements

I	*will be*	*swimming.*
You		
He	*will not be*	
She		
It		
We		
They		

***Yes/No* questions**

Will	*I*	*be swimming?*
	you	
	he	
	she	
	it	
	we	
	they	

***Wh* questions**

What will she be doing?
Where will he be swimming?

Full answers

She will be working.
He will be swimming in the sea.

Short forms: *I/you/he/she/it/we/they will be = I'll be, you'll be, he'll be, she'll be, it'll be, we'll be, they'll be* *will not be = won't be*

Use the future continuous to say that something will be continuing at a certain point in the future.

يستخدم المستقبل المستمر لبيان أن حدثاً سوف يكون مستمراً في وقت محدد في المستقبل.

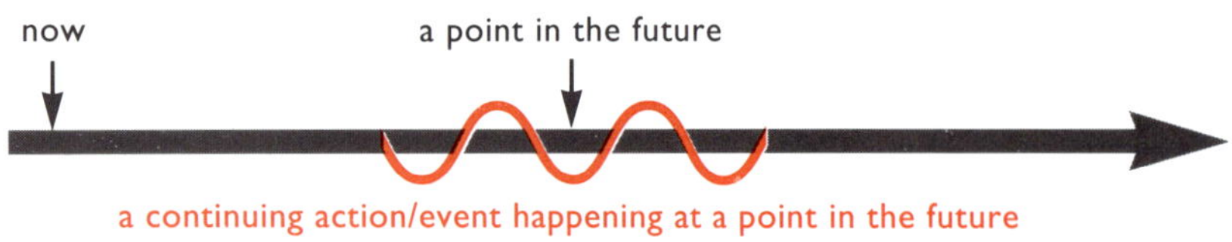

ويوضح الرسم النقطة المستقبلية (السهم الثاني) التي سيكون الحدث عندها مستمراً، في حين يشير السهم الأول الى الوقت الحالي.

- ● *What **will** you **be doing** in five years?*
- ❍ ***I'll be travelling** round the world.*

Use the future continuous to show that something will continue for a long time.

*There's so much to do! **We'll be working** all day.*
*We're having a party tomorrow evening, so **we'll be cooking** all afternoon.*

ويستخدم المستقبل المستمر ليبين ان الحدث سيستمر لفترة طويلة.

These uses of the future continuous are similar to uses of other continuous tenses. Compare the following.

*It's 9.00 now. Harry **is watching** TV.*
*At 9.00 yesterday he **was watching** TV too.*
*At 9.00 tomorrow **he'll be watching** TV again.*

وتشبه هذه الاستخدامات لزمن المستقبل المستمر استخدامات الازمنة المستمرة الاخرى كما توضح الامثلة التالية:

Use the future continuous to talk about something that is already arranged.

- ● *Will you be free after school?*
- ❍ *No, **I'll be playing** basketball then.*

يستخدم المستقبل المستمر للتعبير عن فعل تمّ التخطيط لحدوثه.

This use is like the present continuous for future arrangements and *going to* for expressing plans.

I'll be calling	*at the supermarket on my way home. Can I get you anything?*
I'm calling	
I'm going to call	

واستخدامه هذا يشبه استخدام المضارع المستمر عند التعبير عن ترتيبات مستقبلية، ويشبه استخدام going to عند التعبير عن خطط.

Exercises

1 Read. Then answer the question. Use these verbs.

do, have, learn, study

John's timetable

9.00	9.45	10.30	11.15	12.00	12.45
Science	Art	French	Maths	English	Lunch

What will John be doing at these times?
9.30, 10.00, 10.45, 11.20, 12.20, 1.05

Example: At 9.30 he'll be having Science.

1 ______

2 ______

3 ______

4 ______

5 ______

2 Read Jack's and Lisa's diary pages for next week. Then complete the conversation.

	Jack Hill	Lisa Bell
Mon. 1	Morning – Talk to customers from Japan.	Afternoon – Meet the Sales Manager.
Tues. 2	Morning – Visit the factory.	Afternoon – Have meetings with the sales team.
Wed. 3	Show visitors round London all day.	–
Thur. 4	–	Spend the day in Paris.
Fri. 5	–	–

Company directors Jack and Lisa need to have a meeting next week, but when?

Lisa: *Can we meet on Monday morning?*

Jack: *No, sorry. I* 'll be talking to customers from Japan. *Are you free on Monday afternoon?*

Lisa: *I'm afraid not. I* [1] ______ *Are you free on Tuesday morning?*

Jack: *No, I'm afraid not. I* [2] ______ *Can we meet on Tuesday afternoon?*

Lisa: *No, sorry. I* [3] ______ *Are you free on Wednesday?*

Jack: *No, sorry. I* [4] ______ *Are you free on Thursday?*

Lisa: *I'm afraid not. I* [5] ______ *Can we we meet on Friday?*

Jack: *Yes, I'm free then.*

3 Read. Then write questions and answer them.

Roger Barnes is a traveller. On his next trip he will be travelling round the world by bicycle. He will be flying to Florida next Monday. Then he will be riding across America on his bike for the next two months. He will be arriving in California in ten weeks. From there he will be going up the west coast to Alaska. Then he will be crossing to Asia by ship.

Example: *(How/he/travel/round/the world)*

● How will he be travelling round the world?

○ By bike.

1 *(When/he/fly/Florida)*

● ______

○ ______

2 *(How long/he/ride/across America)*

● ______

○ ______

3 *(Where/he/arrive/in ten weeks)*

● ______

○ ______

4 *(Where/he/go/from there)*

● ______

○ ______

17 Future perfect

We'll have done it by 4.00.

FORMS

Statements			**Yes/No questions**		
I	*will have*	*done it.*	*Will*	*I*	*have done it?*
You				*you*	
He	*will not have*			*he*	
She				*she*	
It				*it*	
We				*we*	
They				*they*	

Short forms: *I/you/he/she/it/we/they will have = I'll have, you'll have, he'll have, she'll have, it'll have, we'll have, they'll have*
will not have = won't have

Form the future perfect with *will* + *have* + past participle.

*We'**ll have cleaned** it by 4.00.*
*We'**ll have done** it before closing time.*

يتكون المستقبل التام من will + have + التصريف الثالث.

Use the future perfect to say that something will happen *before* or *by* a future time. In the negative we often use *not ... until/till.*

*The new manager **will have started** work **before/by** 1st May.*
*The new manager **won't have met** all the staff **before/by** 1st May.*
*The new manager **won't have met** all the staff **until/till** 30th May.*

Do not use *until/till* after a positive future perfect form. Use *before* or *by*.

Yes/No questions are unusual in the future perfect. *Wh* questions in the future perfect are very unusual.

● *We need to arrange a meeting for tomorrow afternoon. **Will** you **have had** your lunch by 1.30?*
❍ *Yes, I **will**.*
● *Good. Let's have the meeting then.*

We often use the future continuous to say that something will be happening at a certain time in the future. We use the future perfect to say that something will happen before a certain time in the future. Compare the following.

***I'll be doing** the work at midday.*
***I'll have done** the work by 1.00.*

يستخدم المستقبل التام للتعبير عن فعل سوف يحدث قبل او مع حلول وقت معين في المستقبل، وغالباً ما تستخدم not في حالة النفي بالإضافة إلى كلمة until او till.

ويوضح الرسم وقت حدوث الفعل المستقبلي بين الوقت الحاضر الذي يشير اليه السهم الاول، وبين نقطة زمنية محددة في المستقبل يشير اليها السهم الثاني.

لا تستخدم اي من كلمتي until او till في حالة الإثبات بل تستخدم كلمتا before او by.

يندر استخدام الاسئلة التي يجاب عنها بِ «نعم» او بِ «لا» في زمن المستقبل التام، اما الاسئلة التي تبدأ باداة استفهام، فإن استخدامها في هذا الزمن نادر جداً.

غالباً ما يستخدم المستقبل المستمر للتعبير عن فعل سوف يحدث في وقت محدد في المستقبل. ويستخدم المستقبل التام للتعبير عن فعل سوف يتم قبل وقت معين في المستقبل.

ويتضح الامر من خلال مقارنة الامثلة.

Exercises

1 Read. Then write statements.

Tessa Black is 16. She wants to be a famous writer. These are her ambitions.

By the age of:

18 – sell some short stories
20 – write a book of short stories
25 – produce a play in London
30 – publish a best-seller novel
35 – win an important international prize
40 – make a lot of money

Example: *By the age of 18, she hopes she* 'll have sold some short stories.

1 *By the age of 20, she hopes she* ______

2 *By the age of 25, she hopes she* ______

3 *By the age of 30, she hopes she* ______

4 *By the age of 35, she hopes she* ______

5 *By the age of 40, she hopes she* ______

2 Write the verbs in positive or negative forms.

Example: ● *Could you record the 9.00 news?*
❍ *All right. I* 'll have mended *the video by then. (mend)* OR
❍ *I'm sorry. I* won't have mended *the video by then. (not/mended)*

1 ● *Could I have the report by 5.00, please?*
❍ *I'm afraid I* ______ *it by then. (not/finish)*

2 ● *Let's buy the red sofa which we saw.*
❍ *The shop* ______ *it by the time we get there. (sell) It was very cheap.*

3 ● *Ask everyone to come here at 6.00.*
❍ *I'm sorry, but they* ______ *by 6.00. (go)*

4 ● *Will she know the results by the 15th?*
❍ *Yes, she* ______ *them before then. (get)*

5 ● *Will Alex bring a present to the party?*
❍ *No, he* ______ *time to get one. (not/have)*

3 Read. Then complete the questions and answer them.

This is a schedule for building a house.

	Schedule
Finish putting up the walls	10/6
Finish putting on the roof	20/6
Finish putting in the windows	12/7
Finish fitting the doors	29/7
Finish doing the wiring	6/8
Finish laying the floors	18/8
Finish plastering the walls	10/9
Finish painting the house	25/9

Example: ● What will they have finished *by 15/6?*
❍ They'll have put up the walls, but they won't have put on the roof.

1 ● ______ *by 15/7?*
❍ ______

2 ● ______ *by 15/8?*
❍ ______

3 ● ______ *by 15/9?*
❍ ______

18 Future review

I'll be 18 next week. *I'm going to have a party.*

FORMS

All of these ways of talking about the future are correct grammatically, and they all give the same information. But each one shows that the speaker is thinking about the information in a different way. Different future forms are correct in different situations.

The party will start at 6.00.
It'll be starting at 6.00.
It's going to start at 6.00.
It's starting at 6.00.
It starts at 6.00.
It'll have started at 6.00.

CROSSCHECK

will

Use *will* to express things that you know or believe will happen.

*Susan **will be** 18 next Sunday.*

Use *will* to say what you decide to do at the time of speaking.

*I know! **I'll have** a party!*

Use *will* to offer, promise or threaten. Use *will* to request or refuse to do it.

- *I'll **pay** you £100 to do the job.*
- *All right. **I'll do** it tonight.*

going to

Use *going to* when it is clear that something must happen soon.

*That's a big shopping list. **It's going to be** an expensive party!*

Use *going to* when you explain future plans.

***I'm going to make** a huge cake.*

نستخدم will للتعبير عن الافعال التي نعرف او نعتقد بانها ستحدث.

وتستخدم going to عندما يكون واضحاً بان شيئاً سوف يحدث حالاً.

تستخدم will للتعبير عمّا نقرر عمله في لحظة التكلم.

وتستخدم going to لعرض الخطط المستقبلية.

تستخدم will عند تقديم عرض معين وعند الوعد او التهديد بالقيام بعملٍ ما. وتستخدم will ايضاً لطلب القيام بعملٍ ما او لرفض القيام به.

Present simple

Use the present simple for facts about future events and times.

*The party **starts** at 6.00.*
*Susan's school **finishes** next Thursday.*
*When **does** school **start** next term?*

Present continuous

Use the present continuous for future plans.

***She's having** a big cake.*
*Susan **is having** a party next Sunday.*
*All her friends **are coming** to the party.*

يستخدم المضارع البسيط للتعبير عن حقائق تتعلق بأحداث وأوقات مستقبلية.

ويستخدم المضارع المستمر للتعبير عن خطط مستقبلية.

will

Use *will* to express a complete action in the future.

*The party **will start** at 6.00.*

Future continuous

Use the future continuous for something continuing in the future.

***They'll be dancing** for hours.*

تستخدم will للتعبير عن حدث متكامل في المستقبل.

ويستخدم المستقبل المستمر للتعبير عن فعل سوف يستمر حدوثه في المستقبل.

Future perfect

Use the future perfect for an action that will be complete before a certain point in the future.

*Don't worry! The party **will have finished** long before midnight.*

Future continuous

Use the future continuous for something continuing at a certain point in the future.

*At lunchtime next day **they'll** still **be cleaning up** after the party!*

ويستخدم المستقبل التام للتعبير عن حدث سوف يكتمل قبل حلول وقت معين في المستقبل.

Exercises

1 Write the verbs in future forms. Use *going to* or *will*.

Example: ● *We 're going to run out of milk soon. (run out of)*
❍ *I 'm going to get a newspaper, so I 'll buy some milk too. (get) (buy)*

1 ● *Slow down! We ______ (crash)*
❍ *Don't worry. We ______ all right. (be) I promise.*

2 ● *______ out this evening? (we/eat)*
❍ *Yes, we ______ to the Café de Paris. (go)*

3 ● *What would you like – tea or coffee?*
❍ *I ______ some coffee, please. (have)*

4 ● *The phone is ringing. ______ it, please? (you/answer)*
❍ *Yes. It ______ Harry. (probably/be)*

5 ● *You ______ 18 soon, so ______ school? (be) (you/leave)*
❍ *Yes, I ______ engineering at college. (study)*

6 ● *What time ______? (the meeting/start)*
❍ *At 6.00 exactly, so be there on time.*
● *I ______ late. (not/be) I promise.*

2 Write the verbs in present tense forms for future meanings.

Examples: *The Stone family are going to Cyprus for their holidays. (go)*
Their train leaves at 18.15. (leave)

1 *They ______ a train to the airport. (take)*

2 *It ______ the airport at 19.45. (reach)*

3 *They ______ with KLM. (fly)*

4 *The plane ______ at 21.30. (take off)*

5 *It ______ in Cyprus at 00.30. (arrive)*

6 *The family ______ in a villa near the beach. (stay)*

3 Write the verbs in future forms. Use *will* or the future continuous.

Example: ● *Will you be at home at 5.00? (you/be)*
❍ *No, I won't. I 'll be playing tennis then. (play)*

1 ● *At this time tomorrow, I ______ to Australia. (fly) What ______ (you/do)*
❍ *I ______ here, as usual. (work)*

2 ● *Do you think she ______ her exams? (pass)*
❍ *I don't know. She certainly ______ very well if she doesn't work harder. (not/do)*

3 ● *What time ______ home from college? (Sam/be)*
❍ *At lunchtime. I expect you and Sam ______ a lot to talk about. (have)*
● *Yes, I expect we ______ all afternoon. (talk)*

4 ● *Hurry up, or we ______ here all day. (wait)*
❍ *Don't worry. I ______ everything ready in five minutes. (have)*

4 Write the verbs in future forms. Use the future perfect or future continuous.

Example: *By this time next week, I 'll have left London, and I 'll be travelling to Africa. (leave) (travel)*

1 *By the time they finish the new offices, 2,000 builders ______ 30 million bricks. (lay)*

2 *In two months from now, 1,000 people ______ in the new offices. (work)*

3 *Don't worry. Your washing machine ______ again in a minute. (work)*

4 *I ______ my exams in June. (take)*

5 *By this time next year, I ______ school, and I ______ as a pilot. (leave) (train)*

6 ● *Could you come soon after 5.00? The others ______ between 5.00 and 5.30. (arrive)*
❍ *I'm sorry, but I ______ work by then. (not/finish)*

19 *have* and *have got*

He has a huge pack. *He's got a huge pack.* *He's having a rest.*

He's got a huge pack.
He's having a rest.

FORMS

***have* and *have got* for possession**

have

Present

I	*have* *do not have*	*a huge pack.*
He	*has* *does not have*	

Past

I He	*had* *did not have*	*a huge pack.*

have got

Present

I	*have got* *have not got*	*a huge pack.*
He	*has got* *has not got*	

Past

I He	*had* *did not have*	*a huge pack.*

***have* for an action**

He is having a rest. *He is having a Pepsi.*

Short forms: *I/you/we/they have got = I've got, you've got, we've got, they've got* *he/she/it has got = he's got, she's got, it's got* *have not got = haven't got* *has not got = hasn't got*

have and *have got*

We use both *have* and *have got* to mean 'own' or 'possess'. Both forms are usually possible, but *have got* is less formal than *have*.

***Does** he **have** a pack?* ***Has** he **got** a pack?*

We use *have* (own) in simple tenses, and not continuous tenses, eg present simple, not present continuous.

● ***Do** you **have** any fruit juice?* ❍ *No, I **don't**. I only **have** Pepsi.*

The verb form *have got* is the present perfect form of *get*, but the meaning is present.

● ***Have** you **got** any coins?* ❍ *No, I **haven't**. I've only **got** notes.*

Auxiliary verb *have* and main verb *have* often go together. Auxiliary verb *have* often shortens, but main verb *have* does not shorten. (See Unit 21 for more information about *have* as a main verb and auxiliary verb.)

*He's **had** that car for 11 years.* *They've **had** that house since May.*

When we use the past simple, we usually use the form *had*, not *had got*. When we use the present perfect, we always use the form *had*.

*He bought that car 11 years ago. He's **had** it for 11 years.*

have for an action

We use this form of *have* in continuous tenses as well as simple tenses.

*He's **having** a rest now.* *He **has** a swim every day.*

We use this form of *have* in a lot of very useful expressions. These are the most common.

have a swim/wash/bath/shower *have a walk/run/ride*
have (a cup of) coffee/tea *have breakfast/lunch/dinner*
have a meal/snack/break/rest *have a look*
have a talk/chat/discussion/fight/an argument

يمكن استخدام صيغتي have و have got للتعبير عن الملكية وتكون الصيغتان ممكنتين عادة، ولكن have got اقل رسمية من have.

وتستخدم have بمعنى الملكية، مع الازمنة البسيطة وليس مع الازمنة المستمرة، اي مع المضارع البسيط، وليس مع المضارع المستمر.

وصيغة have got عبارة عن فعل get في زمن المضارع التام، ولكن المعنى الذي تعبر عنه هو المضارع.

غالباً ما يستخدم فعل have كفعل مساعد وكفعل اساسي في جملة واحدة. وغالباً ما يصير الى استخدام الصيغة المختصرة للفعل المساعد ولكن ليس للفعل الاساسي (انظر unit 21 للمزيد من المعلومات عن have كفعل اساسي وفعل مساعد).

اما في الماضي البسيط فتستخدم had وليس had got.. وتستخدم had بشكل دائم مع المضارع التام.

تستخدم هذه الصيغة من have مع الازمنة المستمرة وكذلك مع الازمنة البسيطة.

كما تستخدم صيغة have في الكثير من التعبيرات اللغوية المفيدة، وهذه اكثرها شيوعاً.

Exercises

1 Write the correct forms of *have got*.

Example: ● *Have you got* any free time later? (you)
❍ No, I *haven't got* a minute. Sorry.

1 ● ____________ *any coins for the phone? (you)*
❍ *No, sorry. I ____________ any money at all. Ask Tom. I think he ________ some.*
● *No, he ____________ any. I've already asked him.*

2 ● *What does your brother look like?*
❍ *He's tall and he ________ red hair.*
● ____________ *a moustache? (he)*
❍ *No, he ________ You're thinking of someone else.*

2 Write the correct forms of *have*.

Example: ● *Do you have* any free time later? (you)
❍ No, I *don't have* a minute. Sorry.

1 ● ____________ *any stamps for this letter? (you)*
❍ *No, sorry. I ____________ any stamps at all. Ask Sue. I think she ______ some.*
● *No, she ____________ any. I've already asked her.*

2 ● *What does your sister look like?*
❍ *She's thin and she ______ dark hair.*
● ____________ *glasses? (she)*
❍ *No, she ________ You're thinking of someone else.*

3 ● ____________ *a bike when you were young? (you)*
❍ *Yes, I ______ , but it was very heavy. I ________ ________ a good bike until I was 15. That was a great bike. It ______ a special light-weight frame.*

4 ● *Alan, what kind of car ____________ (you)*
❍ *I ____________ one. I walk everywhere. I ____________ one for three years. I sold it.*
● *What kind of car ____________ (you)*
❍ *It was a Toyota.*

5 ● *Nick, ______ a holiday home in Spain.*
❍ *Lucky man! How long ____________ it? (he)*
● *I think he ________ it since 1989. But it's sad because he ____________ much time to go there these days.*

3 Write the correct forms of *have* and *have got*. Use *have got* where possible.

Example: *Ann* has got *a new TV. She* 's *only* had *it for a week.*

Tom and Sue [1] ________ *an old French car. It* [2] ________ *a very big engine, so it doesn't go very fast. Tom and Sue don't mind though. They love it. In fact, they* [3] ________ *a name for it – Harold. They* [4] ________ *the car for eight years, and it's the only car they* [5] ______ *ever* ______ *Before that, they were students. They were very poor and they* [6] ________ ________ *a car. They only* [7] ______ *bicycles. Now they* [8] ________ *enough money for a new car, but they don't want to change. They're happy with the car that they* [9] ______ *, even though it* [10] ________ *some engine problems in the last few months.*

4 Write the correct forms of these expressions.

have breakfast, have a chance, have a chat, have coffee, have a game, have a look, have lunch, have a rest, have a run, have a swim, have time

Don and Lyn Blake work hard all week, so at the weekend they like to relax. They have breakfast *at 9.00 instead of 7.30. Then Don* [1] ________ ______ *at the newspaper and Lyn often* [2] ________ ________ *with her mother on the phone. They never* [3] ________ *to do much shopping in the week, so they go to the supermarket and do the week's food shopping. After that they usually* [4] ________ *in a café. Then they go to the sports centre together. Lyn usually* [5] ________ *of tennis with a friend, while Don* [6] ________ *in the indoor pool. When they go home, they are hungry, so they* [7] ________ *and then they* [8] ________ *because they are tired. Later Don often* [9] ________ *round the park and Lyn* [10] ________ *to write all her letters.*

20 Review: main verb forms

talk, talked, talked, talking, talks

FORMS

1	**Infinitive form:**	*look*	*fall*
2	**The *s* form:**	*looks*	*falls*
3	**Past form:**	*looked*	*fell*
4	**Past participle:**	*looked*	*fallen*
5	**Present participle: (the *ing* form)**	*looking*	*falling*

Only use the *s* form with the 3rd person singular of the present simple. (See Unit 2 for the *s/es* difference.)

*He **talks**. She **crashes**. It **falls**.*

تضاف s مع ضمائر المفرد الغائب في زمن المضارع البسيط فقط.

The past and past participle forms of regular verbs are the same.

talked, talked crashed, crashed

لا يختلف شكل تصريف الفعل القياسي في حالة الماضي عنه في حالة التصريف الثالث.

With irregular verbs they are often different. (See Appendix 1 for a list of common irregular verbs.)

fell, fallen took, taken

ولكن في حالة الافعال اللاقياسية، فهما غالباً ما يختلفان. (انظر لائحة بالافعال اللاقياسية الشائعة في الملحق 1).

Use the verb forms as follows.

وتستخدم صيغ الافعال كما هو مبين في الامثلة.

Forms	Uses	Examples
1 Infinitive form	Infinitive	*He tried to **stop.***
	Imperative	***Look** at me!*
	Future with *will*	*He**'ll hurt** himself.*
	Present simple	*Children **make** mistakes.*
2 The *s* form	Present simple (3rd person)	*That boy often **makes** mistakes.*
3 Past form	Past simple	*He **crashed**. He **fell** off.*
4 Past participle	Perfect tenses (present, past, future)	*He**'s damaged** his bike.* *He crashed just after the boy **had warned** him.* *We**'ll have finished** by 3.00.*
5 Present participle (the *ing* form)	Continuous tenses (present, past, present perfect, future)	*The boy **is talking** to an adult.* *He **was going** too fast when he crashed.* *He**'s been crying** ever since he crashed.* *His arm is broken. He **won't be riding** a bike again for a long time!*

We use different forms of the auxiliary verbs *be*, *do* and *have* with main verbs.

be → am, is, are, was, were, been, being

do → do, does, did have → have, has, had, having

تستخدم تصاريف مختلفة للافعال المساعدة be و do و have مضافة إلى الفعل الاساسي.

Together, auxiliary verbs and main verbs form the verb structure of a sentence. Verb structures add extra information to the meaning of the main verbs, including information about the time of the action – present, past or future. (See Unit 21 for more about auxiliary verbs.)

***I'm riding** a bike. **Did** you **know** that boy?*

***Have** you **hurt** yourself?*

ويكوّن الفعل المساعد مع الفعل الاساسي تركيبة الفعل في الجملة التي تضيف معلومات اخرى إلى معنى الفعل الاساسي في الجملة، بما فيها معلومات عن زمن حدوث الفعل - في المضارع أوالماضي أو المستقبل. (انظر unit 21 للمزيد عن الافعال المساعدة).

Exercises

1 Write the verbs in the present simple.

Example: ● *Where does Ann* live? *(live)*
❍ *She* lives *in New York. (live)*

1 ● *Do you* ________ *Joe Lee? (know)*
❍ *Yes, he* __________ *a BMW, doesn't he? (drive)*

2 ● *When does the film* ________ *(start)*
❍ *It* __________ *at 7.45. (begin)*

3 ● *Ann doesn't* ________ *watching TV in the morning. (like)*
❍ *No, but she* __________ *it a lot in the evening. (watch)*

4 ● *What does Peter* ________ *for lunch? (have)*
❍ *He usually* ______ *a sandwich. (have)*

2 Write the verbs in the present simple or present continuous.

Examples: *Steve always* comes *at 8.00. (come)*
Look! He 's coming *now. (come)*

1 *Helen* __________ *work at 5.00 most days. (finish)*

2 *Quiet! I* __________________ *to the news. (listen)*

3 *I* ________ *I'm not late. (hope)*

4 *What* __________________ *with those bits of wood? (he/make)*

5 *How* __________________ *to school every morning? (she/go)*

6 ● __________________________ *the film? (you/enjoy)*
❍ *No, not really. Let's go home.*

3 Write the infinitive, past form and past participle of these irregular verbs.

cost, cut, earn, get, give, hit, let, make, pay, read, ride, see, take, wear

Infinitive	Past form	Past participle
	Verbs with no change	
cost	__________	__________
__________	__________	__________
__________	__________	__________
__________	__________	__________
__________	__________	__________

Infinitive	Past form	Past participle
	Verbs with one change	
learn	__________	__________
__________	__________	__________
__________	__________	__________
__________	__________	__________

Infinitive	Past form	Past participle
	Verbs with two changes	
ride	__________	__________
__________	__________	__________
__________	__________	__________
__________	__________	__________
__________	__________	__________

4 Write the verbs in the past simple.

Example: ● *Who did you* see *at the party? (see)*
❍ *I* saw *Ann and Steve. (see)*

1 ● *Did Mary* ______ *herself? (cut)*
❍ *Yes, she* ______ *her hand with a knife. (cut)*

2 ● *Did you* ________ *any cakes? (make)*
❍ *Yes, I* ________ *two. (make)*

3 ● *Did Tom* ________ *my bike? (ride)*
❍ *No, he didn't* ________ *yours. (ride) He* ________ *his own. (ride)*

4 ● *Why did you* ______ *him go? (let)*
❍ *I didn't* ______ *him go. (let) He* ______ *me and* ______ *away. (hit) (get)*

5 Write the verbs in the present perfect.

Example: ● *What have they* done? *(do)*
❍ *They've* taken *the old car. (take)*

1 ● *What have the children* ________ *(do)*
❍ *They've* ________ *these models. (make)*

2 ● *Has Bob* ________ *the report yet? (see)*
❍ *No, I haven't* __________ *it to him yet. (give)*

3 ● *Have you* ________ *the list of verbs yet? (read)*
❍ *Yes, but I haven't* __________ *them yet. (learn)*

4 ● *Ow! I've* ______ *myself! (hit)*
❍ *Yes, and you've* ______ *yourself too. (cut)*

21 Review: auxiliary verb forms

be, do, have

The forms of main verbs help to form verb structures. (See Unit 20.)

1	2	3	4	5
look	*looks*	*looked*	*looked*	*looking*
know	*knows*	*knew*	*known*	*knowing*

تساعد تصاريف الأفعال الأساسية على تكوين التراكيب الفعلية.

The auxiliary verbs *be*, *do* and *have* also help to form verb structures.

be → *am, is, are, was, were, been, being*
do → *do, does, did*
have → *have, has, had, having*

كذلك تساعد الأفعال المساعدة *be* و *do* و *have* على تكوين التراكيب الفعلية أيضاً.

Together, auxiliary verbs and main verbs form verb structures. Verb structures add extra information to the meaning of the main verb, including information about the time of the action – present, past or future.

وبالتالي فإن التراكيب الفعلية تتكون من الأفعال المساعدة والأساسية معاً. وتضيف التراكيب الفعلية معلومات إضافية لمعنى الفعل الأساسي في الجملة. وذلك فيما يتعلق بزمن حدوث الفعل مضارعاً كان أم ماضياً أم مستقبلاً.

	Auxiliary	Main	
John	***is***	***talking,***	*so please listen.*
Peter	***has***	***found***	*his bag.*
Lyn	***didn't***	***answer***	*the question.*

Use auxiliaries with *not (n't)* to form negative questions. These *Yes/No* question forms show surprise.

Isn't *he winning the match?* (He was champion last year!)
Don't *you like the food?* (Most people love it!)
Haven't *you heard of her before?* (She's famous!)

وتستخدم الأفعال المساعدة مع أداة النفي *not/(n't)* لتكوين صيغة الاستفهام المنفي – والأمثلة هذه للأسئلة التي يجاب عنها بنعم أو بلا تفيد حالة الدهشة.

These *Wh* question forms ask about a non-action. *Why* questions are the most common type of negative *Wh* questions.

Why aren't *you going?* (*You aren't going. Why not?*)
What didn't *we do?* (*We didn't do something. What?*)
Who haven't *we called?* (*We haven't called somebody. Who?*)

الأمثلة التالية للأسئلة التي تبدأ بأداة استفهام تسأل عن حالة امتناع وقوع الحدث... وتعتبر الأسئلة التي تبدأ بكلمة *Why* أكثر شيوعاً بين الأسئلة التي تبدأ بأداة استفهام والتي تفيد الامتناع.

Use auxiliaries to form tag questions. Tag questions can check information. (See also Unit 25.) They expect the listener to agree. Use a falling tone (↘).

You're coming later, ***aren't*** *you?*
You live in Liverpool, ***don't*** *you?*
You ***haven't*** *read the book,* ***have*** *you?*

وتستخدم الأفعال المساعدة لتكوين أسئلة النهاية التي تهدف إلى التحقق من معلومة ما، وتستخدم بحيث تأتي استجابة المستمع المتوقعة بالموافقة.

وهذه الحالة التي يشار إليها باستخدام السهم النازل الذي يفيد انخفاض نغمة الصوت.

Tag questions can also be like a real question. The speaker does not know for sure. Use a rising tone (↗).

You're coming later, ***aren't*** *you?*

ويمكن أن يعمل سؤال النهاية عمل السؤال الحقيقي، وهنا لا يكون السائل متأكداً من الاستجابة وبالتالي يستخدم السهم الصاعد الذي يفيد ارتفاع نغمة الصوت.

The tag question is usually the opposite (positive/negative) of the main verb.

Positive *You've met*	*Harry,*	→	Negative ***haven't** you?*
*She **hasn't** done* Negative	*the job,*	→	***has** she?* Positive

يأتي سؤال النهاية في الغالب عكس حالة الفعل الأساسي في الجملة... فإذا كان الفعل مثبتاً جاء سؤال النهاية منفياً، والعكس صحيح، إذا جاء الفعل الأساسي منفياً جاء سؤال النهاية مثبتاً.

Use auxiliary forms in short answers, and do not repeat the main verb. Use them to reply to ordinary *Yes/No* questions and to tag questions.

- ***Are** you **looking** for your bag?* ❍ *Yes, I **am**.*
- ***Do** you **know** where it is?* ❍ *No, I **don't**.*
- ***Have** you **found** it yet?* ❍ *Yes, I **have**.*
- *You**'re** worried, **aren't** you.* ❍ *Yes, I **am**.*
- *You **haven't** found it, **have** you?* ❍ *No, I **haven't**.*

وتستخدم الأفعال المساعدة عند الإجابات القصيرة ولا يتكرر ذكر الفعل الأساسي. كذلك تستخدم الأفعال المساعدة عند الإجابة على الأسئلة التي يجاب عنها بنعم أو بلا وكذلك في أسئلة النهاية.

Use auxiliary forms with *So, Nor* and *Neither.* Be very careful – the word order looks like a question. (See also Unit 28.)

- *I'm tired.* ❍ ***So am** I.*
- *He doesn't work hard.* ❍ ***Nor does** she.*
- *We haven't finished.* ❍ ***Neither have** they.*

تستخدم الأفعال المساعدة مع *So* و *Nor* و *Neither*. وتجدر الملاحظة هنا بأن ترتيب الكلمات في الجملة يتغير بحيث تبدو وكأنها جملة استفهامية.

Use auxiliary forms for special emphasis in reply to another speaker's words.

- *Please read it.* ❍ *I **am** reading it.*
- *You didn't finish.* ❍ *Actually I **did** finish.*
- *We haven't studied Unit 3.* ❍ *We **have** studied it.*

وتستخدم الأفعال المساعدة للتأكيد وذلك عند الإجابة رداً على كلام من شخص آخر.

be, do and *have* are not only auxiliary verbs. They can also be main verbs. We can use *be, do* and *have* (auxiliary) with *be, do* and *have* (main) in the same sentence.

إن الأفعال *be* و *do* و *have* ليست أفعالاً مساعدة فقط ولكنها أساسية أيضاً. ويمكن استخدام أي منها كفعل مساعد وأساسي في الجملة نفسها.

Use *be* as an auxiliary with a main verb.

*We **were writing** letters.* *__Is__ he **eating** lunch?*

ويستخدم فعل *be* كفعل مساعد مع الأفعال الأساسية.

Use *be* as a link verb with a noun or adjective.

***Is** she **a doctor**.* *They were **clever**.*

ويستخدم فعل *be* كفعل ربط بين الأسماء والصفات.

Use *be* as an auxiliary with *be* as a main verb.

*Why **are** you **being** so stupid?* (behaving stupidly)

ويستخدم *be* كفعل مساعد وكفعل أساسي في الجملة نفسها.

Use *do* as an auxiliary with a main verb in questions and negative statements.

***Do** you **like** football?* *She **doesn't want** to leave.*

ويستخدم *do* كفعل مساعد مع فعل أساسي في الجمل الاستفهامية وفي الجمل المنفية.

Use *do* as a main verb.

*Is he **doing** his homework?* *I **did** my exercises.*

ويستخدم *do* كفعل أساسي أيضاً.

Use *do* as an auxiliary with *do* as a main verb in questions and negative statements.

***Does** he **do** his homework every day?* *I **didn't do** my exercises.*

ويستخدم *do* كفعل مساعد وكذلك كفعل أساسي في الجملة الاستفهامية نفسها وفي الجمل المنفية أيضاً.

Use *have* as an auxiliary with a main verb.

***Have** you **finished** yet?* *When I arrived it **had started**.*

ويستخدم *have* كفعل مساعد مع فعل أساسي آخر.

Use *have* as a main verb.

*When are you **having** lunch?* *I **had** a rest.*

كما يستخدم *have* كفعل أساسي في الجملة.

Use *have* as an auxiliary with *have* as a main verb.

***Have** you **had** this car for long?* *Ann **has had** her lunch.*

وكذلك يستخدم *have* كفعل مساعد وكفعل أساسي في الجملة نفسها.

Exercises

1 Write the correct forms of *be*.

Example: *Lyn* was *working all day yesterday.*

1 *I ______ taking Ann home next week.*

2 *Look! Where ______ Ed going with my bike?*

3 *We ___________ flying to Japan at this time tomorrow.*

4 *Alan ______________ staying in London since last month.*

5 *What ________ you doing at 9.00 last night?*

6 *At last, you're here! I ______________ waiting for hours.*

7 *______ you doing anything at the moment?*

8 *I ______ phoning Pam when Tom arrived.*

2 Write the correct forms of *do*.

Example: ● Does *Peter Speak German?*
❍ *He* doesn't *speak much, but he can read a little.*

1 ● *How ______ you play this game?*
❍ *I'm not sure. We ________ have any instructions.*

2 ● *______ you want to go home, Sue?*
❍ *No, I ________ want to go home just yet.*

3 ● *When ______ you get home last night?*
❍ *I ___________ go home. I stayed at a hotel.*

4 ● *Why ________ he keep looking at us?*
❍ *I ________ know. I'll tell him to stop.*

5 ● *______ you say much at the meeting?*
❍ *No, I ___________ say anything. I kept quiet.*

6 ● *________ Fred play tennis?*
❍ *No, he ___________, but he plays football.*

3 Write the correct forms of *have*.

Example: ● *How much* has *Andy written?*
❍ *He* hasn't *written much. Just a page.*

1 ● *________ the trucks crossed the river yet?*
❍ *No, they ___________ because we ___________ built a bridge yet.*

2 ● *Why were you so angry with Bob?*
❍ *Because he ________ done the work.*

3 ● *________ you found your shoes yet?*
❍ *I ______ found one, but I ___________ found the other one. I don't know where it is.*

4 ● *Why did he come late?*
❍ *Because he ___________ noticed the time.*

5 ● *Will their car be ready by 5.00?*
❍ *Oh, yes. We ___________ finished before then.*

6 ● *How long ______ Fred lived here now?*
❍ *He ______ been here for five years.*

7 ● *I need your report by Friday.*
❍ *I'm sorry. I _______________ finished it by then.*

8 ● *Why didn't the boys have any money?*
❍ *Because they ______ spent it all on sweets.*

4 Re-order the words to make negative questions.

Examples: *(job/didn't/the/finish/you)*
Didn't you finish the job?
(job/didn't/the/finish/you/why)
Why didn't you finish the job?

1 *(Paul/home/hasn't/come/yet)*

____

2 *(they/the/call/didn't/police/why)*

____

3 *(enjoying/film/aren't/you/the)*

____

4 *(you/agree/don't/why/me/with)*

____

5 *(Rosie/the/isn't/wedding/going/to)*

____

6 *(questions/they/yet/answered/which/haven't)*

____

7 *(you/go/have to/home/now/don't)*

____

8 *(parts/don't/have to/we/which/learn)*

____

5 Write tag questions.

Examples: *They're going to crash,* aren't they?
You didn't finish, did you?

1 *You haven't understood,* ____________
2 *He likes her,* ____________
3 *They were angry with you,* ____________
4 *You don't know Tony,* ____________
5 *He arrived late,* ____________
6 *They've done the shopping,* ____________
7 *Alan doesn't like travelling,* ____________
8 *Ann was studying last night,* ____________
9 *You aren't enjoying this,* ____________
10 *Nick didn't get home until midnight,* ____________

6 Agree with the first speaker.

Examples: ● *I'm hungry. (I)*
❍ So am I.
● *She didn't like the film. (he)*
❍ Neither/Nor did he.

1 ● *They don't understand the question. (we)*
❍ ____________

2 ● *Peter likes the new teacher. (Alan)*
❍ ____________

3 ● *I've never been to India before. (I)*
❍ ____________

4 ● *Sam didn't do his homework. (Lisa)*
❍ ____________

5 ● *Sue has called her parents. (her brothers)*
❍ ____________

6 ● *We aren't going to buy the book. (she)*
❍ ____________

7 ● *I'd never seen such a lovely place. (we)*
❍ ____________

8 ● *The car broke down again yesterday. (the van)*
❍ ____________

9 ● *You aren't telling the truth. (you)*
❍ ____________

10 ● *Kate has been to America. (Andy)*
❍ ____________

7 Write questions and answers with *do, have* and *be* as main verbs. Use a) the present continuous, b) the past simple and c) the present perfect.

Examples: (● *Which question/you/do)*
(❍ *we/do/number 2)*
a) ● Which question are you doing?
❍ We're doing number 2.
b) ● Which question did you do?
❍ We did number 2.
c) ● Which question have you done?
❍ We've done number 2.

1 (● *What/you/have/for lunch)*
(❍ *we/have/chicken)*
a) ● ____________
____
❍ ____________
b) ● ____________
____
❍ ____________
c) ● ____________
____
❍ ____________

2 (● *How much work/he/do)*
(❍ *he/do/ten hours)*
a) ● ____________
❍ ____________
b) ● ____________
❍ ____________
c) ● ____________
❍ ____________

3 (● *Why/they/be/so slow with their work)*
(❍ *because they/be/careful)*
a) ● ____________
____
❍ ____________
b) ● ____________
____
❍ ____________
c) ● ____________
____
❍ ____________

22 Short form or full form

I'm angry!   *I am angry!*

FORMS

Short forms			Full forms		
be			***be***		
I'm	*you're*	*he's*	*I am*	*you are*	*he is*
I'm not	*you aren't*	*he isn't*	*I am not*	*you are not*	*he is not*
	you're not	*he's not*			
I wasn't	*you weren't*		*I was not*	*you were not*	
do			***do***		
I don't	*he doesn't*	*they didn't*	*I do not*	*he does not*	*they did not*
have			***have***		
I've	*he's*	*I'd*	*I have*	*he has*	*I had*
I haven't	*he hasn't*	*I hadn't*	*I have not*	*he has not*	*I had not*
will			***will***		
I'll	*we won't*		*I will*	*we will not*	
would			***would***		
he'd	*you wouldn't*		*he would*	*you would not*	

's can mean *is* or *has*, so check the main part of the verb.

*She**'s** coming home.* (***'s*** = *is*)   *She**'s** come home.* (***'s*** = *has*)

Do not confuse *it's* and *its*.

It's** going to sleep.* (It's*** = *It is*)

*The cat is closing **its** eyes.* (***its*** = pronoun)

Also, do not confuse the possessive *'s* and *'s* meaning *is*.

This is Alan***'s*** hat. (***'s*** = possessive)   Alan***'s*** at home. (***'s*** = *is*)

'd can mean *had* or *would*, so check the main part of the verb.

*They**'d** finished by 12.00.* (***'d*** = *had*)

يمكن ان تكون 's اختصاراً لـ is او لـ has، وللتأكد يجب الرجوع الى الفعل الاساسي في الجملة.

ويجب عدم الخلط بين it's وبين its.

كما يجب عدم الخلط بين 's التي تفيد الملكية وبين الاخرى التي تعني is.

كذلك فإن 'd تأتي اختصاراً لـ had وكذلك لـwould الامر الذي يتطلب التعرف على جزء الفعل الاساسي في الجملة.

CROSSCHECK

Short forms

Use short forms for normal speaking.

*They**'re** trying to finish early.*

Use short forms for ordinary statements.

● *He **isn't** working.*

Use short forms for informal writing, eg a letter to a friend.

Dear Sally,
*We**'re** having a great holiday.*

Full forms

Show strong feeling with full forms and stress.

*I **am** sad you **have** to go away!*

Use full positive forms with stress to correct statements.

❍ *Oh, yes, he **is** working!*

Use full forms to ask questions and at the end of sentences.

● ***Are** they working hard?*
❍ *Yes, they **are**.*

Use full forms for most writing, eg a business letter or a report.

Dear Sir,
*We **are** pleased to inform you ...*

تستخدم الصيغ المختصرة في الحديث العادي في حين تستخدم الصيغ الكاملة للتعبير عن المشاعر التي تتسم بالقوة... وكذلك فإنها تستخدم للتأكيد.

وتستخدم الصيغ المختصرة في الجمل الخبرية العادية.

وتستخدم الصيغ المثبتة الكاملة مع النبرة (stress) لتصحيح الجمل الخبرية.

وتستخدم الصيغ الكاملة لتكوين الجمل الاستفهامية وكذلك عندما تأتي في نهاية الجملة.

تستخدم الصيغ المختصرة للكتابة غير الرسمية، رسالة الى صديق مثلاً.

وتستخدم الصيغ الكاملة في الكتابة بشكل عام مثل كتابة الخطابات الرسمية والتقارير.

Exercises

1 Write the short forms.

Example: *(I have)* I've *been here all day.*

1 *(You are)* ________ *right.*
2 *(He has)* ________ *hurt his leg.*
3 *(I am)* ________ *18 next month.*
4 *(What is)* ________ *her name?*
5 *(We will)* ________ *be late.*
6 *If (he is)* ________ *wrong, (he will)* ________ *lose all his money.*
7 *If you were on that plane, (you would)* ________ *be half-way to India now.*
8 *If (she had)* ________ *gone to the interview, (she would)* ________ *have got the job.*
9 *(They have)* ________ *finished their lunch.*
10 *(I would)* ________ *like a cup of tea, please.*

2 Write the negative short forms.

Example: *Mary* hasn't *eaten since yesterday.*

1 *I* ________ *like coffee. I never drink it.*
2 *She* ________ *singing at the moment.*
3 *Peter* ________ *seen Tom for ages.*
4 *We* ________ *be late again tomorrow.*
5 ________ *watch the film, Sam. I saw it at the cinema and I* ________ *enjoy it.*
6 *I* ________ *going to eat at that restaurant again.*
7 *This engine* ________ *much use. It* ________ *work properly.*
8 *If you* ________ *called me yesterday morning, I* ________ *have woken up in time.*
9 *Mike and Sue* ________ *been to Malta before. This is their first time.*
10 *Joe* ________ *at school yesterday because he felt sick.*

3 Write the positive or negative short forms.

Tom is worried about his friend, Ben.

Tom: *What's wrong, Ben? You* don't *look well.*
Ben: *I* 1________ *feel very well either. I* 2________ *ill.*
Tom: *What* 3________ *the matter exactly?*
Ben: *Oh, I* 4________ *got a headache and I feel bad.*
Tom: *You* 5________ *better see the doctor.*
Ben: *I* 6________ *like to do that, but I* 7________ *got any time. I* 8________ *going to an important meeting this morning.*
Tom: 9________ *be stupid. You* 10________ *ill, so if you go to the meeting, you* 11________ *be able to work properly. Can Roger go instead of you?*
Ben: *He* 12________ *really know enough about the project, but perhaps he can. I* 13________ *call him and ask him.*
Tom: *Good. I know he* 14________ *say yes. And then we* 15________ *go to the doctor together.*
Ben: *Thanks. That* 16________ *really kind of you.*

4 Write the full forms.

The bank manager has written an unpleasant letter to a customer.

Dear Mr Morton,
(I'm) I am *writing to you about your company's latest sales figures, which (we've)* 1________ *recently received.*

As you say in your letter, the figures (aren't) 2________ *good and they (don't)* 3________ *seem to be improving. Your figures have been showing losses for three years, and (I'm)* 4________ *very sorry to say that (they're)* 5________ *still showing large losses. As a result, you (won't)* 6________ *be surprised to know that (we're)* 7________ *getting very worried about the business loan which you (haven't)* 8________ *yet been able to start repaying.*

5 Write the full forms.

The letter from the bank continues.

Until your latest sales report, (we'd) 1________ *hoped (you'd)* 2________ *succeed, but (it's)* 3________ *clear now that the company will soon have to close. Our accountant is still studying your sales figures, but (he's)* 4________ *decided that we must now close your loan account with this bank. (He's)* 5________ *sending you a copy of his report in tomorrow's post. (I'd)* 6________ *like to suggest that we meet early this week.*

23 Question forms 1

Are you from Japan?

FORMS

***Yes/No* questions**

● *Is he from Japan?*
❍ *Yes, he is./No, he isn't.*

● *Was she a doctor?*
❍ *Yes, she was./No, she wasn't.*

● *Have we finished?*
❍ *Yes, we have./No, we haven't.*

● *Can they understand?*
❍ *Yes, they can./No, they can't.*

Use *Yes/No* questions to check information.

● ***Is he from America?***
❍ *Yes, he is./No, he isn't.*
● ***Does the film start at 7.30?***
❍ *Yes, it does./No, it doesn't.*

ستخدم الاسئلة التي يجاب عنها بـ «نعم» أو «لا»، للتأكد ن المعلومات.

Form questions from statements in the following ways.
With one auxiliary verb, do this.

***They can** understand.* → ***Can they** understand?*
***He is** working.* → ***Is he** working?*
***They were** reading.* → ***Were they** reading?*

كوّن اسئلة من جمل خبرية تحتوي على فعل مساعد احد، يجري تقديمه على الفاعل.

With two auxiliary verbs (eg *has been, is going to*), do this.

***He has been** working hard.* → ***Has he been** working hard?*
***He is going to** work hard.* → ***Is he going to** work hard?*

ندما تحتوي الجملة على فعلين مساعدين يقدم الاول لى الفاعل.

With no auxiliary verbs, add *do* or *does* in the present simple and add *did* in the past simple. In the present and past simple, use only the infinitive form of the verb.

*I **know** her.* → ***Do** I **know** her?*
*He **knows** her.* → ***Does** he **know** her?*
*He **knew** her.* → ***Did** he **know** her?*

ندما لا تحتوي الجملة على فعل مساعد تضاف do او does في زمن المضارع البسيط، وتضاف did في زمن لماضي البسيط. وتستخدم صيغة المصدر فقط من الفعل لاساسي مع المضارع البسيط ومع الماضي البسيط.

Form *Yes/No* questions with *will* and modal auxilary verbs + infinitive.

***Will** he **win**?*
***Can** she **speak** French?*
***Must** you **go**?*

تكون السؤال الذي يجاب عنه بـ «نعم» أو «لا»، باستخدام wil والافعال المساعدة الدالة على صيغة الفعل الاصلي لمستعمل معها + المصدر من الفعل الاساسي.

Use auxiliaries with *not (n't)* to form negative questions. These *Yes/No* questions show surprise.

***Isn't** he winning the match?* (He was champion last year!)
***Don't** you like the food?* (Most people love it!)
***Haven't** you heard of her before?* (She's famous!)

ستخدم الافعال المساعدة مع not/ n't لتكوين صيغة لنفي من الجمل الاستفهامية... وهنا تأتي الاسئلة التي جاب عنها بنعم او بلا لتعبر عن الدهشة.

Exercises

1 Write questions from the statements.

Examples: *Ed speaks French. (German)*
Does Ed speak German too?
She's having a piano lesson. (he)
Is he having a piano lesson too?

1 *Bob likes basketball. (football)*

2 *Sally is good at cooking. (Lucy)*

3 *The boys have had dinner. (Dad)*

4 *Jim cooked some vegetables. (meat)*

5 *We're going out tonight. (you)*

2 Write questions from the statements.

Example: *Rob can speak Japanese. (you)*
Can you speak Japanese too?

1 *I have to go now. (he)*

2 *She must finish the report. (letters)*

3 *He can run fast. (swim fast)*

4 *We should train every morning. (evening)*

5 *We'll have to write to all our relatives. (friends)*

3 Re-order the words to make questions.

Examples: *(be/married/Liz and Bill)*
● Are Liz and Bill married?
❍ *Yes, they are.*
(in London/live/they)
● Do they live in London?
❍ *No, they don't. They live in Manchester.*

1 *(for long/be/married/they)*
●
❍ *Yes, they've been married for eight years.*

2 *(move/at that time/to Manchester/they)*
●
❍ *No, they moved there a year later.*

3 *(they/any children/have got)*
●
❍ *Yes, they have got one son and one daughter.*

4 *(go/the children/to school)*
●
❍ *The boy does, but the girl is still too young.*

5 *(soon/she/school/start)*
●
❍ *Yes, she's starting school in September.*

4 Write negative questions.

Example: ● *I'm tired. I want to stay at home.*
❍ *Really? (you/not/want to meet Sue)*
Really? Don't you want to meet Sue?

1 ● *Don't buy that car.*
❍ *Why? (it/not/be/a good one)*

2 ● *Let's take the train, not the plane.*
❍ *Really? (you/not/like/flying)*

3 ● *Rod is working at the bank.*
❍ *Why? (he/not/go/to college yet)*

4 ● *The children are starting another game on the computer.*
❍ *Really? (they/not/go/to bed soon)*

5 ● *Pam has just bought a new pen.*
❍ *Why? (she/not/buy/one yesterday)*

24 Question forms 2

Where are you going?

FORMS

***Wh* questions**

● *Where is he going?*
❍ *He is going to London.*

● *How is he travelling?*
❍ *He is travelling by plane.*

● *What are they doing?*
❍ *They are talking.*

● *Why are they travelling?*
❍ *They are travelling because they have business in the UK.*

Use *Wh* questions to get more information.

● ***Where is he going***?
❍ *To London.*
● ***What does he do***?
❍ *He works for IBM.*

تستخدم الاسئلة التي تبدأ بأداة استفهام للحصول على معلومات اضافية.

Form questions from statements in the following ways.
First use a question word.

Where, When, Why, What, Who, Whose, Which, How, How much, How many, How old, etc

تتكون الاسئلة من الجمل الخبرية باستخدام إحدى ادوات الاستفهام كما هو مبين.

Then change the subject and the auxiliary verb.

*Where **are we** going?*
*What **has she** been doing?*
*How **does he** like the town?*
*Why **did they** leave?*

ثم يوضع الفعل المساعد قبل الفاعل.

Who and *What* can ask about the subject or the object of an action.

A car hit the cat. → ● ***What hit** the cat?* (subject) ❍ ***The car** hit the cat.* OR ● ***What did** the car **hit**?* (object) ❍ *The car hit **the cat**.*
Tim called Ken. → ● ***Who called** Ken?* (subject) ❍ ***Tim** called Ken.* OR ***Who did** Tim **call**?* (object) ❍ *Tim called **Ken**.*

اداتا الاستفهام who و what تسألان عن الفاعل او عن المفعول به.

Use auxiliaries with *not (n't)* to form negative questions. Use *Wh* questions to ask about a non-action. *Why* questions are the most common.

***Why aren't** you going?* (*You aren't going. Why?*)
***What didn't** we do?* (*We didn't do something. What?*)
***Who haven't** we called?* (*We haven't called somebody. Who?*)

تستخدم الافعال المساعدة مع اداة النفي not/n't لتكوين اسئلة منفية. وتستخدم الاسئلة المنفية التي تبدأ باداة الاستفهام، لتفيد انعدام وقوع الحدث.. واكثر هذا النوع شيوعاً هو الذي يبدأ بأداة الاستفهام why.

Exercises

1 Write the question words.

Example: ● *When did Liz and Bill get married?*
❍ *Eight years ago.*

1 ● ________ *do they live?*
❍ *In Manchester.*

2 ● ________ *parents live with them?*
❍ *Bill's.*

3 ● ____________ *have they lived in Manchester?*
❍ *For seven years.*

4 ● ____________ *children have they got?*
❍ *Two. A son and a daughter.*

5 ● ________ *one is older?*
❍ *Their son. He's seven.*

6 ● ________ *is their daughter going to start school?*
❍ *This year.*

7 ● ________ *do they live in Manchester?*
❍ *Because Bill has got a good job there.*

8 ● ________ *does he do?*
❍ *He's an engineer.*

2 Re-order the words to make questions. Then write true answers about yourself.

Example: *(your/what's/name)*
● *What's your name?*
❍ *My name's ...*

1 *(you/are/how/old)*
● ____________________
❍ ____________________

2 *(your/address/what's)*
● ____________________
❍ ____________________

3 *(father/do/does/your/what)*
● ____________________
❍ ____________________

4 *(got/and/brothers/have/how many/you/sisters)*
● ____________________
____
❍ ____________________

5 *(you/learning/why/are/English)*
● ____________________
❍ ____________________

3 Write negative questions.

Example: *We didn't finish something. (What)*
What didn't we finish?

1 *Tom hasn't answered my letter. (Why)*
____
____

2 *We haven't done something. (What)*
____

3 *They won't be able to go on holiday. (Why)*
____
____

4 *We didn't go somewhere. (Where)*
____

5 *Ann isn't going to go out tonight. (Why)*
____
____

6 *I don't like this television programme. (Why)*
____
____

4 Write questions with *Who* or *What*.

Example: *Somebody called the manager.*
Who called the manager?
The customer called somebody.
Who did the customer call?

1 *Somebody called the police.*
____

2 *Something went wrong.*
____

3 *Bob found something by the door.*
____

4 *Tom phoned somebody.*
____

5 *The car ran over something.*
____

6 *Somebody saw Peter.*
____

7 *Julie ate something.*
____

25 Tag questions

Alan is finishing college soon, isn't he?

FORMS

Positive statements	Negative statements
Present	**Present**
These shoes are nice, aren't they?	*That jacket isn't very nice, is it?*
He's laughing at me, isn't he?	*You aren't laughing too, are you?*
You love music, don't you?	*He doesn't like music very much, does he?*
Perfect	**Perfect**
You've finished work, haven't you?	*Mrs West hasn't gone home yet, has she?*
He'd found it by 8.00, hadn't he?	*He hadn't expected to find it, had he?*
We'll have gone before 1.00, won't we?	*They won't have come by 1.00, will they?*
Past	**Past**
Rob was on holiday in May, wasn't he?	*You weren't at work either, were you?*
I was going home, wasn't I?	*You weren't going home, were you?*
The plane went on time, didn't it?	*They didn't arrive late, did they?*
Future	**Future**
She's going to be pleased, isn't she?	*They aren't going to complain, are they?*
You'll be at home tomorrow, won't you?	*We won't be out tonight, will we?*
They'll be going on Sunday, won't they?	*You won't be working on Sunday, will you?*
Modal forms	**Modal forms**
You can speak German, can't you?	*We mustn't be late, must we?*
We have to go now, don't we?	*I don't need to buy it, do I?*

The tag question is usually the opposite (positive/negative) of the main verb.

Positive *You've met*	*Harry,* →	**Negative** ***haven't*** *you?*
She ***hasn't*** *done* **Negative**	*the job,* →	***has*** *she?* **Positive**

With one auxiliary verb, use the opposite auxiliary form, eg *is* → *isn't*.

With two auxiliary verbs, use the opposite of the first auxiliary, eg *will have* → *won't have*.

With no auxiliary verbs, in the present and past simple, use a form of *do* (main verb → *don't, doesn't* or *didn't*). *have to* and *need to* also work like this.

Tag questions are not ordinary questions. We can use them to check information. They expect the listener to agree. Use a falling tone (↘).

You're 18, ***aren't you****?* *You live in Liverpool,* ***don't you****?*

We can also use this type of tag question to help a conversation.

● *It's a good film,* ***isn't it****?* ❍ *Yes, it's great. The acting is wonderful.*

Tag questions can be more like ordinary questions – the speaker does not know something for sure. Use a rising tone (↗).

You're 18, ***aren't you****?* *You live in Liverpool,* ***don't you****?*

Note the negative tag after *I am*.

I'm late, ***aren't I****?*

يأتي سؤال النهاية عادةً مخالفاً لحالة الفعل الاساسي في الجملة من حيث كونه مثبتاً او منفياً.

عند احتواء الجملة على فعل مساعد واحد يأتي سؤال النهاية مخالفاً له... (is تصبح isn't).

وعند احتواء الجملة على فعلين مساعدين نعكس حالة الأول منهما (will have تصبح won't have).

وعند خلو الجملة من الافعال المساعدة في زمني المضارع البسيط والماضي البسيط نستخدم تصريفات do كفعل اساسي (don't و doesn't و didn't) ويعامل فعلاً have to و need to بالطريقة نفسها.

ولا تعتبر اسئلة النهاية اسئلة عادية، فهي تستخدم للتحقق من المعلومات بحيث نتوقع من المستمع الموافقة باستخدام نغمة الصوت المنخفضة التي يشار اليها بالسهم النازل.

ويمكن استخدام هذا النوع من الاسئلة ليعين على الحوار اثناء الحديث.

ويمكن ان تعمل اسئلة النهاية مثل عمل الاسئلة العادية تقريباً، وذلك حين لا يكون المتكلم متأكداً من معلومة معينة...

وهنا تستخدم نغمة صوتية مرتفعة يشار اليها بالسهم الصاعد.

وتجدر ملاحظة كيفية استخدام سؤال النهاية مع I am وهي كما هو موضح في المثال.

Exercises

1 Write tag questions.

Examples: *It's hot today,* isn't it?
He won't be working late, will he?

With one auxiliary and most modal verbs

1 *You'll be at home tonight,* ____________
2 *The letter hasn't arrived yet,* ____________
3 *They're doing the shopping,* ____________
4 *It rained last night,* ____________
5 *She isn't at home now,* ____________
6 *Peter wasn't working yesterday,* ____________
7 *Barry can't come to the party,* ____________
8 *He should finish by 5.00,* ____________
9 *We needn't pay now,* ____________
10 *She might arrive tomorrow,* ____________

With two auxiliaries

11 *He'll be working all day,* ____________
12 *You haven't been listening to me,* ____________
13 *The boys will have gone by 4.00,* ____________
14 *The window hasn't been mended,* ____________
15 *Your book isn't being printed yet,* ____________
16 *Tony's car was being serviced yesterday,* ____________

With no auxiliaries and with modal auxiliaries *have to* and *need to*

17 *Bob owns all his land,* ____________
18 *You forgot to post the letters,* ____________
19 *You need to ask the boss,* ____________
20 *Mary had to sell the house,* ____________

2 Write tag questions.

You're interviewing the famous film star, Rocky Reed.

Example: *Mr Reed, you've made nearly 40 films,* haven't you?

1 *Your last film earned $30 million,* ____________
2 *Your early films weren't so successful,* ____________
3 *You're going to make your next film in Mexico,* ____________
4 *You don't like being away from your home and family,* ____________
5 *Your wife isn't interested in films,* ____________
6 *You've got four children,* ____________
7 *They won't be going into the film industry,* ____________

These tag questions check information. Mark the tags with a falling tone (↘).

3 Write tag questions.

You're at a party.

Example: *It's a lovely house,* isn't it?

1 *The food is wonderful,* ____________
2 *There aren't many people here yet,* ____________
3 *Bob and Celia aren't coming,* ____________
4 *I haven't seen you since last year,* ____________
5 *You met my wife at the last party,* ____________
6 *We'll be seeing you next week,* ____________

These tag questions encourage the listener to speak. Mark the tags with a falling tone (↘).

4 Write tag questions.

Lucy and her daughter, Emma, are going to the airport. Emma is very worried, but Lucy is calm.

Emma: *Mum, you didn't forget to bring the passports,* did you?
Lucy: *Don't worry. I told you I'd brought them,* 1____________
Emma: *Yes, that's right. I forgot. And you've got the tickets,* 2____________
Lucy: *Yes, don't you remember? They were on the table with the passports,* 3____________
Emma: *Yes, I suppose so. But Mum, what's the time? We're going to be late,* 4____________
Lucy: *Calm down, Emma. It's 10.30 now and the flight doesn't leave until 12.30,* 5____________ *And we only have to go another 30 kilometres,* 6____________
Emma: *I guess you're right.*
Lucy: *Well, then, there's nothing to worry about,* 7____________

Emma is unsure. Mark her tags with a rising tone (↗).
Lucy is sure. Mark her tags with a falling tone (↘).

26 Short answers

Yes, I am. *No, I can't.*

FORMS

- *Are you upstairs now?*
- *Yes, I am. I'm going into the bedroom.*
- *Is the room on fire?*
- *No, it isn't, but there's a lot of smoke.*
- *Can you see the boy now?*
- *No, I can't ... Ah, wait. Yes, I can.*
- *Is he all right?*
- *I don't know yet.*

A short answer can be a *Yes* or a *No* answer. The verb in the answer matches the verb in the question.

يمكن ان تكون الاجابات المختصرة إجابات كاملة بِـ «نعم» أو «لا». ويكون الفعل في الاجابة نظيراً للفعل في السؤال.

- ***Is the room** on fire?*
- *Yes, **it is**.*
- ***Can you** see the boy now?*
- *No, **I can't**.*

We always use full forms in *Yes* answers, when the verb is the last word.

*Yes, **I am**.* *Yes, **it is**.* *Yes, **I can**.*

وتستخدم الصيغ الكاملة دائماً، عند الاجابة بـ «بنعم» وعندما يكون الفعل آخر كلمة في الجملة.

We usually use short forms in *No* answers.

*No, it **isn't**.* *No, I **can't**.* *No, they **didn't**.*
(But *No, **I'm not**.*)

وتستخدم الصيغ المختصرة عادة، عند الاجابة المنفية بِـ «لا».

Here are some more examples.

والیك مزيداً من الامثلة توضح الافكار السابقة الذكر.

Present

- ***Are they** at home?* ○ *Yes, **they are**./No, **they aren't**.*
- ***Is Ann** going home?* ○ *Yes, **she is**./No, **she isn't**.*
- ***Do you** like Italian food?* ○ *Yes, **I do**./No, **I don't**.*

Perfect

- ***Has Peter** posted the letter?* ○ *Yes, **he has**./No, **he hasn't**.*
- ***Had the film** started by 8.00?* ○ *Yes, **it had**./No, **it hadn't**.*

Past

- ***Were the children** at home?* ○ *Yes, **they were**./No, **they weren't**.*
- ***Was the cat** eating?* ○ *Yes, **it was**./No, **it wasn't**.*
- ***Did you** see Susan last night?* ○ *Yes, **I did**./No, **I didn't**.*

Future

- ***Are we** going to be late?* ○ *Yes, **we are**./No, **we aren't**.*
- ***Will Joe** be at home tonight?* ○ *Yes, **he will**./No, **he won't**.*

In conversation, we often give extra information after a short answer. This helps the conversation to continue.

غالباً ما يعطى مزيد من التفاصيل بعد الاجابات القصيرة اثناء الحوار وهذا يساعد على استمرار المحادثة.

- *Do you know Helen?*
- *Yes, I do. **I've known her for years**.*
- *Have you finished work yet?*
- *No, I haven't. **I still have to write a report**.*

Exercises

1 Complete the answers.

Some people are talking at a wedding party.

Example: ● *Are you a member of the family?*
❍ No, *I'm not.* *I'm a friend.*

1 ● *Have you met Tony?*
❍ *No,* ____________ *Hello.*

2 ● *Do you know Mary?*
❍ *Yes,* ________ *We're old friends.*

3 ● *Are you from London?*
❍ *No,* __________. *I'm from Liverpool.*

4 ● *Should we go and get some food now?*
❍ *Yes,* ________________ *It's in the next room.*

5 ● *Would you like some more wedding cake?*
❍ *Yes,* ____________ *It's delicious.*

6 ● *Are there any more sandwiches?*
❍ *No,* ________________ *They're all gone.*

7 ● *Have you known Susie for long?*
❍ *No,* ____________ *But I know Ian well.*

8 ● *Is Ian going to give a speech?*
❍ *Yes,* ________ *He's standing up now.*

9 ● *Can you hear what Ian is saying?*
❍ *No,* __________ *It's too noisy.*

10 ● *Did you enjoy the wedding?*
❍ *Yes,* ________ *It was lovely.*

11 ● *Must you go already?*
❍ *Yes,* __________. *I'm sorry.*

2 Complete the answers in the game, *Who am I?*

The answer to 10 is *Yes, I was.*

1 ● *Are you alive?*
❍ *No,* ____________

2 ● *Have you died recently?*
❍ *No,* ____________

3 ● *Were you a woman?*
❍ *No,* ____________

4 ● *Did you come from Britain?*
❍ *No,* ____________

5 ● *Were you European?*
❍ *Yes,* ____________

6 ● *Were you a soldier?*
❍ *Yes,* ____________

7 ● *Did you lead your country?*
❍ *Yes,* ____________

8 ● *Were you like a king?*
❍ *Yes,* ____________

9 ● *Did you live about 200 years ago?*
❍ *Yes,* ____________

10 ● *Were you Emperor Napoleon of France?*
❍ *Yes,* ____________

3 Write true short answers about yourself.

Example: ● *Are you studying English?*
❍ *Yes, I am.*

1 ● *Are you a full-time student?*
❍ ________________

2 ● *Do you ever speak English outside class?*
❍ ________________

3 ● *Is English a difficult language to learn?*
❍ ________________

4 ● *Are you learning any other language?*
❍ ________________

5 ● *Do most people learn English in your country?*
❍ ________________

6 ● *Do a lot of people in your country use English in their work?*
❍ ________________

7 ● *Do you think you will use your English in the next year?*
❍ ________________

8 ● *Will you travel abroad in the next year?*
❍ ________________

9 ● *Have you ever been to Britain or the USA?*
❍ ________________

10 ● *Would you like to visit an English-speaking country?*
❍ ________________

27 Indirect forms

Could you tell me what time it is?

FORMS

What time is it? →	*Could you tell me what time it is?*
Is there a bank? →	*Do you know if there is a bank?*
Where does she live? →	*Do you have any idea where she lives?*
Did he go home? →	*Can you tell me if he went home?*

Indirect questions are a polite form, and we often use them to ask for information or opinions. There are several common ways of starting indirect questions.

Could you tell me ...? *Do you know ...?*
Do you have any idea ...? *Can you tell me ...?*

تعتبر الاسئلة غير المباشرة اسلوباً متأدباً في اللغة وغالباً ما تستخدم بغرض الوصول الى معلومات او آراء. وهناك العديد من الطرق الشائعة لبدء هذا النوع من الاسئلة.

A *Wh* question continues like this.

*Could you tell me **what** (or **when**, **where**, **why**, **how**, etc) ...?*

ويجري طرح السؤال الذي يبدأ بأداة استفهام في هذا السياق كما هو مبين.

A *Yes/No* question continues like this.

*Do you know **if** (or **whether**) ...?*

كما يجري طرح السؤال الذي يجاب عنه بِـ «نعم» أو «لا»، كما هو مبين.

The following subjects and verbs are not in question form. They are like subjects and verbs in a statement.

*Could you tell me what time **it is**?* *Do you know if **he went**?*

الفاعل والفعل فيما يلي، ليسا في صيغة السؤال، بل مثل الفعل والفاعل في الجملة الخبرية.

Be careful about *do*, *does* and *did*. We use them in ordinary present simple and past simple questions, but not in indirect questions.

*What time **does** the bank **close**?* → *Could you tell me what time the bank **closes**?*
***Did** the bank **close** at 4.30?* → *Can you tell me if the bank **closed** at 4.30?*

وتجدر الملاحظة بان استخدام do وdoes وdid يكون في الاسئلة العادية في زمني المضارع البسيط والماضي البسيط ولكن ليس في الاسئلة غير المباشرة.

We can use indirect forms in statements too.

I know/don't know	*what time it is.*
I can/can't tell you	*when the bank closes.*
I've no idea	*if the bank opens late.*
I wonder	*whether it's open now.*

يمكن استخدام صيغ الاسئلة غير المباشرة مع الجمل الخبرية ايضاً.

Indirect forms are similar to reported forms. (See Unit 47.)

***Where can I get** some stamps?* → ***Do you know where I can get** some stamps?* OR ***He wants to know where he can get** some stamps.*

وتشبه صيغ الاسئلة غير المباشرة صيغ الكلام غير المباشر (انظر unit 47).

We often use the form *Do you think ...?* to ask for an opinion.

***Is it** going to rain?* → ***Do you think it is** going to rain?*

غالباً ما تستخدم صيغة ?...Do you think للاستفسار عن وجهة نظر ما.

A *Yes/No* question does not take *if* or *whether*.

***Do you think she went** home?* ***Do you think she was** angry?*

ولا تتطلب الاسئلة التي يجاب عنها بِـ «نعم» أو «لا»، استخدام if او whether.

The question word is at the beginning in a *Wh* question.

***Where** do you think she went?*
***How long** do you think he'll stay?*

وتستخدم اداة الاستفهام في بداية الجملة الاستفهامية التي تبدأ بها.

Exercises

1 Write indirect questions with *Wh* forms.

Example: *What time is it? Can you tell me?*
Can you tell me what time it is?

1 *What date is it today? Do you know?*

2 *When is Ann coming home? Could you tell me?*

3 *Why has Tom gone? Do you have any idea?*

4 *How long will you be away? Can you say?*

5 *Where have they gone? Can you tell me?*

2 Write indirect questions with *Yes/No* forms.

Example: *Is the shop open? Can you tell me?*
Can you tell me if/whether the shop is open?

1 *Have they had lunch? Do you know?*

2 *Will you be home tonight? Can you say?*

3 *Are the team going to win? Do you have any idea?*

4 *Are we having a test this week? Can you tell us?*

3 Write indirect questions with *do/did* forms.

Example: *Did they leave at 1.00? Do you know?*
Do you know if/whether they left at 1.00?

1 *Does Tom go to school? Can you tell me?*

2 *Did the ring cost a lot? Can you say?*

3 *Do they play tennis? Do you have any idea?*

4 *When did the bus go? Could you tell us?*

5 *How does the engine work? Do you know?*

6 *Where do they always go? Can you tell me?*

4 Write indirect questions with ... *do/Do you think ...* ?

Examples: *Will it rain?*
Do you think it'll rain?
When did he go?
When do you think he went?

1 *Why does he arrive late?*

2 *Are they going to finish today?*

3 *How far did they walk?*

4 *Have we made a mistake?*

5 *Where will you live when you go to college?*

28 So and Neither/Nor so and not

So am I. Neither/Nor do I. I think so. I'm afraid not.

FORMS

So and Neither/Nor

Positive	Negative
● *I'm thirsty.*	● *I don't understand.*
❍ *So am I.*	❍ *Neither/Nor do I.*

so* and *not

Positive	Negative
● *Is there any milk?*	● *Do you understand?*
❍ *I think so.*	❍ *I'm afraid not.*

So and *Neither/Nor*

So follows a positive statement. *Neither* or *Nor* follow a negative statement.

- ● *I'm hungry.* ❍ ***So** am I.*
- ● *I'm not hungry.* ❍ ***Neither/Nor** am I.*

تبع كلمة so جملة خبرية مثبتة، أما neither او nor يتبعان جملة خبرية منفية.

The next word is a verb. It matches the verb in the first statement. It may be a form of *be*, *do* or *have*, or it may be a modal verb, eg *can*, *should*, *ought to*.

- ● *I'**m** thirsty.* ❍ *So **am** I.*
- ● *I **can't** do it.* ❍ *Neither **can** we.*

كلمة التي تلي أياً من هذه الكلمات تكون فعلاً يماثل فعل المستخدم في الجملة الخبرية الاولى، ويمكن ان كون احد تصاريف be او do او have او أحد الافعال لساعدة الناقصة مثل can..الخ.

do or *does* follow a positive present simple statement. *did* follows a positive past simple statement.

- ● *She **likes** TV.* ❍ *So **does** he.*
- ● *He **watched** the news.* ❍ *So **did** she.*

تتبع do او does جملة خبرية مثبتة في زمن المضارع لبسيط. في حين تتبع did جملة خبرية مثبتة في زمن لماضي البسيط.

The subject comes after the verb.

*So am **I**. Neither did **we**. So will **they**.*

يأتي الفاعل بعد الفعل.

Use these forms to agree with another speaker's statement. Compare the replies.

● *I often go out on Saturday.*	● *He didn't arrive on time.*
❍ *I often go out on Saturday **too**.*	❍ *We **didn't** arrive on time **either**.*
OR ***So do I**.*	OR ***Neither did we**.*

تستخدم هذه الصيغ للموافقة على ما يقوله المتحدث. يتضح الامر من خلال مقارنة الاجابات المبينة.

so and *not*

You can use *so* after *hope*, *think*, *believe*, *expect*, *suppose*, *guess* and *be afraid*. Verb + *so* shows a positive feeling.

- ● *Is this answer right?* ❍ *I **hope so**.* OR *I **think so**.*

ويمكن استخدام so بعد الأفعال المبينة. ويدلّ استخدام الفعل + so على مشاعر ايجابية.

There are two negative forms – positive + *not* and negative + *so*.

- ● *Perhaps the bus isn't coming.* ❍ *I **guess not**.* OR ***I'm afraid not**.*
- ● *Are you going to be rich?* ❍ *I **don't imagine so**.*

هناك صيغتان للنفي: فعل مثبت + not وفعل منفي + so.

With *believe*, *expect* and *suppose*, we can use either positive + *not* or negative + *so*.

- ● *Is Tom arriving tomorrow?*
- ❍ *I **believe not**.* OR *I **don't believe so**.*

عند استخدام اي من الافعال الثلاثة المبينة يمكن استخدام لصيغة المثبتة متبوعة بـ not او الصيغة المنفية متبوعة بـ so.

Exercises

1 Complete the conversation. Use *So* ... or *Neither/Nor* ...

Two people on a train journey are talking.

Examples: Tony: *I'm travelling to Glasgow.*
Nick: So am I.
Tony: *I don't like long journeys much.*
Nick: Neither/Nor do I.

Tony: *I don't come from Glasgow.*
Nick: 1____________ . *I'm from London.*
Tony: 2____________ . *I'm going to a meeting.*
Nick: 3____________ *You know, I had to get up at 6.30 this morning to catch this plane.*
Tony: 4____________ . *I didn't enjoy that at all.*
Nick: 5____________ . *I wanted to have the meeting in London.*
Tony: 6____________ . *I couldn't understand why they didn't want a meeting in London?*
Nick: 7____________ . *I was told I had to go to the Head Office in Glasgow.*
Tony: 8____________ *Where's your meeting?*
Nick: *It's at Northern Technical.*
Tony: 9____________ *That's amazing. What time does your meeting start? Mine starts at 10.00.*
Nick: 10____________ *That's even more strange! My meeting is about their new steel pipe project.*
Tony: 11____________ *Tell me, who are you meeting?*
Nick: *Dr Tony Blair.*
Tony: *That's me!*

2 Look at the table. Then complete the statements.

	Ken	Sally	Ted	Claire
Tennis	✗	✗		
Judo	✗			✗
Swimming		✗	✗	
Computer games			✗	✗

Examples: *Ken does judo, and* so does Sally.
Ted can't play tennis, and neither/nor can Claire.

1 *Sally isn't interested in judo, and* ____________
2 *Ken is very good at tennis, and* ____________
3 *Ted loves playing computer games, and* ____________
4 *Sally hates computer games, and* ____________
5 *Sally can swim very well, and* ____________
6 *Ken can't swim at all, and* ____________

3 Complete the answers.

Examples: ● *Does the bank open on Saturday morning?*
❍ I think so. *(think) Most big banks do.*
● *I think it's going to snow.*
❍ I hope not. *(hope) I haven't got a coat.*

1 ● *Will Tessa get home late again tonight?*
❍ ____________ *(expect) She usually gets home late.*

2 ● *I think they're going to build the new road.*
❍ ____________ *(suppose) Everybody says they are.*

3 ● *Are you going to wear the blue shirt?*
❍ ____________ *(not/think) I don't like it any more.*

4 ● *Do you think Alex passed her exam?*
❍ ____________ *(be afraid) She didn't do any work.*

5 ● *I don't think Tom is coming.*
❍ ____________ *(guess) He should be here by now.*

6 ● *I wonder if we'll get to the shop in time.*
❍ ____________ *(think) It doesn't close until 6.00.*

29 Modal auxiliary verbs 1

can, could, be able to *can't have, could have, couldn't have*

FORMS

can

The sea is warm now. We can go swimming.
Mary can swim very well.
The child cannot swim.

could* and *be able to

Mary could swim when she was five.
She was able to swim 100 metres when she was six.
The other day a child fell in the sea. He could not swim, but Mary was able to rescue him.

can

Use *can* to express ability and possibility in the present and future. The negative form is one word – *cannot*. The short form is *can't*.

*She **can swim** very well.* *It's warm, so we **can go** swimming.*
*The boy **cannot swim**.* *Help! I **can't swim**.*

ستخدم can للتعبير عن القدرة وعن الاحتمالية في حاضر والمستقبل.. وتنفي في كلمة واحدة cannot تختصر على شكل can't.

could

Use *could* to express ability and possibility in the past.

*She **could swim** when she was five.*
*It was warm, so we **could go** swimming.*

ستخدم could للتعبير عن القدرة وعن معنى الاحتمال ي الماضي.

Use *could not (couldn't)* for an impossible action in the past.

*He was underwater. He **couldn't breathe**.*

ستخدم could not (couldn't) للتعبير عن استحالة نوع حدث في الماضي.

Use *could* for an action in the past with these verbs: *feel, hear, see, smell, taste, remember, understand*. (For most other verbs see below.)

*I **could hear** his call for help.* *I **could see** that he needed help.*

ستخدم could مع حدثٍ ما في الماضي مصحوبةً باحد فعال المبينة.

be able to

You can use *be able to* for ability and possibility in the present and past, but it is more formal than *can* and less common.

*She's **able to swim** ten kilometres.*

ستخدم be able to للتعبير عن القدرة ومعنى حتمال في زمني المضارع والماضي ولكنها تعتبر اكثر سمية من can واقل شيوعاً.

Use *be able to* instead of *can* in the present perfect.

*I've had some free time, so **I've been able to write** some letters.*

ستخدم be able to عوضاً عن can مع زمن المضارع ام.

Use *be able to* instead of *could* for a past action with most verbs.

*We had some free time, so we **were able to look** round town.*

ستخدم be able to عوضاً عن could مع معظم فعال في الماضي.

can't have, could have and *couldn't have*

Use *can't have* or *couldn't have* when something was impossible in the past. (See also Unit 34.)

*He **can't/couldn't have been** in Tokyo yesterday. I saw him in London.*

ستخدم صيغتا can't have وcouldn't have للتعبير ن استحالة وقوع الحدث في الماضي.

Use *could have* to talk about a missed opportunity in the past.

*You **could have visited** Ann in hospital. Why didn't you?*

ستخدم could have للتعبير عن ضياع فرصة كانية عمل شيء ما في الماضي.

We often use *could have* when something was possible in the past.

*The thief **could have entered** through the door or the kitchen window. We don't know which.*

الباً ما تستخدم could have عند توفر إمكانية القيام مل ما في الماضي.

Exercises

1 Complete the statements. Use *can* or *can't* and these verbs.

catch, go, hear, see, walk

Example: *Please speak up. I* can't hear *very well.*

1 *I* ________ *Lucy now. Look!*

2 *I've finished, so I* ________ *home.*

3 *Tim is only a baby. He* ________ *yet.*

4 *You* ________ *me! I'm too fast for you.*

2 Complete the statements. Use *can/can't* or *could/couldn't*.

Example: *I* can *speak French well now, but I* couldn't *speak it at all five years ago.*

1 *Poor old Mr Black* ________ *play football now, but he* ________ *play well when he was young.*

2 *Sally* ________ *read now, but she* ________ *read at all when she was five.*

3 *I* ________ *understand the game last time, and I still* ________ *understand now. It's very difficult.*

4 *Fifty years ago, you* ________ *buy a house for £500, but you certainly* ________ *do that now.*

3 Complete the statements. Use *could* and choose from these verbs.

feel, hear, remember, see, smell, taste, understand

Example: *I woke up suddenly. I* could smell *something burning downstairs.*

1 *The waterfall was huge. You* ________ *the noise a kilometre away.*

2 *I thought about the girl. I* ________ *her face, but not her name.*

3 *Ann* ________ *the words, but she still wasn't sure what the French girl wanted.*

4 *I* ________ *the rain running down my neck. It was horrible.*

4 Complete the statements. Use *could* or *be able to*. Use *could* where possible.

Example: *The door was open, so we* were able to *go straight in.*

1 *Lucy* ________ *hear somebody outside.*

2 *Lisa* ________ *read when she was four.*

3 *The police* ________ *stop the two men.*

4 *The plane crashed, but the pilot* ________ *get out.*

5 *Dan* ________ *see the mountains 20 kilometres away.*

5 Complete the story. Use *can/can't* or *could/couldn't* or *be able to*.

Luckily, we were able to *hire a four-wheel drive vehicle quite easily. Next day we started early, and we* [1] ________ *travel fast across the open country. Later we climbed into the hills and stopped for a rest. From there, we* [2] ________ *look back across the flat land to the city. Maria pointed. 'Look, Rod,' she said. 'You* [3] ________ *still see the castle.' Rod looked, but he wasn't wearing his glasses and he* [4] ________ *see it. 'Let's go,' I said. 'If we hurry, we may* [5] ________ *reach the valley by 6.00. Later we ran into some deep mud. 'It's no good,' I said. 'We* [6] ________ *go forward or back.' Then we got out and pushed. In the end we* [7] ________ *move the vehicle, but we were covered in mud. Rod and I looked at ourselves and laughed, but Maria was upset. She* [8] ________ *see what was funny at all.*

6 Complete the statements. Use *can't have* or *could have*.

Example: *Peter* can't have *bought a car. He hasn't got any money.*

1 *You* ________ *finished already. Nobody can work as fast as that.*

2 *Lucy* ________ *gone to the party, but she decided to stay at home.*

3 *Ed* ________ *been at the restaurant because I was there and I didn't see him.*

4 *We don't know how Steve went, but he* ________ *by train or bus.*

30 Modal auxiliary verbs 2

can, could, would, may

FORMS

can, could, would* and *may

Bob, can you answer the phone for me?
Could you meet me at 4.00, please?
Miss Evans, would you book me a flight to New York, please?
Can I use your pen, Ann?
May I speak to Mr Evans, please?
● *Could I borrow the car tonight, Dad?*
❍ *Yes, of course you can. You can have the car keys now. Here you are.*

Can/Could/Would you ...?

Use these verbs for requesting + 2nd or 3rd person.

ستخدم هذه الافعال لصيغة الطلب + ضمير المخاطب او
فرد الغائب.

***Can you help** me for a moment?* (informal)
***Could you give** me your name, please, Sir?* (polite/formal)
***Would guests kindly leave** their rooms by midday?* (more formal)

Can/Could/May I ...?

Use these verbs for requesting + 1st person.

ستخدم هذه الافعال لصيغة الطلب + ضمير المتكلم.

***Can I borrow** your pen for a second?* (informal)
***Could I have** your phone number, Sir?* (polite/formal)
*Ladies and gentlemen, **may I have** your attention, please?* (more formal)

Yes, you can/may.

ستخدم هذه الافعال للتعبير عن منح الاذن.

Use these verbs for permission.

● *Could I borrow some money, Sam?*
❍ ***Yes**, of course **you can**. How much?* (informal/formal)
● *Could I talk to the King, please?* ❍ ***Yes. You may see** him at 10.00 tomorrow.* (very formal/old-fashioned)

ند الرفض لا نستخدم عادة نفي can او may.

When we refuse permission, we do not usually use the negative of *can* or *may*.

● *Can I borrow your jacket tonight?*
❍ ***No, I'm sorry**. I need it tonight.*

عند استخدام صيغة النفي cannot (can't) او may not
انها تدل على الرفض الشديد.

If we use *cannot (can't)* or *may not*, it shows very strong feeling.

● *Dad, could I have this week off school?*
❍ *No, **you certainly can't**!* OR *No, **you most certainly may not**!*

can/may

Use these verbs for offering.

ستخدم الافعال المبينة لعرض شيء على الآخرين.

***You can ride** my bike if you want.* (informal)
***Can I help** you, Mr Hill?* (informal)
*Good morning, Barclays Bank. How **may we help** you?* (more formal)
***Regular customers may open** a monthly account if they wish.* (more formal)

Exercises

1 Complete the requests with suitable modal verbs.

Example: You're speaking to an old friend.
Ed, can you pass the dictionary?

1 You're speaking to an old friend.
Ed, ___________ you tell me what this means?

2 You're speaking to a foreign visitor at your firm.
___________ you come with me, Mr Hoffman?

3 A stewardess is speaking to the passengers.
___________ all passengers kindly return to their seats?

4 You're speaking to an old friend.
Jim, ___________ I use your bike for ten minutes?

5 You're speaking to a foreign visitor at your firm.
___________ I have your name, Sir?

6 A stewardess is speaking to a passenger.
___________ I take your cup, if you've finished?

2 Complete the requests with suitable modal verbs.

Example: A stewardess wants all passengers to fasten their seat belts.
Would all passengers kindly fasten their seat belts?

1 You want to borrow your friend's book.

____

2 You want your friend to lend you his pen.

____

3 You want to know the company visitor's address.

____

4 You want the company visitor to take a seat for a moment.

____

5 A stewardess wants to put a passenger's bag away.

____

6 A stewardess wants all passengers to remain in their seats until the plane stops.

____
____
____

3 Write the answers. Use *Yes, you can ...* or *No, you can't ...*

Example: ● *Can I turn right here?*
❍ *No, you can't turn right here. It says NO ENTRY.*

1 ● *Can I go now?*
❍ ___________________________ *The lights are green.*

2 ● *Can I park here?*
❍ ___________________________ *It says NO PARKING.*

3 ● *Can I pass this bus?*
❍ ___________________________
There are no cars coming.

4 ● *Can I turn round here?*
❍ ___________________________
It's dangerous.

4 Complete the conversation. Use suitable modal forms for requesting, permitting and offering.

Simon Bell has brought a German businessman, Franz Hoffman, home for dinner.

Simon: *Come in, Franz. Can I take your coat for you?*
Franz: *Thanks very much.*
Simon: *Now, [1]___________ you like to meet the family?*
Franz: *Please.*
Simon: *This is my wife, Carol, and these are the children– Luke and Lisa.*
Carol: *It's nice to meet you Mr Hoffman.*
Franz: *And it's very good to meet you too. But one thing. [2]___________ you just call me Franz?*
Carol: *Yes, of course. Now [3]___________ you all come and eat? Dinner's getting cold.*

Ten minutes later

Simon: *[4]___________ you pass the salt, please?*
Carol: *Yes, of course. Here you are.*
Lisa: *Dad, [5]___________ you help me with my German homework after dinner?*
Simon: *No, I [6]___________ My German isn't very good.*

31 Modal auxiliary verbs 3

should, ought to, had better *should have, ought to have*

FORMS

should
She should stop now.
She should not go on.

ought to
She ought to go to bed.
She ought not to stay up.

had better
She had better put her books away.
She had better not study any more.

should and *ought to*

These are nearly the same, but *ought to* is a little stronger and more formal. Use *should* and *ought to* for advising the right thing to do in a particular situation.

> *That hat looks terrible, Tom! You* ***should try*** *this one.*
> *You look very ill, Mr Jones. I think you* ***ought to see*** *the doctor.*

ناك تشابه كبير في استخدام الصيغتين، الا ان ought t تعتبر اكثر قوة ورسمية. وتستخدم الصيغتان لتقديم نصح في مواقف معينة.

Also use *should not (shouldn't)* and *ought not to (oughtn't to)* for advising what not to do.

> *You* ***shouldn't wear*** *those shoes, Tom. They're not very nice.*
> *You* ***oughtn't to work*** *today. Really! Please go and see the doctor.*

ستخدم الصيغتان ايضاً في صيغة النفي وذلك للنهي ن القيام بعملٍ ما.

Use *should* and *ought to* for saying what is always the right or wrong thing to do.

> *Parents* ***should teach*** *their children to be polite.*
> *People* ***oughtn't to play*** *loud music at night.*

ستخدم should و ought to للتعبير عن عمل يتصف ئماً بالصواب او الخطأ.

Use *should* and *ought to* for saying what is wrong and what is necessary.

> *Excuse me. The bill* ***shouldn't be*** *£5.50. It* ***ought to be*** *£3.70.*

ستخدم should وought to للتعبير عن الشيء الخطأ كذلك عن الشيء الضروري.

had better

had better ('d better) is like *should* and *ought to* (first use) for advising the right thing to do in a particular situation.

> *That hat looks terrible, Tom! You'****d better try*** *this one.*
> *You look very ill, Mr Jones. I think you'****d better see*** *a doctor.*

يشبه استخدام had better ('d better) استخدام should و ought to الاول وذلك بغرض تقديم النصح ي ما يجب عمله في مواقف معينة.

Also use *had better not ('d better not)* for advising what not to do.

> *You'****d better not wear*** *those shoes.* *You'****d better not work*** *today.*

تستخدم had better not او اختصارها، للنهي عن قيام بعمل ما.

You cannot use *had better* for the other uses of *should* and *ought to.* But *had better* can be much stronger than *should* or *ought to.* It can be a threat.

> *You'****d better work*** *a lot harder, or you're going to lose your job!*
> *You'****d better not say*** *that again, or I'll be angry!*

يمكن استخدام had better مثل الاستخدامات الاخرى should او لـ ought to ولكن had better يمكن ان تكون قوى منهما. وقد يفيد استخدام had better مفهوم تهديد.

should (not) have and *ought (not) to have*

Use these past forms when somebody did the wrong thing.

> *Tom crashed the car. He* ***shouldn't have driven*** *so fast.* OR *He* ***should have driven*** *more slowly.*
> *Susie has broken all the plates. She* ***ought to have been*** *more careful.* OR *She* ***oughtn't to have carried*** *so many.*

ستخدم صيغة الماضي should (not) وought (not) ند قيام شخص ما بعمل خطأ.

Exercises

1 Complete the conversation. Use *should* or *ought*.

Eve and Sam are getting ready for a party.

Eve: *What time* should *we go?*

Sam: *We* ought *to leave here at 7.30. And it's 6.30 now, so we* 1__________ *to hurry now. What do you think I* 2__________ *wear?*

Eve: *I think you* 3__________ *to wear a jacket and tie. Do you think I* 4__________ *wear my red dress?*

Sam: *Yes, you* 5__________ *It looks very good.*

2 Complete the conversation. Use *should/shouldn't* or *ought/oughtn't*.

Tina and Steve are going to visit his parents.

Tina: *Do you think we* should *go by train?*

Steve: *No, we* oughtn't *to do that. We'll have too much to carry. We* 1__________ *to go by car.*

Tina: *Well, OK, but we* 2__________ *to take too much. We're only going for two days.*

Steve: *All right, but I think we* 3__________ *take some warm clothes. The weather may be cold. And* 4__________ *we to take some toys for the children? They may be bored.*

Tina: *No, we* 5__________ *do that. I think we* 6__________ *just take one or two books for them to read. Now what time do you think we* 7__________ *leave?*

Steve: *Well, it takes five hours by car, so we* 8__________ *to leave here after 2.00.*

3 Complete the statements. Use *had better* or *had better not*.

Example: *You* 'd better not *play with those matches. They're dangerous.*

1 *You look ill. You* __________ *see a doctor.*

2 *Ed has got a lot of homework to do. He* __________ *go out this evening.*

3 *We've only got a little food. We* __________ *waste it.*

4 *The children are tired. They* __________ *go to bed.*

4 Give advice.

Example: ● *I'm overweight. (should/not/eat/so much)*
❍ You shouldn't eat so much.

1 ● *I'm unfit. (ought/do/more exercise)*
❍ __________

2 ● *I've got a bad toothache. (better/see/a dentist)*
❍ __________

3 ● *I've got a lot of work to do. (should/not/watch/TV/so much)*
❍ __________

4 ● *I've got a huge phone bill. (ought/not/use/the phone/so much)*
❍ __________

5 ● *It's still raining. (better/not/go out/yet)*
❍ __________

6 ● *It's nice and sunny now. (should/go/to the beach)*
❍ __________

5 Write the replies.

Example: ● *Andy felt really ill this morning. (ought/not/go/to work)*
❍ He oughtn't to have gone to work.

1 ● *Tim was ill this morning. (should/go/to the doctor)*
❍ __________

2 ● *The boys got wet in the rain. (should/not/play/outside)*
❍ __________

3 ● *We're on the wrong road. (ought/turn/left/the traffic lights)*
❍ __________

4 ● *Maria doesn't like her new jacket. (ought/not/buy/it)*
❍ __________

32 Modal auxiliary verbs 4

must, have to

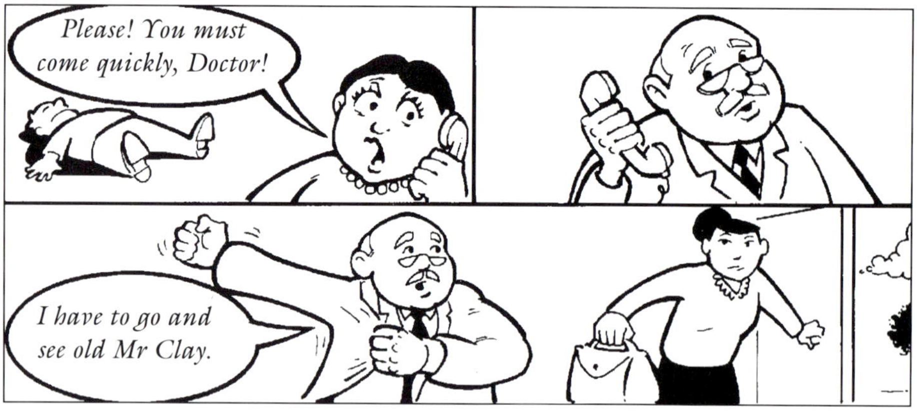

FORMS

must

You must help my husband! Please!
Stop those boys! They must not play with that knife!

have to

Dr Bell often has to visit people.
I have to go now.
He had to visit Mr Clay last night.

We use *must* and *have to* for saying something is necessary now or very soon.

*It's late. You **must stop** work and **go** to bed now, Tom.*
● ***Must** you **drive** so fast?*
❍ *Yes, or we'll miss the plane.*
*He **has to start** work at 8.00 tomorrow.*
*I **have to go**. My boss is calling me.*

تستخدم must او have to للقول بان شيئاً ما ضروري الآن او في اسرع وقت.

Use *have to* for other times. (*have to* has tenses, but *must* does not.)

● *Did you **have to work** late?* ❍ *Yes, we **had to stay** until midnight!*
● *Has Ann **had to go** to hospital?* ❍ *Yes, she has. She's very ill.*
*We can't finish now. We'**ll have to come back** next week.*

وتستخدم have to للتعبير عن ظروف اخرى. وتجدر الملاحظة ان have to تُصرّف حسب الازمنة ولكن must لا تُصرّف.

We often use *have got to* instead of *have to*. Use *have got to* in conversation. Use it for saying something is necessary now or very soon.

*I'**ve got to go** or Dad will be angry.*
● ***Have** we **got to do** all this?*
❍ *Yes, you **have**. It's part of the job.*

غالباً ما تستخدم صيغة have got to بديلاً من have to. وتستخدم have got to اثناء المحادثة وذلك للدلالة على ان شيئاً ما ضروريٌ الآن، او في القريب العاجل.

CROSSCHECK

must

Use *must* when the speaker feels a strong need inside.

*Quick! We **must run** for the bus!*
*You **must come** quickly, Doctor!*

have to

Use *have to* when the speaker expresses a need from outside, eg from a boss or teacher or parent.

*I **have to go** and **see** old Mr Clay.*
*I **have to do** some Maths for Mr Davis.*

تستخدم must عندما يشعر المتحدث ' بحاجة داخلية ملحة. وتستخدم have to عندما يعبر المتحدث عن حاجة خارجة عن نطاقه (من قبل رئيس او مدرس او والد).

must not

Use *must not* for necessity not to do something. Use the short form *mustn't* in conversation. (Do not pronounce the *t* in the middle.)

*Stop! You **mustn't drink** that! It'll make you ill.*

We often use *can't* like *mustn't*.

*You **can't hold** the ball. It's against the rules.*

not have to

Use *not have to* for no necessity to do something. (See Unit 33 for information on *didn't need to* and *didn't have to*.)

*You **don't have to take** the exam if you don't want to.*

تستخدم must not للتعبير عن ضرورة عدم القيام بعمل ما. وتستخدم الصيغة المختصرة mustn't اثناء الحوار والنقاش (حرف t الواقع في وسطها لا يُنطق)

وتستخدم not have to عند عدم وجود ضرورة للقيام بعمل ما. (انظر unit 33 لمعلومات حول didn't need to و if you don't want to).

غالباً ما تستخدم can't مثل استخدام mustn't.

Exercises

1 Complete the questions with *have to*.

Example: *Paul has had to buy a car.*
Why has Paul had to buy a car?

1 *Paul has had to pay a lot of money for it.*
How much ________________________________

2 *Emma will have to go to London soon.*
When ________________________________

3 *The Smith family had to go last week.*
Where ________________________________

4 *Ann has to change all her plans.*
Why ________________________________

5 *Ed and Sue have had to live in the flat for years.*
How long ________________________________

2 Complete the statements. Use *must* or *have to*.

Examples: *He said, 'You must finish by 5.00, Ann.'*
So Ann has to finish by 5.00.
The children have to go to bed now.
Mum said, 'You must go to bed now, children.*'*

1 *Old Mr Robbins has to rest for a week.*
The doctor said, 'You ________________________________

2 *The bill says they must pay immediately.*
So they ________________________________

3 *We have to check in one hour before the flight.*
The air tickets say: 'Passengers ________________________________

4 *The hotel sign says: 'All guests must complete a registration form.'*
So all guests ________________________________

5 *Jimmy has to be home by 6.00.*
His mother said, 'You ________________________________

6 *The policeman said, 'You must go to the police station, Mr Reece.'*
So Mr Reece ________________________________

3 Complete the statements. Use *must* or *have to*.

Examples: *We* had to *work all day yesterday.*
The fireman said, 'Quick! You must *leave the building immediately.'*

1 *I* __________ *read Ian York's new book. I love his writing.*

2 *Alan* __________ *go to the shop for some milk. Do you want anything?*

3 *You* __________ *listen to what I tell you. It's very important.*

4 *Last week we* __________ *wait for hours at the airport because of bad weather.*

5 *We really* __________ *buy a new TV. This old one is terrible.*

6 *Our new trainer is tough. We* __________ *run ten kilometres every morning.*

7 *This job looks interesting. I* __________ *ask for an application form.*

4 Complete the statements. Use *mustn't* or *not have to*.

Examples: *You* don't have to *buy a new pen. You can use mine.*
Bob mustn't *go out. He's ill.*

1 *You* ____________________ *be late or you won't get into the cinema.*

2 *Students* ____________________ *wear a uniform at this school.*

3 *You* ____________________ *talk like that. It's rude.*

4 *I* ____________________ *be late home. I've got a lot of homework to do.*

5 *Ruth* ____________________ *go to work tomorrow. She's on holiday.*

6 *I* ____________________ *eat it if I don't want to.*

33 Modal auxiliary verbs 5

needn't, mustn't, didn't need to, needn't have

FORMS

needn't* and *mustn't

We needn't buy any food. We've got lots.
I mustn't forget his phone number. I have to phone him tonight.
She doesn't need to do any housework. She's got a maid.

didn't need to* and *needn't have

I didn't need to buy any meat as there was some in the fridge.
I needn't have gone to the meeting. Nobody else was there!

CROSSCHECK

needn't

Use *need to* (or *have to*) for saying something is necessary.

*Come on! We **need to hurry**.*

Use *need not* (or *not need to/not have to)* for no necessity to do something.

*We **needn't go** to the cinema to see it. We can get the video.*
*We **don't need to buy** the video. We can rent it.*
*We **don't have to rent** it. We can borrow it from Peter.*

mustn't

Use *must* for saying something is necessary.

*We **must get** there by 11.00.*

Use *mustn't* for necessity not to do something.

*You **mustn't play** with that knife. You'll cut yourself.*
*You **mustn't cross** the road when the lights are red.*

didn't need to

Use *didn't need to* (or *didn't have to*) + infinitive when something was not necessary.

*She's very clever, so she **didn't need to work** for the test.*

didn't need to (or *didn't have to*) usually means that an action was not necessary, so it did not happen.

*Tom **didn't need to arrive** until 8.00, but he was there at 7.00. He likes being early.*

But we can use it when an action was not necessary, but it still happened – like *needn't have*.

*You **didn't have to pay** him any money. He was happy to work for nothing.*

needn't have

Use *needn't have* + past participle when something happened, but it was not necessary.

*Poor Sam **needn't have worked** so hard for the test. It was cancelled!*

تستخدم need to (أو have to) للقول بان شيئاً ما ضروري.

وتستخدم must للتعبير عن ضرورة القيام بعملٍ ما ايضاً.

تستخدم need not او not need to او not have to عند انتفاء ضرورة القيام بعمل ما.

وتستخدم mustn't للتعبير عن ضرورة عدم القيام بعمل ما.

تستخدم didn't need to (أو didn't have to) + مصدر عند التعبير عن ان القيام بعمل لم يكن ضرورياً.

وتستخدم needn't have + التصريف الثالث للفعل للتعبير عن حدث حصل ولكنه لم يكن ضرورياً.

يعني استخدام didn't need to (او didn't have to) عادةً ان القيام بعملٍ مّا لم يكن ضرورياً، ولهذا فهو لم يحصل.

ولكن يمكن ان تُستخدم ايضاً للتعبير عن ان القيام بعملٍ ما لم يكن ضرورياً ولكنه حدث رغم ذلك.

Exercises

1 Complete the statements. Use *needn't* or *mustn't*.

Examples: *We* needn't *hurry. We've got lots of time.*
We mustn't *swim here. It's dangerous.*

1 *Don't you like it? Well, you* ________ *drink it if you don't want to.*

2 *Listen! You* ________ *be late again or you'll be in bad trouble.*

3 *You* ________ *make so much noise. This is a library.*

4 *You* ________ *finish the report today, but please can I have it tomorrow?*

5 *Children* ________ *play with knives. They're dangerous things.*

6 *Ann* ________ *stay. Carol can do everything.*

2 Re-order the words to make positive and negative statements and questions.

Examples: *(there/he/go/to/have/doesn't)*
He doesn't have to go there.
(need/what/buy/we/do/to)
What do we need to buy?

1 *(work/to/I/late/have)*
____

2 *(they/go/to/where/have/do)*
____

3 *(she/need/go/does/to/so soon)*
____

4 *(tomorrow/you/do/to/have/work)*
____

5 *(need/I/homework/don't/do/my/to)*
____

6 *(learn/why/to/they/French/do/need)*
____

3 Complete the conversation. Use *need to*, *needn't* or *mustn't*.

Neil is telling his parents about his school trip to France.

Neil: *On the day we go I* need to *be at school at 7.45. The bus goes at 8.00.*

Mum: *What clothes do you* need to *take with you?* 1 ________ *wear your school uniform? (you)*

Neil: *No, we* 2 ________ *do that. We can wear our ordinary clothes. We also* 3 ________ *take clothes for outdoor activities – jeans, boots and anoraks. You* 4 ________ *look at this list of clothes and equipment and this letter from school.*

Dad: *How much is it going to cost?*

Neil: *It's £200, but you* 5 ________ *pay it all yet. The letter says you only* 6 ________ *pay half now.*

Dad: *Good. We* 7 ________ *spend too much now because we haven't got much money this month. How soon* 8 ________ *give the school the first £100? (we)*

Neil: *I* 9 ________ *take it by next weekend.*

Mum: *It sounds great fun.*

Neil: *Yes, but they've made a special rule. As soon as we get on the bus we* 10 ________ *speak English any more. We can only speak French for a whole week!*

4 Complete the statements. Use *didn't need to* or *needn't have*.

Examples: *I* needn't have *gone to the meeting. Nobody else was there.*
Yesterday was a holiday, so I didn't need to *go to work.*

1 *At my school we* ________ *wear a uniform. People just wore their ordinary clothes.*

2 *They* ________ *worked so hard. Nobody even noticed all the work they did.*

3 *We* ________ *hurried. Everybody else was late too.*

4 *Sally* ________ *buy a coat. Her brother gave her a very nice one.*

5 *I* ________ *send the money. Mr Brant came for it.*

6 *You* ________ *written to them. I'd already told them your answer.*

34 Modal auxiliary verbs 6

may, might, could, may be, must be, can't be, may have, must have, can't have

FORMS

may, might* and *could

It may/might rain. There are some clouds over there.
It could snow, but it seems unlikely.

may be, must be* and *can't be

He can't be at home. Nobody is answering the phone.
He must be at work.

may have, must have* and *can't have

Tom can't have made enough money to buy that car.
His father must have given it to him.

may, might and *could*

Use *may* or *might* to say something is possible in the future.

*The score is 3-3, so either side **may/might win**.*

تستخدم may او might للقول بان شيئاً ما ممكن في المستقبل.

Use *could* to say something is possible, but not likely.

*The score is 3-1 against City. They **could win**, but I don't think so.*

وتستخدم could للتعبير عن امكانية حدوث شيء ما، ولكن حدوثه امر مستبعد.

may not and *might not* mean something negative is possible.

*I'm very busy, so I **may not/might not have** time to go to the match.*

ويعني استخدام may not و might not وجود احتمال بنفي شيء ما.

cannot (can't) and *could not (couldn't)* mean something negative is impossible.

*City **can't/couldn't win** against Rangers. Rangers are too good.*

ويعني استخدام cannot (can't) و could not (couldn't) أستحالة حدوث شيء سلبي.

may be, might be, must be and *can't be*

Use *may be* or *might be* when something is not certain in the present.

*Bill isn't in his office. He **may be** in Room 303, or he **might be seeing** Mr Bell.*

تستخدم may be او might be عندما يكون الامر غير مؤكد في الوقت الراهن.

must be and *can't be* are opposites. Use them when something is certain in the present. *must be* means certain (negative).

*Look at that car! It **must be doing** 250 kph. The driver **must be** crazy.*
*This boy says he's 16, but he looks so young. He **can't be telling** the truth. He **can't be** more than 14.*

تأتي must be لتعني عكس can't be، ويستخدمان عندما يكون الامر مؤكداً في الوقت الراهن. ويفيد استخدام must be التأكد (السلبي).

may have, must have and *can't have*

Use these (and *might have* or *could have*) when something is certain or uncertain in the past.

*Jerry **must have left** his bag somewhere because he hasn't got it now.*
*He **can't have left** it at school because he's checked and it isn't there.*
*He **may have left** it somewhere on the way home.*

تستخدم هذه الصيغ (أضافة الى might have او could have) عندما يكون شيءٌ ما مؤكداً او غير مؤكد في الماضي.

Exercises

1 Complete the statements. Use *may (not)/ might (not)*.

Example: *We're very late for the plane. We* may/might *miss it.*

1 *I ______ be late home tonight, so don't worry if I'm not back at the usual time.*

2 *Dr Jones ______ have time to see you, but I don't think so. Ask his secretary.*

3 *If we go on playing this badly, we ______ win the game.*

4 *I ______ catch the 9.00 train, but I'll probably get the one at 9.30.*

5 *We ______ have enough milk. Could you buy some, please?*

6 *I'll try and get a green sweater in town, but I ______ be able to find one.*

2 Write statements. Use *may (not) be/might (not) be, must be* or *can't be.*

Examples: ● *Do you know where Paul is?*

❍ *(It's late, so he isn't at school.)*
He can't be at school.

● *(Perhaps he's at home.)*
He may/might be at home.

❍ *(He's always with his friends in the evening.)*
He must be with his friends.

1 ● *How old do you think Mr Lee is?*

❍ *(I'm sure he isn't under 60.)*

______

● *(Perhaps he's about 64 or 65.)*

______

❍ *(I know he's 65 because he's just retired from work.)*

______

______

2 ● *Is that Rod coming across the beach.*

❍ *(I'm sure it's Julian because that looks like his jacket.)*

______

______

● *(Perhaps it isn't him. He's walking towards some other people.)*

______

______

❍ *(I'm sure it isn't Rod. Rod is taller.)*

______

3 Complete the conversation. Use *may be/ might be, must be* or *can't be* + present participle.

? = may be/might be, ✓ *= must be,* ✗ *= can't be*

Tina: *Do you know what Dave is doing?*

Nick: *I'm not sure. He* may/might be riding *his bike. (? ride)*

Tina: *No, he* [1] ______ *that.* (✗ *do*) *His bike is still in the garage.*

Nick: *Well, he* [2] ______ *upstairs.* (✗ *play*) *The house is too quiet.*

Tina: *Oh, look. His baseball bat has gone. He* [3] ______ *baseball in the park.* (✓ *practise*)

4 Complete the conversation. Use *may have/ might have, must have* or *can't have* + past participle.

? = may have/might have, ✓ *= must have,* ✗ *= can't have*

Dave: *Mum, have you seen my wallet in the dining-room?*

Tina: *No, you* can't have put *it there.* (✗ *put*) *I've just tidied the dining-room and I didn't see it.*

Dave: *And I* [1] ______ *it in the park because I didn't take my money.* (✗ *drop*)

Tina: *You* [2] ______ *it upstairs in your bedroom. (? leave)*

Dave: *I'm not sure.*

Nick: *Wasn't your wallet in your jeans pocket yesterday?*

Tina: *And didn't you throw your jeans in the washing machine this morning?*

Dave: *Oh, so I* [3] ______ *my wallet in the washing machine too.* (✓ *put*) *I'll have to hang my money out to dry!*

35 Modal auxiliary verbs 7: past forms

could, had to, needed to, may have, must have, can't have, could have, etc

FORMS

Grandad: *I could run 100 metres in ten seconds when I was young.*
Grandson: *Wow! You must have been the fastest in the country.*
Grandad: *Yes, I should have been in the Olympic team, but I was ill. I couldn't go.*

could, had to and *needed to*

Use *had to* and *needed to* to talk about past necessity and need. (*must* has no past form.) (See Units 32/33 for more information.)

> *I was late for the meeting. I* ***had to run****.*
> *We* ***needed to get*** *some milk, so I went to the shop.*

تستخدم had to وneeded to للتعبير عن ضرورة وحاجة في الماضي. وتجدر الملاحظة بأنه لا توجد صيغة في الماضي لـ must. (انظر units 32/33 للمزيد من المعلومات).

Use *could* and *could not* to talk about ability and possibility in the past.

> *I* ***could run*** *30 kilometres when I was 20.*
> *He* ***couldn't swim*** *when he was five.*

وتستخدم could و could not للتعبير عن القدرة وعن الامكانية في الماضي.

Use *could not* for an action that did not happen.

> *I was so tired that I* ***couldn't walk*** *any more.*

وتستخدم could not للتعبير عن عمل لم يحدث.

We usually use *be able to* instead of *could* for a past action. But you can use *could* with verbs of feeling (*see, hear,* etc) and thinking (*remember, forget,* etc). (See Unit 29.)

> *After a long sleep, I* ***was able to get up*** *and* ***start*** *walking again.*
> *After a long while I* ***could see*** *a farm ahead of me.*

تستخدم صيغة be able to عادةً عوضاً عن could عند التعبير عن حدث في الماضي. ويمكن استخدام could مع الافعال التي تتعلق بالحواس مثل (see و hear... الخ) وكذلك مع الافعال التي تتعلق بالتفكير مثل (remember و forget). (انظر unit 29).

may have, must have and *can't have*

Use these (and *might have* or *could have*) when something seems certain or uncertain in the past. (See Unit 34 for more information.)

- ● *There's nobody at home. They* ***must have gone out****.*
- ❍ *They* ***may have gone*** *to the beach.*
- ● *No. They* ***can't have done*** *that. Their car is still here.*

تستخدم هذه الصيغ اضافة لـ might have او could have عندما يبدو شيءٌ ما مؤكداً او غير مؤكد في الماضي (انظر unit 34 للمزيد من المعلومات).

could have, should have and *would have*

Use these (and *ought to have* or *might have*) when somebody did something wrongly or differently.

> *You* ***could have called*** *earlier. Why didn't you?*
> *I'm sorry. I can't pay. I* ***should have brought*** *more money.*

وتستخدم هذه الصيغ اضافة الى ought to have او might have عندما يكون الشخص قد اخطأ في عملٍ ما او ان يكون قد اتى بعمل مخالف.

would have is the same form as in Type 3 conditionals. (See Unit 45.) Use these negative forms in the same way: *should not have, ought not to have, would not have, need not have.* (See Units 31/33.)

> *We* ***would have visited*** *you, but we didn't know you were at home.*
> *He* ***shouldn't have shouted*** *at her. Look! She's crying now!*
> *You* ***needn't have gone*** *to town for a newspaper. You can get them near here.*

ان صيغة would have هي نفسها صيغة النوع الثالث من الجمل الشرطية (انظر unit 45) . وتستخدم الصيغ المنفية المبينة بالطريقة نفسها: مثل should not have ... الخ. (انظر units 31/33).

Compare *needn't have* and *didn't need to.*

> *I* ***didn't need to go*** *to work, so I stayed in bed.*

لاحظ الفرق بين صيغتي needn't have و didn't need to.

Exercises

1 Complete the story. Use past forms of *can, be able to, have to, need* or *need to.*

When Larry's boat hit a rock, he didn't need to *look below. He* [1]__________ *hear the water rushing in, and he knew the boat was going down. He also knew he* [2]__________ *get off the boat in two or three minutes. He* [3]__________ *pull out the orange life-raft and he threw it quickly into the water, where it filled with air. Next, he ran to the cabin. He* [4]__________ *collect as many things as possible – food, water medicine, a map, and so on. The only thing he* [5]__________ *take was petrol – the life-raft had no motor. Soon water was coming into the cabin, and he* [6]__________ *get out quickly. He looked round for the raft. He* [7]__________ *see it! Then he did. It was ten metres away. Larry dropped his supplies on top of the cabin and jumped into the sea. He* [8]__________ *get that raft! He reached it, climbed in and started rowing back for his supplies. As he rowed, he* [9]__________ *see the boat sinking. He rowed harder. He* [10]__________ *those supplies as much as the life-raft itself. He* [11]__________ *let those supplies go down with his boat.*

Complete these possible endings.

But he [12]__________ *get there in time. He lost everything.* OR
He got there just in time, and he [13]__________ *save everything.*

2 Complete the conversation. Use *may have* (or *might have/could have*), *must have* or *can't have.*

Bob and Lucy are looking for their son, Joe, at the beach.

Bob: *He* can't have *gone into the water. He's still wearing his T-shirt and shorts.*

Lucy: *And he* [1]__________ *gone to the ice-cream van or the beach shop because he hasn't got any money.*

Bob: *He* [2]__________ *gone to the beach shop just to look around.*

Lucy: *Yes, he* [3]__________ *done that. He was asking me to buy a ball before. He's crazy about volleyball.*

Bob: *Talking about volleyball, there are some people playing volleyball over there, and there are some people watching. He* [4]__________ *gone to watch the game. What do you think?*

Lucy: *You're wrong. He isn't watching. He's playing. He* [5]__________ *gone and asked to join the game.*

3 Complete the conversation. Use *could have, would have ('d have), shouldn't have, should have, wouldn't have* or *needn't have.*

The Green family are coming back from a terrible holiday in the south of France. It rained all the time and it was very cold.

Mum: *Well, nobody* could have *guessed the weather would be so bad.*

Dad: *Yes, if we'd known about the weather, we certainly* [1]__________ *gone there.*

Tim: *We* [2]__________ *taken our raincoats, rubber boots, hats, gloves and scarves.*

Jo: *And I* [3]__________ *bought that new summer dress. I didn't wear it once. I'm so disappointed.*

Dad: *We* [4]__________ *chosen a holiday in Greece as easily as the one in France. It* [5]__________ *been the same price. In fact, I* [6]__________ *chosen Greece except that we can all speak French, but not Greek.*

Mum: *We* [7]__________ *listened to the travel agent. She said the weather was always wonderful in the south of France.*

Dad: *We* [8]__________ *done better to stay at home and save our money.*

Mum: *Well, next year we'll go somewhere else – somewhere warm and dry.*

36 Review: modal auxiliary verbs

can, could, would, be able to, should, ought to, must, have to, etc

Ability (See Unit 29.)

*Most birds **can fly**.*
*Some people **can't swim**.*
*Ann **could write** when she was three.*
*I **was able to finish** the test in an hour.*

Requests, offers and permission (See Unit 30.)

***May I speak** to Mr Hill, please?*
***Could you keep** the noise down, please?*
***Would you post** this for me, please?*
***Would you like** a part-time job?*
● ***May I go** home early today?*
❍ ***Yes**, of course **you can**.*

Advice (See Unit 31.)

*You **shouldn't eat** so much.*
*You **oughtn't to play** computer games so much.*
*You look tired. You**'d better go** home.*

Obligation and necessity (See Unit 32.)

*You **mustn't copy** his work. That's wrong.*
*At my new job I **have to start** at 9.00.*
*I**'ve got to go** now, or my parents will be angry.*
*You **can't walk** on the grass. Look! The notice says: 'Keep off the grass.'*
*If you want a licence, you **need to fill in** this form.*

Non-obligation (See Unit 33.)

You ***needn't do*** *this work now. You can finish it tomorrow.*
We ***didn't have to work*** *at the weekend, but we wanted to help as much as we could.*

Certainty and uncertainty (See Unit 34.)

He ***might come****, but I don't think so.*
She ***definitely will/won't be*** *at the wedding.*
They ***could arrive*** *this evening, but I don't think so.*
He ***can't be*** *at the office. He never works this late.*
He ***must be visiting*** *a friend.*

Past forms of modals (See Unit 35.)

We ***should have gone*** *to school, but we went to the football match.*
You ***oughtn't to have used*** *the money. Now we haven't got any to buy food.*
They ***couldn't stay****. They* ***had to go*** *home.*
Nobody answered the phone, so they ***can't have been*** *at home. They* ***must have been*** *out.*

Exercises

1 Complete the statements and questions. Use *can, can't, could, couldn't* or *be able to*.

Examples: *I'm tired. I* can't *go on any longer.*
At last, we were able to *escape.*

1 *I* ________ *understand the problem.* ________ *you?*

2 *Alex* ________ *already swim when he was three.*

3 *I tried to move, but I* ________

4 *You were near the accident, Mr Jones.* ________ *you see what happened?*

5 *In the end, we* ________________ *save enough money to buy a car last year.*

6 *What happened when he got lost?* ________ ________ *find his way of the woods? (he)*

2 Write requests. (You can often give more than one answer.)

Example: A business caller wants to talk to the manager.
● May I speak to the manager, please?

1 A girl wants to borrow her friend's book.
● ________________________________

2 A shop assistant offers to help a customer.
● ________________________________

3 A manager asks his assistant to get the red file.
● ________________________________

4 Somebody offers a friend a cup of tea.
● ________________________________

5 A receptionist asks a business visitor his name.
● ________________________________

6 Somebody asks a friend to lend him some money.
● ________________________________

7 An office worker asks her boss for a day off next week.
● ________________________________

8 A visitor asks if he can park his car outside the entrance.
● ________________________________
____

3 Give advice. (You can often give more than one answer.)

Examples: ● *I feel ill. (see the doctor)* OR *(not go to work today)*
❍ You'd better see the doctor. OR You oughtn't to go to work today.

1 ● *I've got a terrible toothache. (go to the dentist)*
❍ ________________________________

2 ● *The boys have got a lot of work tonight. (not watch TV)*
❍ ________________________________

3 ● *I can't see very well. (get some glasses)*
❍ ________________________________

4 ● *My brother wants to make more money. (find a better job)*
❍ ________________________________

5 ● *Tom wants a good grade in Maths. (not miss the next test)*
❍ ________________________________

6 ● *Sam wants to play outside, but it's still raining. (not go out yet)*
❍ ________________________________

4 Complete the statements. Use *must, mustn't, have to* or *can't*.

Examples: Mary's new contract: *Employees* must *work 38 hours a week*
Mary to her parents: *I* have to *work 38 hours a week.*

1 Teacher to a new student: *Tony, you* ________ *come late again. You* ________ *always be here on time.*

2 Friend to Tony: *We* ________ *come to school late. If we do, we* ________ *stay behind for an hour after school.*

3 Notice on a beach: *DANGER! Visitors* ________ *remain close to the beach at all times. When the red flag is up, swimmers* ________ *leave the water.*

4 Swimmer to friend: *Look! The red flag is up. That means we* ________ *stay in the water. We* ________ *get out.*

5 Complete the statements. Use the present form *needn't* and the present and past forms of *(not) need to* or *(not) have to.*

Example: *There is a holiday next week, so we* don't have to *come to work.*

1 *You* ____________ *go shopping. I've been already.*

2 *I* ____________ *write a report last month. There was nothing to write about.*

3 *We* ____________ *wear a uniform at work, but the boss always says we* ____________ *dress smartly.*

4 *When I was at school, we* ____________ *wear the school uniform until the last year, but in the last year, we* ____________ *wear the uniform any more.*

5 *I* ____________ *use the car again this week, so you can have it. But I* ____________ *have it again by Monday morning.*

6 ● *How many questions did you* ____________ *answer in the exam?*

❍ *We* ____________ *answer five questions.*

6 Complete the conversation. Choose from *will, won't, could, may (not)* or *might (not).*

Two friends are waiting at the station for another friend, Ted, and for a train.

Tony: *I hope Ted isn't going to be late. The train* will *be here in a minute.*

Lisa: *Don't worry. Ted* 1 ____________ *be here in a minute. He promised.*

Tony: *I don't know. He's often late. He* 2 ____________ *get here, but he* 3 ____________ *Look! The train is coming. It* 4 ____________ *be here in a minute.*

Lisa: *You* 5 ____________ *be right. But he still* 6 ____________ *come. There's still a chance.*

Tony: *No. He* 7 ____________ *get here in time now. It's too late. The train is here.*

Ted: *Hi, Tony. Hi, Lisa. I'm here.*

7 Read Ann Green's diary for today. Then answer her colleague's questions. Use *can't be, may be* or *must be.*

9.00 – 10.30	visit GLA
10.30 – 12.00	travel to Birmingham
12.00 – 1.00	meet Stephen Fisher
1.00 – 2.00	have lunch with Eric Ross at the City Hotel or the Ritz Grill
2.00 – 3.30	travel to Liverpool or Manchester

Examples: ● *What's she doing at the moment?* (It's 9.30.)

❍ *She* must be visiting GLA.

● *Is she in Birmingham now?* (It's 11.15.)

❍ *No, she* can't be in Birmingham. *She* must be travelling there.

1 ● *What's she doing now?* (It's 12.30.)

❍ *She* ____________

2 ● *Where's she having lunch?* (It's 1.15.)

❍ *She* ____________

or she ____________

3 ● *Is she in Birmingham now?* (It's 2.45.)

❍ *No, she* ____________

She ____________

____

8 Complete the statements with past forms. Choose from these modals.

could have, should have, ought to have, would have ('d have), can't have, couldn't have, shouldn't have, oughtn't to have, needn't have.

Examples: *Jean* needn't have *cooked so much. Nobody was very hungry.*

1 *I* ____________ *said thank you, but I forgot.*

2 *They* ____________ *crossed the desert. They had no water.*

3 *You* ____________ *made your little brother cry.*

4 *We* ____________ *taken our coats. It was warm.*

5 *I* ____________ *given you the money if I'd known you needed it.*

37 Passive verb forms 1

Every bike is checked.

FORMS

Statements

I	*am* *am not*	*checked.*
He *She* *It*	*is* *is not*	*checked.*
We *You* *They*	*are* *are not*	*checked.*

***Yes/No* questions**

Am	*I*	*checked?*
Is	*he* *she* *it*	*checked?*
Are	*we* *you* *they*	*checked?*

***Wh* questions**

Where are they checked?
When is it done?

Full answers

They are checked at the factory.
It is done all the time.

Short forms: *I am = I'm* *he is = he's* *we are = we're*
I am not = I'm not *he is not = he isn't, he's not*
we are not = we aren't, we're not *was not = wasn't*
were not = weren't

Form the present simple passive with *am, is, are* + past participle, eg *am checked, is checked* and *are checked.* (See Appendix 1 for a list of common irregular participle forms.)

Active: *Our workers* ***check*** *all the bikes.*
Passive: *All the bikes* ***are checked*** *by our workers.*

Form the past simple passive with *was, were* + past participle eg *was made,* and *were made.*

The first bike ***was made*** *100 years ago.*
The first bikes ***were made*** *100 years ago.*

Form negative passives and passive questions like active sentences.

● ***Are*** *all these cars* ***sold*** *in Europe?*
❍ *No, they* ***aren't****. Some cars* ***are sold*** *in America.*
● *How many* ***are sent*** *to America?* ❍ *About 500 a month.*

Use the passive to focus on the object of an active sentence, eg we are more interested in the cars than who built them – the agent.

The first plane ***was built*** *by somebody nearly 100 years ago.*

You can leave out the agent if it is not important.

The first planes ***were built*** *nearly 100 years ago.*

Sometimes, we use the passive because we do not know the agent.

The wheel ***was invented*** *thousands of years ago.*

We often use the passive in technical English to explain how we do something. (Who does it is not important.)

The engines ***are put*** *together in 85 separate steps.*

We often use the passive in formal English, eg in business agreements.

Under this agreement it ***is understood*** *that both parties* ***are committed*** *to completing the project by 31st December, 1999.*

يتكون المضارع البسيط المبني للمجهول من am أو is أو are، إضافة للتصريف الثالث للفعل، مثلما هو موضح في الأمثلة. (انظر لائحة بصيغ التصريف الثالث للفعل اللاقياسية الشائعة، في الملحق رقم ١).

يتكون الماضي البسيط المبني للمجهول من was أو were إضافة إلى التصريف الثالث للفعل.

تتكوّن الجمل المبنية للمجهول النافية وكذلك الأسئلة المبنية للمجهول مثل الجمل المبنية للمعلوم.

تستخدم صيغة المبني للمجهول للتركيز على المفعول به في الجملة المبنية للمعلوم. ويوضح المثال أن اهتمامنا منصب على السيارة وليس على من صنعها.

ويمكن الاستغناء عن الفاعل عندما لا يضيف شيئاً إلى المعنى.

وأحياناً نستخدم صيغة المبني للمجهول لأن الفاعل غير معروف لدينا.

وغالباً ما تستخدم صيغة المبني للمجهول في المجال التقني لشرح كيفية عمل الأشياء حيث لامجال للاهتمام بالفاعل.

وغالباً ما تستخدم صيغة المبني للمجهول في اللغة الرسمية مثل الاتفاقات التي تتعلق بالأعمال التجارية.

Exercises

1 Write the verbs in the present simple passive.

The European Airbus A320 is built *by a group of European aeroplane makers. (build) The nose of the plane* [1] ________ *by the French. (make) The body of the plane* [2] ________ *by the Germans. (produce) The wings* [3] ________ *by the British. (provide) Then of all the parts* [4] ________ *to one factory in France where the plane* [5] ________ *together. (brought) (put) The finished A320 planes* [6] ________ *to their customers. (deliver)*

2 Write the verbs in the past simple passive.

One of the first flying machines was designed *by Leonardo da Vinci. (design) The first real plane* [1] ________ *by the Wright brothers in 1903. (build) Planes soon became more common, and they* [2] ________ *in World War 1. (use) In 1919 letters* [3] ________ *across the Atlantic for the first time. (fly) Other ways of using planes* [4] ________ *too. (find) Passengers* [5] ________ *on regular flights, also in 1919. (carry) In the same year, the first international passenger flights* [6] ________ *between London and Paris. (begin) Airline services developed fast. In 1925 the first hot meals for passengers* [7] ________ *by a French airline. (provide) The first stewardess* [8] ________ *by an American airline in 1937. (employ)*

3 Change the active statements into passive statements. Leave out the agents.

Example: *They didn't tell people about the plan.*
People weren't told about the plan.

1 *First the company built the new factory.*

____

2 *Then the engineers designed the new Superbike 2,000.*

____

____

3 *They didn't show the design to anyone.*

____

____

4 *People bought 1,000 in the first year.*

____

4 Read. Then write questions and answers.

Examples: *(What/oil/need/for today)*

● What is oil needed for today?
❍ It's needed for modern transport and industry.

(oil/know/in ancient times)

● Was oil known in ancient times?
❍ Yes, it was.

Our modern world needs large amounts of oil for industry and modern forms of transport. But oil was first known and used thousands of years ago. In ancient times, it was burned in oil lamps for light at night. Boats were also covered with it to keep water out. It was also used as a surface for roads by the Chinese.

About 100 years ago, far more oil was suddenly needed as modern transport and industry developed. Oil wells were drilled and large amounts of oil were found in many parts of the world, including the Middle East and the USA.

Today, oil is less easy to find, but new supplies are still discovered. Nearly 50 million barrels of oil are pumped from the ground every day.

1 *(When/oil first/use)*

● ________
❍ ________
____

2 *(it/burn/for light)*

● ________
❍ ________

3 *(When/far more oil/need)*

● ________
❍ ________

4 *(more oil/find/at that time)*

● ________
____
❍ ________

5 *(How many barrels/oil/pump/every day now)*

● ________
____
❍ ________
____

38 Passive verb forms 2

It's being checked. *It's been checked.* *It can be checked.* *Get it checked.*

FORMS

Simple tense forms
The roof was finished last week.

Continuous tense forms
The doors are being put in now.

Perfect tense forms
The electrics have been checked.

Modal/auxiliary forms
Everything can be finished next month.

***have/get* something done**
I want to have everything finished fast.

Tense forms

Form the different passive tenses like this.

يتم تحويل أزمنة المبني للمجهول على أختلافها كما هو مبين:

Active	Passive
*They **check** everything.*	*Everything **is checked**.*
*They **checked** everything.*	*Everything **was checked**.*
*They **are checking** everything.*	*Everything **is being checked**.*
*They **were checking** everything.*	*Everything **was being checked**.*
*They **have checked** everything.*	*Everything **has been checked**.*
*They **had checked** everything.*	*Everything **had been checked**.*
*They **will have checked** everything.*	*Everything **will have been checked**.*

قارن بين صيغ تصاريف فعل be في الأزمنة المستمرة وفي الأزمنة التامة.

Compare the different forms of *be* in continuous tenses and perfect tenses.

*It **is being** finished.* *They **are being** finished.*
*It has **been** finished.* *They have **been** finished.*

Future and modal passive forms

Use the following with *be* + past participle: *will, would, going to, can, could, may, might, must, should, have to, ought to*, etc.

تستخدم الأفعال المساعدة الناقصة المبينة هنا، مع فعل الكينونة be + التصريف الثالث.

Form the different future and modal passives like this.

تتكون أزمنة المستقبل المبنية للمجهول على اختلافها وكذلك الأفعال المساعدة الناقصة في صيغة المبني للمجهول على النحو الذي توضحه الأمثلة.

Active	Passive
*They **will finish** everything.*	*Everything **will be finished**.*
*They **are going to finish** everything.*	*Everything **is going to be finished**.*
*They **must finish** everything.*	*Everything **must be finished**.*
*They **have to finish** everything.*	*Everything **has to be finished**.*

have/get something done

Use this form when you give somebody else some work to do for you. Form it with *have* or *get* + object + past participle.

تستخدم هذه الصيغة عند إسناد عمل ما إلى شخص ما ليقوم به. وتتكون من have أو get + المفعول به + التصريف الثالث.

*I'm **going to have the car checked** by a mechanic.*
*They **got the work done** for £10,000.*

Use *had*, not *got*, in the present perfect.

وتستخدم had عوضاً عن got في زمن المضارع التام المبني للمجهول.

*We've **had the room decorated** and we've **had new curtains made** too.*

Exercises

1 Write statements with verbs in continuous passive tenses.

Example: *The boy shouted for help. (he/carry/out to sea)*
He was being carried out to sea.

1 *We heard a noise and turned. (we/call/by somebody)*

2 *The towers are dangerous. (they/pull/down/next week)*

3 *The boss was angry. (the work/not/do/efficiently)*

4 *I didn't see little Ann yesterday. (she/look after/by Sue)*

5 *I haven't got my car. (it/service/at the garage)*

2 Write statements with verbs in perfect passive tenses.

Example: *I couldn't open the door. (it/lock/on the inside)*
It had been locked on the inside.

1 *The village is different now. (many new houses/build)*

2 *I managed to start the old car. (it/not/drive/for 20 years)*

3 *The bus has gone. (we/leave/behind)*

4 *We were angry about the plan. (we/not/tell/about it)*

3 Write the official rules.

Example: *Read this. It says we must pay bills within 30 days.*
Bills must be paid within 30 days.

At the library

1 *It says we can borrow up to five books.*

2 *It says we should return books on time.*

At work

3 *It says you must wear protective clothing at all times.*

4 *It says we mustn't eat food in the office.*

4 Write statements. Use *have/get* + object + past participle.

Example: *The door needs painting soon.*
Let's get the door painted soon.

1 *The window needs mending now.*
Let's __________

2 *These films need printing soon.*
Let's __________

3 *This wall needs rebuilding tomorrow.*
Let's __________

5 Change the active statements into passive statements. Leave out the agent if it is not important.

Examples: *The police are checking the house.*
The house is being checked by the police.
They haven't cleaned this room.
This room hasn't been cleaned.

1 *They built this castle in 1760.*

2 *Somebody was pulling Tony along the road.*

3 *Alan won't win the match. Jim will win it.*

4 *People should always read contracts before they sign them.*

5 *Bob has written a memo and the staff are reading it.*

39 Verb + *to* + infinitive or verb + *ing* form 1

I want to go. *I love going on the rides.*

FORMS

Verb + *to* + infinitive

Mum: *I want to go home now. It's late.*
Tim: *Please, Mum! I want to stay.*

Verb + *ing* form

Mum: *We can't keep going round the fair. It's expensive!*
Tim: *But, Mum! I love going on the rides!*

CROSSCHECK

Verb + *to* + infinitive

Some verbs take this form. These are the most common.

agree, aim, appear, arrange, ask, attempt, can't afford, can't wait, choose, decide, expect, fail, happen, hesitate, hope, learn, manage, offer, plan, prepare, pretend, promise, refuse, seem, tend, threaten, train, want, wish

*I **agreed to go** with the others.*
*We **aim to get** home by 9.00.*
*Has Ed **promised not to spend** any more money?*

هناك مجموعة من الأفعال تتخذ صيغة الفعل + to + المصدر، وهذه قائمة بأكثرها شيوعاً.

Verb + *ing* form

Some verbs take this form. These are the most common.

admit, avoid, can't face, can't help, can't stand, carry on, consider, delay, deny, detest, dislike, enjoy, fancy, finish, give up, imagine, involve, keep, keep on, mention, mind, miss, postpone, practise, put off, quit, regret, risk, suggest

*Steve **avoided seeing** Bob for months.*
*Have you **finished writing** that letter?*
*I **enjoy not getting up** early at the weekend.*

وهناك مجموعة أخرى تتخذ صيغة الفعل مضافاً له ing. وهذه قائمة بأكثرها شيوعاً.

Some verbs take either a *to* + infinitive or an *ing* form, eg *continue, love* and *start*. (See Unit 40.)

*It **continued to rain** all day.* *It **continued raining** all day.*
*Tom always **loves to win**.* *Tom always **loves winning**.*
*She **started to run**.* *She **started running**.*

تتخذ بعض الأفعال إما to + المصدر أو إضافة ing إلى المصدر مثل أفعال continue، love و start. (انظر unit 40).

Some verbs take an object + *to* + infinitive, eg *ask, persuade* and *remind*. (See Unit 41.)

*The manager **asked us to wait**.*
*Tom **persuaded me to go**.*
*Could you **remind me to call** Mr Hill at 4.00?*

تتخذ بعض الأفعال المفعول به + to + المصدر مثل أفعال ask، persuade و remind. (انظر unit 41).

Some verbs take a preposition + *ing* form, eg *think of* and *blame ... for*. (See Unit 42.)

*We're **thinking of buying** a new car.*
*I can't **blame her for leaving** that boring job.*

تتخذ بعض الأفعال حرف جر + مصدر مضافاً له ing مثل think of و blame... for. (انظر unit 42).

Exercises

1 Write these verbs in the correct forms.

climb, finish, get, give, learn, move, play, see, win

Example: *I've managed* to finish *the report in time.*

1 *Tom agreed* ______________ *for our team.*

2 *Sandra refused* ______________ *her son any more money.*

3 *I can't wait* ______________ *my cousins again. They've been away for a long time.*

4 *Bob promised* ______________ *here on time. He's late.*

5 *She's hoping* ______________ *the competition.*

6 *My parents have decided* ______________ *to a house in the country.*

7 *We're preparing* ______________ *the mountain.*

8 *I've chosen* ______________ *German this term.*

2 Write these verbs in the correct forms.

buy, crash, eat, lose, say, smoke, wait, walk, watch

Example: *Drive slowly. We don't want to risk* crashing *Dad's new car.*

1 *I can't stand* ______________ *that TV programme.*

2 *They can't deny* ______________ *the money. It's gone.*

3 *We've delayed* ______________ *a car. We're short of money.*

4 *I enjoy* ______________ *breakfast in the garden.*

5 *Don keeps on* ______________ *he's clever, but he seems stupid to me.*

6 *Do you mind* ______________ *here? Mr Price will be here soon.*

7 *I've given up* ______________ *. I feel fitter already.*

8 *We'll have to carry on* ______________ *We can't stop here.*

3 Write the verbs in the correct forms.

Jean: *I hate all these bills – gas, electricity, phone, the garage.*

Joe: *I detest* dealing with *them too. (deal with) But we can't afford* to pay *them any longer. (pay)*

Jean: *We seem* [1]______________ *all our money as fast as it comes in. (spend)*

Joe: *That's right. The bills keep on* [2]______________ *(arrive)*

Jean: *Do you think we can afford* [3]______________ *a holiday this summer? (have)*

Joe: *Maybe. If we try hard, I think we'll manage* [4]______________ *enough. (save)*

Jean: *We should give up* [5]______________ *(smoke) That would save a lot of money.*

Joe: *You're right. Anyway, where do you fancy* [6]______________ *(go)*

Jean: *I've always wanted* [7]______________ *Italy. (see) Would you mind* [8]______________ *that? (do)*

Joe: *No, that's a good idea. And I suggest* [9]______________ *in June. (go) I can get some free time then.*

Jean: *Fine. Let's plan* [10]______________ *then. (go) I can imagine* [11]______________ *around the streets of Venice and Rome already! (walk)*

4 Complete the statements with negative forms.

Examples: *Are you sorry that you didn't pass the exam?*
Do you regret not passing the exam?
Please don't break the contract.
Please agree not to break the contract.

1 *Jean looks as if she doesn't mind what he said.*
Jean seems ______________________________

2 *Please don't make so much noise.*
Would you mind ______________________________

3 *'It's true. I don't have the money to repay Sam,' Tom said.*
Tom admitted ______________________________

4 *'I'm not going to go out with the others,' Suzie said.*
Suzie decided ______________________________

5 *'I'm not going to talk to Bill any more,' Ann said angrily.*
Ann threatened ______________________________

40 Verb + *to* + infinitive or verb + *ing* form 2

I started to race. *I started racing.*

FORMS

Verb + *to* + infinitive or verb + *ing* form (no change of meaning)

Reporter: *When did you start racing?*
Driver: *I first started to race when I was 17.*

Verb + *to* + infinitive or verb + *ing* form (change of meaning)

Tony went on racing European Formula One cars for years. Later, he went on to race in the USA.

Verb + *to* + infinitive or verb + *ing* form (no change of meaning)

Some verbs can take either form with no change of meaning, eg *begin, start, continue, intend, propose* and *bother.*

تأتي بعض الأفعال بأي من الصيغتين دون أن يتغير المعنى ... مثلا begin و start، الخ.

> *It **began raining** at 10.00.* *It **began to rain** at 10.00.*
> *I **intend visiting** my mother this weekend.*
> *I **intend to visit** my mother this weekend.*
> *Only 20 people **bothered coming** to the garden party.*
> *Only 20 people **bothered to come** to the garden party.*

Do not put two *ing* forms together.

لا يمكن استخدام صيغتين من صيغ ing معاً.

> *People **were starting to leave** when the sun suddenly came out.* (not *leaving*)

These verbs also take the *ing* or the *to* + infinitive form: *like, love, hate, prefer.*

تتخذ الأفعال المذكورة صيغة المصدر مضافاً له ing أو صيغة to + المصدر.

> *Tony **loves driving** fast.* *Tony **loves to drive** fast.*
> *I **prefer drinking** tea.* *I **prefer to drink** tea.*

Note the difference between *like* + *ing* and *like* + *to* + infinitive.

تجدر ملاحظة الفرق بين استخدام like + فعل مضاف له ing وبين استخدام صيغة like + to + المصدر.

> *He **likes driving** classic racing cars.* (He enjoys this.)
> *He **likes to check** the oil and tyres before he drives anywhere.* (He thinks this is the right thing to do.)

Note the differences between *hate/would hate, like/would like, love/would love* and *prefer/would prefer.*

تجدر ملاحظة الفروق في المعنى عند استخدام أفعال hate و love و prefer بمفردها وعند استخدامها مع would.

> *I **love** my mother and father very much.*
> *I'm really thirsty. **I'd love** a cup of tea.*
> *I always **prefer driving to going** by bus.*
> ***I'd prefer to drive** there tonight. The bus might be late.*

Some verbs can take either verb + *ing* form or object + *to* + infinitive with no change of meaning, eg *advise, allow, encourage, permit* and *recommend.*

تأتي بعض الأفعال إما مع فعل مضاف له ing أو مع مفعول به + to + مصدر دون تغيير في المعنى .. ومنها الأفعال المذكورة.

> *Bill **advised doing** some exercise.*
> *Bill **advised me to do** some exercise.*
> ***I don't allow smoking** in my house.*
> ***I don't allow people to smoke** in my house.*

Verb + *to* + infinitive or verb + *ing* form (change of meaning)

Some verbs can take either verb + *to* + infinitive or verb + *ing* form, but with a change of meaning.

تأتي بعض الأفعال إما مع فعل + *to* + مصدر أو مع فعل مضاف له *ing* ولكن بمعنى مختلف في كل صيغة.

CROSSCHECK

Verb + *to* + infinitive	Verb + *ing* form
remember/forget + *to* + infinitive (for necessary actions) *Please* ***remember to buy*** *a newspaper.* *Please* ***don't forget to buy*** *some milk.*	*remember/forget* + verb *ing* (for memories of the past) *I* ***remember climbing*** *that mountain in 1985.* *I'll never* ***forget reaching*** *the top. It was great!*
stop + *to* + infinitive (stop one thing and do something else for a short time) *On our way home we* ***stopped to buy*** *some stamps.*	*stop* + verb *ing* (end an action) *Let's* ***stop fighting*** *and start talking.*
try + *to* + infinitive (make a strong effort, do your best) *We* ***tried to mend*** *the engine all night, but we failed.*	*try* + verb *ing* (do something in a new way) *I don't like the table here. Let's* ***try putting*** *it over there.*
mean + *to* + infinitive (1 plan to do something, 2 be required to do something) 1) *I* ***meant to call*** *you, but I was busy.* 1) *I'm very sorry! I* ***didn't mean to hit*** *you.* 2) *You're* ***meant to sign*** *the papers here. Then they'll give you your money.*	*mean* + verb + *ing* (one thing makes another thing necessary) *I want to go to college, but that* ***means working*** *really hard.* *The bus has broken down. That* ***means waiting*** *for an hour for the next one.*
regret + *to* + infinitive (for showing you are sorry about what you are saying) *We* ***regret to tell*** *you that Mr Briggs has died.*	*regret* + verb *ing* (for showing you are sorry about doing something) *I* ***regretted leaving*** *my money at home. I needed it in town.*
need + *to* + infinitive (has to do) *Harry* ***needs to fly*** *to Cairo tonight as he has a meeting there tomorrow.*	*need* + verb *ing* (for something that is necessary) *Look at that dirty floor. It really* ***needs cleaning****.*
go on + *to* + infinitive (do something new after finishing another thing) *She* ***went on to become*** *a famous artist.*	*go on* + verb *ing* (continue doing) *Sally* ***went on working*** *hard, even after her terrible accident.*

يعني استخدام *remember* و *forget* + *to* + المصدر ضرورة القيام بشيء ما.

واستخدام الفعلين مع فعل آخر مضاف له *ing* بما يفيد استحضار الذكريات.

يعني استخدام صيغة فعل stop + to+ مصدر التوقف عن القيام بعمل ما لبرهة قصيرة من أجل القيام بعمل آخر.

ويعني استخدام الفعل stop + فعل مضاف له ing بما يفيد التوقف عن القيام بعمل ما نهائياً.

يعني استخدام فعل try + to + المصدر القيام بجهد كبير

ويعني استخدام فعل try + الفعل مضافاً له ing القيام بعمل ما بطريقة جديدة .

يعني استخدام فعل mean + to + المصدر (١) التخطيط للقيام بعمل ما (٢) وجوب القيام بعمل ما.

أما استخدام فعل mean + فعل مضاف له ing فيعني ان أمراً ما يجعل أمراً آخر ضرورياً.

يبين استخدام فعل *regret* + *to* + مصدر الأسف على ما سيقال.

ويبين استخدام فعل *regret* + فعل مضاف له *ing* أسف المتحدث على ما بدر منه.

يبين استخدام فعل *need* + *to* + المصدر معنى الإلزام ووجوب القيام بالفعل.

ويبين استخدام فعل *need* + فعل مضاف له *ing* أن القيام بعمل ما أمر ضروري.

تستخدم صيغة *go on* + *to* + المصدر لتفيد القيام بعمل جديد يتلو أمراً آخر جرى الانتهاء منه.

ويفيد استخدام *go on* + فعل مضاف له *ing* استمرار القيام بعمل ما.

Exercises

1 Write these verbs in the correct forms.

ask, be, come, form, provide, take

Someone is making a speech.

Ladies and gentlemen,

Thank you for bothering to come *to this meeting on a cold, wet December evening. I know most of us would prefer* [1]____________ *at home. I don't intend* [2]____________ *much of your time, but I have an important proposal to make. I'm proposing* [3]____________ *a group of us to collect money for our local hospital. For many years, the hospital has continued* [4]____________ *us all with a great service. Recently, though, the hospital has not been getting enough money for things such as children's toys. That's why the staff have started* [5]____________ *for help from us, the local community.*

2 Write the verbs in the correct forms.

Example: *Ed loves* going *on holiday. (go)*
Ed would love to go *away this year. (go)*

1 *Alan hates* ____________ *early in the morning. (get up)*

2 *Would you like* ____________ *out to the cinema this evening? (go)*

3 *I like* ____________ *that all the windows and doors are shut at night. (check)*

4 *We always prefer* ____________ *in the sea to* ____________ *in a pool. (swim)*

5 *Ben doesn't like* ____________ *very much. (read)*

6 *Which would you prefer* ____________ *tomorrow – stay at home or go out? (do)*

7 *I'd love* ____________ *London and see Buckingham Palace. (visit)*

8 *When Emma was small, she loved* ____________ *with her doll's house. (play)*

9 *Ann always likes* ____________ *exactly where her children are. (know)*

10 *I'd hate* ____________ *alone. (live)*

3 Write the verbs in the correct forms.

Tina: *Did you remember* to post *the letters and buy the new TV licence? (post)*

Bob: *Well, I remembered* [1]__________ *the letters. (post) But I didn't get the licence.*

Tina: *Oh, no. You really forgot* [2]____________ *the licence? (buy) I clearly remember* [3]____________ *you to do that when you went out this morning. (ask)*

Bob: *Well, I don't remember* [4]___________ *you. (hear) Perhaps I was too far away.*

Tina: *That's wrong. I remember you* [5]___________, *'I'll get it on the way home.' (say)*

Bob: *Don't be silly. People don't forget* [6]__________ *things like that. (say)*

Tina: *Well, you did. Anyway, please don't forget* [7]__________ *it tomorrow. (get)*

Bob: *All right. I'll remember* [8]___________ *that. (do) I promise.*

4 Write the verbs in the correct forms.

1 At a cleaners

Customer: *Can you try* to clean *this jacket for me, please? (clean) I've tried* ___________ *these marks out, but I can't. (get)*

Assistant: *Have you tried* ___________ *Vanish? (use) It's very good.*

2 At a hotel

Clerk: *Excuse me, Sir. Could you complete this form, please? It just means* ___________ *your home address and* ___________ *at the bottom. (write) (sign)*

Guest: *Oh, yes, of course. I meant* ___________ *it when I arrived, but I had to make a quick phone call. (do)*

3 In an office

Manager: *This report needs* ____________ *(correct)*

Secretary: *When would you like me to do it?*

Manager: *Oh, you don't need* ___________ *it now. (do) Tomorrow is all right.*

5 Join each pair of statements to make one statement.

Example: *Bob didn't get the licence. He forgot.*
Bob forgot to get the licence.

1 *Ian said some terrible things to Emma. He didn't mean it.*
Ian didn't ______________________

2 *I thought I could develop a new kind of engine. I tried for years.*
For years I tried ______________________

3 *They say I had fights with other children. I don't remember them.*
I don't ______________________

4 *They shouldn't make so much noise late at night. They should stop.*
They should ______________________

5 *I hate telling you this, but your son has done badly in his exams. I regret that.*
I regret ______________________

6 *What about buying some things for dinner? Let's stop at this supermaerket.*
Let's ______________________

7 *Throw your work away and start again. That's what this mistake means.*
This mistake means ______________________

8 *I'm sorry. I didn't telephone you this morning. I meant to.*
I'm sorry. I meant ______________________

9 *We should paint the dining-room. It really needs it.*
The dining-room really ______________________

6 Write the verbs in the correct forms.

Alan Jones is talking to a careers adviser about starting a new career.

Adviser: *We need* to work out *a plan for your future. (work out) What have you done up to now?*

Alan: *Well, I tried* working *in a shop. (work) I also tried* 1 ________ *as an office worker. (train) But I've stopped now. I need* 2 ________ *something more interesting. (find)*

Adviser: *How long did you go on* 3 ________ *those jobs? (do)*

Alan: *For two years. Now what I need* 4 ________ *is to change completely. (do) I want to become a doctor.*

Adviser: *That's a very big change. It needs* 5 ________ *about. (think) First of all, it means* 6 ________ *a lot of exams. (pass) It's a pity you left school early. You must really regret* 7 ________ *without doing your final school examinations. (leave)*

Alan: *Yes, I do. I meant* 8 ________ *them. (take) But my dad suddenly got very ill, I regret* 9 ________ *(say) And I had to leave school and get a job to help support the family. Anyway, now I'm studying hard and I'm trying* 10 ________ *(catch up) If I do well enough in my exams next summer, I'll go on* 11 ________ *at medical college after that. (study)*

Adviser: *Well, I certainly hope you succeed.*

41 Verb + object + *to* + infinitive

Dad has invited us to stay. *He wants us to go.*

FORMS

Verb + object + *to* + infinitive

Dad has invited us to stay with him.
He has asked me to phone you.

Verb (+ object) + *to* + infinitive

He wants us to go on Saturday.
He wants to go to the theatre with us.

Verb + object + *to* + infinitive

Some verbs take an object + *to* + infinitive, eg *cause, enable, force, get* (persuade), *instruct, invite, let, make, order, permit, persuade, remind, teach, tell* and *warn*.

The officer ***ordered his men to start****.*
I ***told the children not to play*** *with matches.*

تطلب بعض الأفعال وجود مفعول به + to + مصدر، منها الأفعال المذكورة.

After *let* and *make* use an infinitive without *to*.

We ***let students go*** *home at 4.00.* *The boss* ***made us work*** *late.*

يستخدم مصدر الفعل بدون to بعد فعلي let و make.

Verb (+ object) + *to* + infinitive

Some verbs work with, and also without, an object, eg *ask, beg, expect, help, intend, mean* (intend), *want, (would) hate, (would) like, (would) love* and *(would) prefer*.

She ***asked to meet*** *the President.*
She ***asked us to meet*** *the President.*
Steve ***expects to pass*** *his driving test.*
Ann ***expects everybody else to do*** *the work for her.*

قد يأتي مفعول به مع بعض الأفعال وقد لا يأتي... ومثال ذلك الأفعال المبينة.

After *help* use either a *to* + infinitive or an infinitive without *to*.

I ***helped*** *(them)* ***to make*** *dinner.* *I* ***helped*** *(them)* ***make*** *dinner.*

بعد فعل help يمكن استخدام to + المصدر كما يمكن استخدام المصدر بدون to أيضاً.

The verbs *hate, like, love* and *prefer* can take all these forms.

I ***hate going****.* *I* ***hate you going****.*
I ***hate to go****.* *I* ***hate you to go****.*

ويمكن أن تأتي الأفعال hate و like و love و prefer بأي من الصيغ المبينة.

Note the difference in meaning between forms of *like*.

He ***likes us visiting*** *him.* (He enjoys this.)
He ***likes to call*** *him first.* (He feels this is the right thing to do.)

وتجدر ملاحظة الفرق في المعنى بين صيغتي فعل like كما هو موضح في المثالين.

These verbs can take an object + *to* + infinitive or the *ing* form: *advise, allow, encourage, permit, recommend.*

We ***don't allow people to smoke****.* *We* ***don't allow smoking****.*

يمكن للأفعال التالية أن تتعدى إلى مفعول به + to + مصدر أو فعل مضاف له ing.

After *suggest* do not use an infinitive or an object + infinitive. Use one of these forms.

I ***suggest going*** *to the park.* *I* ***suggest (that) we go*** *to the park.*

لا يجدر استخدام مصدر بعد فعل suggest ولا مفعول به + مصدر بل تستخدم أي من الصيغتين المبينتين.

After *offer* and *promise* do not use an object + infinitive. Use one of these forms.

I ***promised Tim*** *a new book.* (verb + object only)
I ***promised to buy Tim*** *a new book.* (verb + *to* + infinitive only)
I ***promised (that) I would buy Tim*** *a book.* (verb (+ *that*) + *will/would*)

ولا يجدر استخدام مفعول به + مصدر بعد فعلي offer و promise، بل يجب استخدام أي من الصيغ التالية المبينة.

Exercises

1 Complete the statements.

Example: *'Be careful, Steve!' John said.*
John warned Steve to be careful.

1 *'Be quiet, Alan,' the teacher said.*
The teacher told ____________

2 *The weather was bad and Ann said, 'Rob, don't drive so fast.'*
Ann warned ____________

3 *'Don't take photos,' the soldier said to me.*
The soldier ordered ____________

4 *Lucy always says to her son, 'Take your medicine after lunch.'*
Lucy always reminds ____________

5 *Nick said, 'Try this cake, everybody.'*
Nick invited ____________

6 *'Stop!' the policeman said to the man.*
The policeman instructed ____________

2 Join each pair of statements to make one statement.

Example: *I went out last night. Bill persuaded me.*
Bill persuaded me to go out last night.

1 *Tina didn't buy the dress. Suzie persuaded her.*
Suzie persuaded ____________

2 *The climbers turned back. The bad weather forced them.*
The bad weather forced ____________

3 *Our boat rolled over. A wave caused it.*
A wave caused ____________

Be careful these are different!

4 *You can buy now and pay later. This credit card lets you.*
This credit card lets ____________

5 *The boys ran five kilometres. The new trainer made them.*
The new trainer made ____________

6 *We didn't go out. Dad didn't let us.*
Dad didn't let ____________

3 Complete the statements.

Example: *'Can I listen, please?' Julie said.*
Julie wanted to listen.
'Listen, everybody,' Julie said.
Julie wanted everybody to listen.

1 *It would be great to buy that car.*
I'd love ____________

2 *I'll be very angry if Tom gets the job.*
I would hate ____________

3 *'Could you leave your cases there, Mrs Jones?' he said.*
He asked ____________

4 *Tony said, 'Can I see the contract, please?'*
Tony asked ____________

5 *Our friends cut down a tree. We helped.*
We helped ____________

6 *You saw your present. We didn't want that yet.*
We didn't mean ____________

4 Write the verbs in the correct forms.

Examples: *I suggest* going *home. (go)*
I suggest we go *home. (go)*

1 *He doesn't allow people* ________ *in the river. (swim)*

2 *Our dentist likes everybody* ________ *a check-up every six months. (have)*

3 *The taxi driver offered* ________ *Lucy with her luggage. (help)*

4 *The doctor advised Bob* ________ *more exercise. (get)*

5 *I don't recommend you* ________ *that car. (buy)*

6 *I suggest you* ________ *to your teacher about the problem. (talk)*

42 Verb/adjective + preposition + *ing* form

I dream of winning. I'm bored with television.

FORMS

Verb/adjective + preposition (+ *ing* form)
Rick was thinking about the race.
He was bored with television.

Verb + preposition + *ing* form
He was dreaming of winning the race.

Verb + object + preposition + *ing* form
His boss accused him of wasting company time.

Adjective + preposition + *ing* form
Rick isn't very keen on working hard, but he's very enthusiastic about windsurfing.

Verb/adjective + preposition (+ *ing* form)

Some verbs and adjectives can take a preposition. If there is a verb after the preposition, it takes an *ing* form.

*I'm **thinking about** the race.*
*I'm **bored with** television.*
*I **don't feel like doing** any more.*
*I'm **tired of working** all the time.*

يمكن أن تأتي أدوات الجر مع بعض الأفعال والصفات.
وإذا جاء فعل بعد أداة الجر يضاف له ing

Verb + preposition + *ing* form

Some verbs can take this form. These are the most common: *apologize for, approve/disapprove of, believe in, decide against, dream of, feel like, insist on, object to, rely on, think of, succeed in.*

*I **apologized for arriving** late.* *They **don't approve of smoking**.*
*I **decided against buying** the car.* *We **can't rely on winning**.*

تأتي بعض الأفعال مع أداة جر + فعل مضاف له ing .
وهذه قائمة بأكثر هذه الأفعال شيوعاً.

We can also use *about* + *ing* with these verbs: *ask, complain, dream, speak, talk, think, wonder.*

*I **thought about going**.* *We **talked about buying** a car.*

يمكن استخدام about + فعل مضاف له ing مع الأفعال المذكورة.

Be careful about the different meanings of *think about* and *think of.*

*I'm **thinking about** the problem.* (ideas going through your mind)
*I'm **thinking of going** to Spain, but I'm not sure yet.* (ideas going through your mind about a future action)

وتجدر ملاحظة الفرق في المعنى بين think about وبين think of.

Verb + object + preposition + *ing* form

Some verbs can take this form. These are the most common: *accuse ... of, blame ... for, congratulate ... on, discourage ... from, forgive ... for, prevent ... from, stop ... from, punish ... for, suspect ... of, thank ... for, warn ... against.*

*I **blame Tom for causing** the crash.* *I **thanked her for coming**.*

يمكن أن تتخذ بعض الأفعال صيغة الفعل + مفعول به + أداة جر + فعل مضاف له ing.

وهذه قائمة بأكثر هذه الأفعال شيوعاً.

Adjective + preposition + *ing* form

Some adjectives can take this form. These are the most common: *annoyed at, bored with, capable of, enthusiastic about, excited about, fed up with, fond of, good/bad at, grateful for, guilty of, interested in, keen on, pleased about, tired of.*

*Rick **was annoyed at losing**.* *I'm **good at dancing**.*

يمكن أن تتخذ بعض الصفات صيغة الصفة + أداة جر + فعل مضاف له ing.. وهذه قائمة بأكثرها شيوعاً.

Exercises

1 Write the verbs in the correct forms and use these prepositions.

about, for, in, like, of, on, to

Example: *Tom tried nine times, but he never succeeded* in winning. *(win)*

1 *Mike apologized* ______________________ *the vase. (break)*

2 *He insisted* ______________________ *for a new one. (pay)*

3 *We often wonder* ______________________ *house. (move) Is it a good idea?*

4 *I object* ______________________ *out in this terrible weather. (go)*

5 *What do you feel* ______________________ *today? (do)*

6 *We're thinking* ______________________ *a sports club next year. (join)*

2 Join each pair of statements to make one statement.

Example: *She got the job. Her brother congratulated her.*
Her brother congratulated her on getting the job.

1 *I'm going to win. You can't prevent me.*

____

____

2 *Ben broke the window. His father punished him.*

____

____

3 *Don't go sailing in this wind. I must warn you.*

____

____

4 *She hit my child. I can't forgive her.*

____

____

5 *He's left that terrible job. You can't blame him.*

____

____

6 *The dogs are fighting. We can't stop them.*

____

____

3 Write the adjectives and verbs in the correct forms.

Example: *The ship was* capable of crossing *the Atlantic in three days. (capable/cross)*

1 *She's very kind. She isn't* ______________________ *anybody. (capable/hurt)*

2 *Are you* ______________________ *on holiday? (excited/go) It's very soon.*

3 *I'm very* ______________________ *this village. (fond/visit) I love the old place.*

4 *Which are you* ______________________ *next year – Art or Music? (interested/study)*

5 *Is Sam* ______________________ *his exams? (pleased/pass) He got very good marks.*

6 *We're* ______________________ *the same music all the time. (fed up/hear)*

7 *Tom is* ______________________ *(bad/cook) He always burns things.*

4 Write the verbs in the correct forms.

Mary: *Do you remember the other night? We* talked about going *away for a week. (talk/go) And we* [1] ______________________ *to Scotland for a week. (think/go)*

Bill: *Yes, but we* [2] ______________________ *that in the end. (decide/do) You* [3] ______________________ *Scotland as it's cold at this time of year. (discourage/us/choose)*

Mary: *That's right, but I mentioned the idea when I called Sheena in Edinburgh this evening. She's* [4] ______________________ *us again. (enthusiastic/see) She says we must come, and she's really* [5] ______________________ *us Edinburgh. (look forward/show)*

Bill: *That's really nice of her. I must say I'm* [6] ______________________ *all the time. Let's go. (tired/work)*

Mary: *OK, I'll phone her and* [7] ______________________ *us. (thank/her/ask) She'll be very pleased.*

43 Conditional forms: type 0 and type 1

If the wind is strong, the waves are dangerous.

FORMS

Type 0 conditionals

***If* + present simple,**	**present simple**
If the wind is strong,	*the waves are dangerous.*

OR *The waves are dangerous if the wind is strong.*

Type 1 conditionals

***If* + present simple,**	**future with *will***
If it's sunny tomorrow,	*we'll go to the beach.*

OR *We'll go to the beach if it's sunny tomorrow.*

Put a comma after the *If* part when it comes first.
If the wind is strong, the waves are dangerous.

Do not use a comma when the *If* part comes second.
We'll stay at home if it rains.

Type 0 conditionals

These express things which always happen. If one thing happens, then another thing always happens. This is similar to *When* + present simple, present simple.

> ***If** the wind **is** strong, the waves **are** dangerous.*
> ***If** you **shout** at her, she always **cries**.*
> ***When** the wind **is** strong, the waves **are** dangerous.*
> ***When** you **shout**, she always **cries**.*

يستخدم هذا النوع من الجمل الشرطية للتعبير عن الأحداث التي تقع بشكل دائم... فإذا حدث أمرٌ ما، يحدث امر آخر دائماً.

و هذا يشبه الصيغة التي تستخدم when + المضارع البسيط في الشطر الأول والمضارع البسيط في الشطر الثاني.

We can also use *If* with instructions.

> ***If** Ann **phones**, please **take** a message.*
> ***If** your son still **feels** ill tomorrow, **call** me again.*

ويمكن استخدام if الشرطية لإعطاء التعليمات.

Type 1 conditionals

We also use *If* sentences to talk about a probable future action or condition. Both parts of the sentence are about the future, but the *If* part is in the present simple, not the future.

> ***If** it's sunny tomorrow, **we'll go** to the beach.*
> ***If** we **hurry**, **we'll catch** the bus. **If** we **don't hurry**, **we'll miss** it.*

تستخدم جمل if الشرطية للتعبير عن احتمال حدوث فعل أو شرط مستقبلي. ويتعلق جزءا الجملة بالمستقبل رغم ان الجزء الشرطي الذي يحوي أداة الشرط if يكون في المضارع وليس في المستقبل.

The *If* part of the sentence is about something which may or may not happen. The result – the other part of the sentence – follows from the *If* part.

***If* part**	**The result**
If it's sunny, ...	*... we'll go to the beach.*
If it rains, ...	*... we'll stay at home.*
If we hurry, ...	*... we'll catch the bus.*
If we don't hurry, ...	*... we'll miss the bus.*

يتعلق الجزء الشرطي الذي يحوي أداة الشرط if في الجملة بحدث يمكن أن يقع أو لا يقع. ويحدد الجزء الشرطي جواب الشرط في الجزء الآخر من الجملة والذي يأتي كنتيجة للجزء الشرطي.

unless means *if not.*

> *I'll fail the test **unless I learn** these words. (if I don't learn)*

كلمة unless تعني if not.

as long as and *provided (that)* mean *If* with a special emphasis.

> *You can borrow the car **as long as/provided (that) you bring** it back this evening. (if, and only if, you bring it back)*

تعمل عبارة as long as وعبارة provided (that) عمل if الشرطية ولكن بما يفيد مزيداً من التأكيد.

Exercises

1 Complete the Type 0 conditionals. Use these endings.

it becomes ice. *it soon goes bad.*
the machinery soon breaks down. *the oil light comes on.*
the lights come on. *you get orange.*

Example: *If you mix red and yellow,* you get orange.

1 *If the car needs oil,* ______
2 *If you cool water to 0°C,* ______
3 *If you don't keep food cool,* ______
4 *If you press this switch,* ______
5 *If the engineers don't check every month,* ______

______

2 Choose the correct form of the verbs.

Example: *If Ann* doesn't call *me, I'll call her. (doesn't call/won't call)*

1 *If the money* ______ *I'll put it in the bank. (arrives/will arrive)*
2 *Peter* ______ *us if he hears any news. (tells/will tell)*
3 *If you don't finish your homework, I* ______ *you watch TV. (don't let/won't let)*
4 *You won't know what it tastes like if you* ______ *it. (don't try/won't try)*
5 *If the neighbours don't stop that noise, I* ______ *the police. (call/'ll call)*
6 *I'm sure Tom* ______ *you some money if you ask him. (lends/will lend)*
7 *If you shout like that again, Helen* ______ *to you. (doesn't listen/won't listen)*
8 *If the climbers* ______ *down before the storm, they'll be in great danger. (don't come/won't come)*

3 Join each pair of statements to make one statement.

Example: *Tom may call. If so, I'll talk to him.*
If Tom calls, I'll talk to him.

1 *The police may come. If so, they'll ask about Tom.*

______

______

2 *Enter the race. You'll probably win.*

______

______

3 *The party may go on till late. If so, we'll go home early.*

______

______

4 *Call the office at 2.00. Tony will be there.*

______

______

5 *Ann may not call. I'll be worried.*

______

______

6 *Finish the job today. Then you won't have to come tomorrow.*

______

______

4 Write the verbs in the correct forms.

Bob is reading the college newspaper.

Bob: *Look. Here's an advert for a water-ski weekend. If we* have *a group of ten, we* 'll get *a special price. (have) (get)*

Steve: *It sounds good. But I* 1______ *to go if it* 2______ *in May. (not/be able) (be)*

Bob: *No, the offer starts in June. We can go just after the exams.*

Steve: *Yes, if we* 3______ *to go then, everybody* 4______ *(decide) (come) Let's ask some people. Ask Alan.*

Bob: *Alan,* 5______ *us if we* 6______ *a water-ski weekend in June? (you/join) (organize)*

Steve: *If we* 7______ *just after the exams, we* 8______ *a great time. (go) (have)*

Alan: *OK, I* 9______ *if it* 10______ *too expensive. (come) (be/not)*

Steve: *There's a special group rate.*

Bob: *If we* 11______ *another seven people, it* 12______ *just £30 each. (find) (cost)*

Steve: *We'd better hurry. If we* 13______ *fast, somebody else* 14______ *the offer and we* 15______ *the chance. (not/act) (take) (miss)*

44 Conditional forms: type 2

If someone found him, he would have a huge meal.

FORMS

Type 2 conditionals

If **+ past simple,** ***would*** **+ verb**

If someone found him, he would have a huge meal.
OR *He would have a huge meal if someone found him.*

Put a comma after the *If* part when it comes first. Do not use a comma when the *If* part comes second.

In conversation we often use *'d* for *would* and *wouldn't* for *would not*, eg *I'd buy ...*, *He wouldn't buy ...*

Type 2 conditionals express future conditions which are not probable and present conditions which are not true.

يعبر النوع الثاني من الجمل الشرطية عن شروط مستقبلية غير مرجحة وشروط حاضرة غير صحيحة.

> ***If*** *he* ***won*** *the prize, he****'d buy*** *some new clothes.* (But he probably won't win.)
> ***If*** *they* ***had*** *some money, they****'d stay*** *at a hotel.* (But they don't have any money.)

We use the past simple in the *If* part of the sentence. In the other part we usually use *would* (from *will*) + verb.

يستخدم الماضي البسيط في الجزء الشرطي من الجملة، ويستخدم عادة would + فعل في الجزء الآخر.

> ***If*** *he* ***won*** *£10,000, he* ***would visit*** *Rome.* (sure)

We also use *could* (from *can*) and *might* (from *may*).

وتستخدم ايضاً صيغة الماضي من can وهي could، والماضي من may وهي might.

> *... he* ***could visit*** *Rome.* (able to) *... he* ***might visit*** *Rome.* (unsure)

We can make statements with *would*, *could* and *might*, but without the *If* part. The words *would*, *could* and *might* show that the statement is about something unlikely or impossible.

تستخدم الكلمات would و could و might في جمل خبرية بدون الجزء الشرطي الذي يضم if. وهذا يعني أن الجمل الخبرية تفيد أن وقوع الحدث أمر غير متوقع أو أنه مستحيل.

- ● *Let's invite Bill and Luke.*
- ❍ *No, they hate each other. They****'d fight****.* (... if we invited them.)
- ● *I dream of going to Paris.*
- ❍ *We* ***could have*** *a wonderful time there.* (... but it's only a dream.)
- ● *It's a pity Sally and Helen hardly ever meet.*
- ❍ *Yes, they* ***might become*** *friends.* (... but they don't meet.)

We often give advice with Type 2 conditionals, and we can use these special expressions. Note the special form of *be* in Type 2 conditionals.

غالباً ما يستخدم النوع الثاني من الجمل الشرطية لإبداء النصح وذلك باستخدام الصيغ المبينة في الأمثلة، ويجدر ملاحظة الصيغة الخاصة من فعل be المستخدمة في هذا النوع.

> ***If I were you, I'd get*** *a new job.*
> ***If I were in your position, I'd tell*** *the police what happened.*

wish and *If only*

We use the forms *wish* + *would/could* and *If only* + *would/could* to show that we want a change in the future (but we do not really expect the change to happen).

تستخدم صيغة wish +would أو could وكذلك صيغة if only + would أو could للتعبير عن تمني حدوث تغيير مستقبلي ولكنه تغيير غير متوقع الحدوث.

> *I* ***wish*** *that boy* ***would do*** *his work properly!*
> *I* ***wish*** *I* ***could take*** *a holiday, but I'm very busy.*
> ***If only*** *he****'d answer*** *the phone, but it just keeps ringing!*
> ***If only*** *the neighbours* ***wouldn't make*** *so much noise!*

We use the forms *wish* + past and *if only* + past to show that we want a change in the present (but we know it is impossible).

تستخدم صيغتا wish + ماضٍ و if only + ماضٍ للتعبير عن التمني بأن يكون الحاضر مختلفاً مع العلم مسبقاً باستحالة ذلك.

> *I* ***wish*** *things* ***didn't cost*** *so much.*
> ***If only*** *that man* ***did*** *his work properly, we* ***wouldn't have to do*** *the work all over again now.*

Exercises

1 Write the verbs in the correct forms.

Examples: *If I* had *enough money, I'd buy that car. (have)*

You 'd have *enough money if you got a better job. (have)*

1 *If we ________ a bigger house, we could invite people to stay. (have)*

2 *I ________ out of business if we cut our prices. (go)*

3 *If I ________ my job, I wouldn't know what to do. (lose)*

4 *If we ____________ the plan exactly, we'd never finish the job. (follow)*

5 *I think she ________ angry if I didn't invite her this evening. (be)*

6 *You ______________________ me if I told you the whole story. (not/believe)*

7 *If we decided to go to London, we __________ with my brother. (stay)*

8 *He's so good that I'd be very surprised if he ________________ into the team. (not/get)*

2 Write Type 2 conditionals.

Examples: *(we/be/surprised/Ann/come)*

We'd be surprised if Ann came.

(Tom/have/time/he/be/here)

If Tom had time, he'd be here.

1 *(Ann/be/pleased/Tom/call)*

____

____

2 *(you/not/visit/us again/we/be/very sad)*

____

____

3 *(I/get/fit quite fast/I/work out/at the gym)*

____

____

4 *(Barry/not/argue/so much/he/have/more friends)*

____

____

5 *(the team/win/more games/they train/harder)*

____

____

3 Write the verbs in the correct forms to complete the answers without *if*.

Example: ● *It'd be great if we had a million pounds.*

❍ *Yes, we* could do *anything. (can/do)*

1 ● *Let's give Larry some money.*

❍ *No, he ______________ it all. (waste)*

2 ● *If you could change jobs, what would you do?*

❍ *I ______________ a film star. (become)*

3 ● *I don't want to go out tonight.*

❍ *Why not? You ______________ yourself. (enjoy)*

4 ● *If I could, I'd love to travel through time.*

❍ *But you ____________________ your friends and family again. (may/never/see)*

4 Write questions and answer them without *if*.

Example: *You might lose your money. (What/you/do) (go/to the police)*

● What would you do if you lost your money?

❍ I'd go to the police.

1 *They might visit Turkey. (Where/they/stay) (stay/in cheap hotels)*

● ____

____

❍ ____

2 *We could complain at the Head Office. (Who/we/see) (talk/to the Sales Manager)*

● ____

____

❍ ____

3 *I might visit Scotland. (How/you/travel) (go/by car)*

● ____

____

❍ ____

4 *They could leave school now. (What/they/do) (get/jobs)*

● ____

____

❍ ____

45 Conditional forms: type 3

If he'd bought a present, she'd have been happy.

Yesterday was Mr and Mrs Carter's wedding anniversary. She remembered it, but he didn't. If he'd bought a present, she'd have been happy!

FORMS

Type 3 conditionals

If **+ past perfect** — ***would have*** **+ past participle**

If he had bought a present, — *she would have been happy.*

OR *She would have been happy if he had bought a present.*

Put a comma after the *If* part when it comes first. Do not use a comma when the *If* part comes second.

In conversation we often use *'d* for *had* and also *'d* for *would*, eg *If he'd got* ... and *she'd have* ...

Both *'d* forms sound the same, but their meanings are different.

Type 3 conditionals express something past which was not true.

> ***If** he**'d got** a present, she**'d have been** happy.*
> (... but he didn't!) (... and she was angry!)

يستخدم النوع الثالث من الجمل الشرطية للتعبير عن أمرٍ ما في الماضي لم يكن حقيقياً.

Form Type 3 conditionals like this.

> ***If** he **hadn't forgotten** the present, she **wouldn't have been** angry.*
> (... but he did!) (... and she was angry!)

تتشكل حالة النفي للنوع الثالث من الجمل الشرطية هكذا:

In the *If* part of the sentence we use the past perfect. In the other part we usually use *would have* + past participle.

> *If he**'d remembered** to buy a present, ...*
> *... she**'d have been** very pleased.* (sure)

يستخدم زمن الماضي التام في الجزء الشرطي من الجملة في حين يكون جواب الشرط عادة مكوناً من would + have التصريف الثالث.

But we also use *could have* and *might have*.

> *... he **could have got it** on the way home.* (possible)
> *... he **might have decided** to get some flowers.* (unsure)

ولكن يمكن استخدام صيغتي could have و might have أيضاً.

We can make statements with *would have*, *could have* and *might have*, but without the *If* part. The words *would have*, *could have* and *might have* show that the statement is about something past and impossible.

> *I'm sorry that you didn't visit Harry. He**'d have loved** to see you.*
> (... if you'd visited him.)
> *I wanted to go to New York. We **could have seen** Manhattan.*
> (... if we'd gone to New York.)
> *He was stupid not to work. He **might have passed** his exams.*
> (... if he'd worked harder.)

ويمكن استخدام جمل خبرية مع would have وcould و might have دونما حاجة إلى استخدام الجزء الشرطي الذي يحتوي على if. وتبين تلك الصيغ أن الموضوع يتعلق بحدث ماضٍ ومستحيل.

wish and *If only*

We use the forms *wish* + past perfect and *If only* + past perfect to show that we would have liked a change in the past (but we know that it did not happen).

> *Most people **wish** they**'d done** a few things differently when they were younger.*
> *I **wish** I **hadn't wasted** so much time yesterday.*
> ***If only** they**'d called** the doctor immediately, they could have saved his life.*
> ***If only** we **hadn't spent** our money, we could have gone out last night.*

تستخدم صيغتا wish + ماضٍ تام و if only + ماضٍ تام تبينا التمني لو أن تغييراً حدث في الماضي مع العلم بأن ذلك لم يحدث.

Exercises

1 Write the verbs in the correct forms.

Examples: *If I* 'd driven *faster, I'd have arrived in time. (drive)*

We wouldn't have gone *to the show if Alan hadn't recommended it. (not/go)*

1 *If you'd seen the film, you* ______ *it. (love)*

2 *If she* ______ *earlier, she'd have seen Pat. (go)*

3 *We wouldn't have noticed the house if you* ______ *it to us. (not/show)*

4 *If the weather* ______ *better yesterday, we'd have gone out. (be)*

5 *If she* ______ *some money, she* ______ *enough for those shoes. (save) (have)*

6 *We* ______ *for help that night if we* ______ *desperate. (not/ask) (not/be)*

2 Write Type 3 conditionals.

Examples: *(you/come/to the party/you/enjoy/it)*

If you'd come to the party, you'd have enjoyed it.

(we/be/very sad/John/not/marry/Suzie)

We'd have been very sad if John hadn't married Suzie.

1 *(Jim/ask/us/we/lend/him our car)*

______

2 *(I/not/write down/her phone number/I/forget)*

______

3 *(the car/not/crash/Tom/keep/to the speed limit)*

______

4 *(I/forget/to buy/Ann's present/you/not/remind/me)*

______

3 Write Type 3 conditionals.

Example: *The plane didn't crash because the pilot landed on a road.*

If the pilot hadn't landed on the road, the plane would have crashed.

1 *We didn't find the house as we didn't have a map.*

______

2 *The bus arrived late, so we didn't miss it.*

______

3 *They found the books when they opened the last box.*

______

4 *The tree didn't fall on the car, so the driver wasn't hurt.*

______

5 *I got lost on the mountain because I didn't turn back.*

______

4 Write answers without *if*.

Example: ● *I wanted to go to New York. (we/can/see/the Manhattan skyline)*

❍ *Yes,* we could have seen the Manhattan skyline.

1 ● *It's a pity Tom's car broke down. (he/might/win/the race)*

❍ *Yes,* ______

2 ● *Why didn't she call the police? (they/can/catch/the thieves)*

❍ *Yes,* ______

3 ● *I should have taken the other road. (we/get/home an hour ago)*

❍ *Yes,* ______

46 Reported speech 1: statements

He said (that) he was late.

FORMS

He said, 'I'm late.' → He said (that) he was late.

He said, 'I'll call you from New York.' → He said (that) he would call us from New York.

'I'm in New York now.' → He says (that) he's in New York now.

'I'm eating dinner here at my hotel.' → He says (that) he's eating dinner there at his hotel.

You can report a person's exact words in quotation marks (' ... '). This is common in stories.

*He said, **'I'm late.'*** ***'What time is it?'** he asked.*

يمكن نقل حديث شخص ما بشكل حرفي بوضعه بين علامات تنصيص «...»، وهو أمر شائع في القصص.

In conversation we usually express the speaker's idea in reported speech after a reporting verb such as *say, tell, shout* and *whisper*.

*He **said** (that) he was late.* *He **told** us (that) he would call us.*
*He **shouted** (that) ...* *She **whispered** (that) ...*

وفي حالة الحوار فإننا عادة ما نعبر عن فكرة المتحدث بطريقة تقريرية بعد فعل تقريري مثل الأفعال المذكورة، أي بالتحويل إلى الكلام غير المباشر.

The reporting verb *say* is usually in the past. But it is sometimes in the present, eg when we report a telephone conversation as we listen.

*He **says** (that) he's in New York now.*

ويوضع فعل التقرير say عادة في الماضي ولكنه يأتي في المضارع احياناً، عند نقل محادثة تليفونية أثناء الاستماع إليها على سبيل المثال.

After *say*, we do not usually mention the listener. After *tell* we always mention the listener.

*He **said** he was working late.*
*He **told me** he was working late.*

يغفل ذكر المستمع عادةً بعد فعل say ولكنه يذكر دائماً بعد فعل tell.

that after the reporting verb is formal. You can leave it out.

*He **said that** he was tired.* OR *He **said** he was tired.*

يعتبر استخدام that بعد فعل التقرير رسميا، ويمكن إغفال ذكرها.

There are word changes to show changes of person and place.

*... call **you** from New York. → ... call **us** from New York.*
*... **here** at **my** hotel. → ... **there** at **his** hotel.*

وهناك تغييرات للكلمات لاظهار تغيير الشخص والمكان.

There are word changes to show time changes between the statement and reporting the statement.

*He said, 'I'm flying **tomorrow**.' → He said he **was** flying the **next day**.*

وهناك تغييرات للكلمات لاظهار تغيّر الزمن بين الجملة الخبرية المباشرة وبين الجملة المنقولة.

A main verb in the present simple, eg *call* or *calls*, changes to the past simple, *called*. Remember these other common verb changes.

am/is → was, are → were, have/has → had, have/has got → had,
do/does → did, will → would, can → could, may → might

يتغير الفعل الأساسي في الجملة من المضارع البسيط إلى الماضي البسيط... تذكّر تغيرات الأفعال الشائعة المبينة.

Unlike *can* and *may*, these modal verbs do not change.

must, might, could, would, should, ought

لا تتغير صيغة الأفعال المساعدة الناقصة المذكورة وذلك على النقيض من فعلي can وmay.

Remember these other common ways of showing time changes.

tomorrow → the next day/the day after
yesterday → the previous day/the day before
this Saturday → last Saturday/the following Saturday

تذكّر هذه الطرق الشائعة الاخرى التي تظهر تغيّرات الزمن.

Exercises

1 Report the telephone conversation.

Nick is in Australia and Alan is in Britain.

Nick: *It's hot here, and I'm sitting by our new pool.*
Alan: *It's really cold here, and we're sitting by our fire.*

They're telling their wives about the conversation.

Nick to Suzie: *Alan says* it's really cold there, and ______________________
____

Alan to Celia: *Nick says* ______________________
____
____

2 Write the statements in reported speech. Use *He said ...* and *He told me ...*

You met an old school friend, Jim, last year

Examples: *'I've got a flat in London.'*
He said he had a flat in London.
'I'm visiting my parents this weekend.'
He told me he was visiting his parents that weekend.

1 *'I'm working outside London this month.'*
____
____

2 *'I finished my college course a year ago.'*
____
____

3 *'I haven't been to see my parents for ages.'*
____
____

4 *'I arrived home with my family yesterday.'*
____
____

5 *'We're going to go back to London tomorrow.'*
____
____

6 *'We can't stay for long as I have to get back to work.'*
____
____
____

7 *'We may come back next year. I don't know.'*
____
____
____

8 *'I'll write soon and send you a photo of the family.'*
____
____

9 *'You should stay with us when you have time.'*
____
____

3 Write replies to the comments. Use *But you said ...* and *But you told me ...*

Example: ● *I'm going home. (stay/here)*
❍ But you said you were staying here.

1 ● *I don't like this music. (love)*
❍ ______________________
____

2 ● *Tom has sold his bike. (not/sell)*
❍ ______________________
____

3 ● *I'm not going to call her. (call)*
❍ ______________________
____

4 ● *The film is on tomorrow. (today)*
❍ ______________________
____

5 ● *They won the match. (lose)*
❍ ______________________
____

6 ● *Lisa will be at home tomorrow. (tonight)*
❍ ______________________
____

7 ● *They have sent me a present. (not/send/anything)*
❍ ______________________
____

8 ● *The children can swim very well. (cannot/swim/at all)*
❍ ______________________
____

47 Reported speech 2: questions

They asked if I was staying long.

FORMS

'Are you staying long?' → They asked if I was staying long.

'Did you have a good journey?' → They wanted to know if I had had a good journey.

'How are your parents?' → They wanted to know how you were.

'When will you go?' → They asked when I would go.

Reported questions usually start with *ask* or *want to know*.

*They **asked** how long I was staying.*
*They **wanted to know** how you were.*

تبدأ صيغة الاستفهام في الكلام غير المباشر عادةً بـ ask و want to know.

Reported *Yes/No* questions need *if* or *whether*.

*They asked **if** I had had a good journey.*
*They wanted to know **whether** I liked London.*

يستدعي تحويل صيغ الأسئلة التي يجاب عنها بـ «نعم» و «لا» إلى الكلام غير المباشر استخدام if أو whether.

Reported *Wh* questions need a question word, eg *how, when, what*, etc.

*They wanted to know **how** you were.*
*They asked **what** I wanted to do.*

ويستدعي تحويل الأسئلة التي تبدأ بأداة استفهام مثل how و when، الخ... الاحتفاظ بأداة الاستفهام في الجملة غير المباشرة.

The verb after *if* or *whether* or question word is not in question form. It is like a verb in a statement.

*They asked **if** I **was** hungry.*
*They asked **what** I **wanted** to do.*

يوضع الفعل بعد if وبعد whether وكذلك بعد أداة الاستفهام، في صيغة الجملة الخبرية وليس في الصيغة الاستفهامية.

Be careful about *do, does* and *did*. We use them in ordinary present and past simple questions, but not in reported questions.

*Where **do** you **want** to go? → They asked me where I **wanted** to go.*
*How long **did** the journey **take**? → They asked me how the journey **had taken**.*

وتستخدم do و does و did في الجمل الاستفهامية العادية، في زمني المضارع والماضي البسيطين ولكنها لا تستخدم في الجمل الاستفهامية المحولة إلى الكلام غير المباشر.

The reported question form is similar to the form of indirect questions. (See Unit 22.)

*Why does he like London? → They wanted to know **why he likes London**.* OR *Could you tell me **why he likes London**?*

تشبه الجمل الاستفهامية المحولة إلى الكلام غير المباشر صيغة الأسئلة غير المباشرة (انظر unit 22).

The rules for word changes for change of person, place and time are the same as for reported statements. (See Unit 46.)

*'How **are you**?' → They asked how **I was**.* (change of person)
*'When will you get **here**?' → They asked when I would get **there**.* (change of place)
*'Did you call **yesterday**?' → They asked if I had called **the previous day**.* (change of time)

تتطابق قواعد تغيير الكلمات لتغيير الشخص والمكان والزمان مع قواعد تحويل الجمل الخبرية إلى الكلام غير المباشر. (انظر unit 46).

Exercises

1 Report the telephone conversation.

Nick is in Australia and Alan is in Britain.

Nick: *What are you and Celia doing this winter? Are you taking a skiing holiday again?*

Alan: *No, we're staying at home this year. Where are you and Suzie going for your holiday? Are you going to visit us again?*

They're telling their wives about the conversation.

Nick to Suzie: *Alan is asking where* ____________

____

____________ *He wants to know*

____

____

Alan to Celia: *Nick is asking what* ____________

____________ *He wants to know*

____

____

2 Write the *Yes/No* questions in reported speech.

You met your old school friend, Jim, last year.

Examples: Jim: *Are you still at college?*

Jim asked me whether I was still at college.

You: *Do you remember Joe?*

I asked him if he remembered Joe.

1 Jim: *Have you sold your terrible old car?*

____

2 Jim: *Do you still live with your parents?*

____

3 Jim: *Are you going to visit London soon?*

____

4 You: *Is there room for me to stay with you?*

____

5 You: *Can I have your phone number?*

____

6 You: *Did you meet your wife at college?*

____

3 Write the *Wh* questions in reported speech.

Some students are talking to a new French student.

Example: *'What subjects are you going to do?'*

They asked him what subjects he was going to do.

1 *'Where do you come from?'*

____

2 *'How long have you been in Britain?'*

____

3 *'Why did you decide to come here?'*

____

4 *'How long are you going to stay?'*

____

5 *'Where are you living?'*

____

4 Write the questions in reported speech.

At a language school

Example: A German student: *How can I renew my my passport?*

A German student asked me how he could renew his passport.

1 A Swedish student: *Do you know the way to the station?*

____

2 A Turkish student: *Can you help me find a flat?*

____

3 A Lebanese student: *Which is the best travel agency?*

____

48 Reported speech 3: orders, promises, etc

They told him to be quiet.

FORMS

Reported orders

'Be quiet!' → They told him to be quiet.

Reported requests

'Could you turn it down, please?' → She asked him to turn it down.

'Would you mind not making so much noise, please?' → She asked him not to make so much noise.

Reported orders, invitations, etc

tell, invite, remind, warn and *use* take *to* + infinitive after the object. In the negative form add *not* before the *to* + infinitive.

Subject	Verb	Object	*to* + Infinitive
They	***told***	*him*	***to be** quiet.*
They	***warned***	*her*	***not to do** it again.*

الأفعال التقريرية التالية tell و invite و remind و warn و use، تأخذ to + مصدر الفعل بعد المفعول به. وفي حالة النفي نأتي بأداة النفي not قبل المصدر مع to.

Reported promises, offers, etc

promise, offer, refuse, agree and *threaten* do not take an object before the *to* + infinitive. In the negative form add *not* before the *to* + infinitive.

Subject	Verb	*to* + Infinitive
He	***promised***	***to turn** it **down**.*
They	***agreed***	***not to make** so much noise.*

لا تتعدى الأفعال التقريرية promise و offer و refuse و agree و threaten ، إلى مفعول به قبل المصدر مع to، وفي حالة النفي نأتي بأداة النفي not قبل المصدر مع to.

Reported suggestions, apologies, etc

suggest, apologize for, admit and *insist on* take an *ing* form.

Subject	Verb	*ing* form
Nick	***suggested***	***turning** it **down**.*
They	***apologized***	***for making** so much noise.*

نأتي بالفعل مضافاً له ing عند استخدام الأفعال suggest و apologize for و admit و insist on .

With *suggest* it is possible to use this form.

*Nick **suggested that they turn** it **down**.*

من الممكن استخدام صيغة الفعل بدون ing مع الفعل التقريري suggest.

Other reporting verbs

Reporting verbs like *invite, promise, suggest, warn*, etc, tell us much more than the basic reporting verbs *say, tell* and *ask*. They express the speaker's aim – the type of communication that the speaker produced. In fact, the reporting verb can summarize some or all of the actual words that the speaker used. Similar reporting verbs include *accuse, complain, correct, deny* and *recommend*.

The police to Mr Saunders: *'We have reason to believe that you took the car, Mr Saunders.' → The police **accused** Mr Saunders of taking the car.*

A neighbour to a teenager: *'Do you have to make that terrible noise?' → The neighbour **complained** to the teenager about the terrible noise.*

Mr MacLaren to a reporter: *'I'm sorry, but you've got my name wrong. It's M-a-c, not M-c.' → Mr MacLaren **corrected** the spelling of his name.*

Mr Saunders to the police: *'I certainly didn't take the car.' → Mr Saunders **denied** taking the car.*

بعض الأفعال التقرنرية مثل invite و promise و sug- gest و warn ... تفيدنا معلومات اكثر بكثير من الافعال التقريرية الأساسية say و tell و ask. فهي تعبّر عن غرض المتحدث وبالتالي نوعية المعلومات التي اعطاها المتحدث. في الواقع، يمكن للفعل التقريري ان يختصر بعض الكلمات التي استخدمها التكلم، أو كلها. ومن الأفعال التقريرية المماثلة، accuse و complain و cor- rect و deny و recommend.

Exercises

1 Put the direct speech into reported speech.

Example: *'Give me your books,' the teacher told us.*
The teacher told us to give him/her our books.

1 *'Could you open the door?' the girl asked me.*

2 *'Don't use this photocopier,' Carol instructed the new asssistant.*

3 *'Come for dinner on Saturday,' Tom invited us.*

4 *'Don't be late for the party,' Celia reminded me.*

5 *'Could you please not make so much noise?' Ann asked everybody.*

6 *'Give your name to the receptionist,' Mrs Davis told Tony.*

7 *'Don't touch the red button,' Bob warned Emma.*

8 *'Remember to post the letters,' the manager reminded her assistant.*

2 Report the conversation. Use these reporting verbs.

agree, offer, promise, threaten

Bill is always late for appointments. His sister, Jean, is tired of it.

Example: *'Can we meet outside the cinema?' Bill said.*
'All right. Outside the cinema,' Jean agreed.
They agreed to meet outside the cinema.

1 *'And can we meet at 7.30?' he said.*
'Fine. 7.30,' she agreed.

2 *'This time I'll be there on time,' he promised.*

3 *'I'm not going to wait for you if you're late,' she threatened.*

4 *'Look, if you like, I'll get there an hour early!' he offered.*

5 *'You don't need to do anything silly like that, but I'll leave if you aren't there at 7.30,' she threatened again.*

6 *'I won't be late. Believe me,' he promised.*

3 Report the statements and questions. Use these reporting verbs.

admit, apologize for, insist on, suggest

Example: *'Let's do something exciting,' Bob suggested.*
Bob suggested doing something exciting.

1 *'Why don't we go parachuting?' Maria suggested.*

2 *'Good idea, but it's getting late. If we're going to go parachuting, we must go right now,' Barry insisted.*

Later, 3,000 metres up in the sky ...

3 *'I feel scared,' Barry admitted.*

4 *'I don't want to jump either. I'm sorry, Barry. I was stupid to suggest parachuting,' Maria apologized.*

5 *'Look we can't go back now. Even if you aren't going to jump, I am!' Barry insisted. 'Bye!'*

49 Singular and plural

a girl, an apple, two boys, some chairs

FORMS

a

a girl, a table

an

an apple, an umbrella

number

two boys, five books

some

some chairs, some books

All the things in the picture are countable nouns – we can count them, eg *two boys, three chairs* and *five books.*

They have a singular form (for one), eg *boy*, and a plural form (for more than one), eg *boys.*

We can use *a/an* before the singular form. Use *a* before a hard sound (consonant), eg *a girl, a desk* and *a table* (but *an old table*).

Use *an* before a soft sound (vowel), eg *an apple, an orange* and *an olive* (but *a green olive*).

Compare *a hat* and *an hour*. Use *an* when the *h* is silent.

Compare *an umbrella* and *a university*. Use *a* when the *u* sounds like *you*.

Do not use a singular countable noun by itself. It needs a determiner. (See Unit 52 for more information about *a, an* and *the.*)

*I want **a book**.* *I want **my book**.*
*I want **that book**.* *I want **the book** over there.*

We use *a/an* to say what a thing or a person is.

- *What's that?* ❍ *It's **a map**.*
- *What's her job?* ❍ *She's **an actress**.*

If we talk about more than one thing or more than one person in this way, use the noun alone.

- *What are those?* ❍ *They're **maps**.*
- *What are their jobs?* ❍ *They're **actresses**.*

We can use the singular or the plural form to make general statements. In both these examples we mean 'all horses'.

***A horse** is an animal with four legs.*
***Horses** are animals with four legs.*

We often want to talk about more than one thing, but we do not know exactly how many. For this use *some*. (See Unit 55 for more information about *some* and *any.*)

*I'd like a beefburger and **some fries**, please.*

Be careful. *fries* and *some fries*, etc, have different meanings.

*I love **fries**.* (all fries, at any time, anywhere)
*I'd like **some fries**.* (a number of fries now)

جميع الأشياء التي تحويها الصورة من نوع الأسماء التي يمكن عدها وبالتالي فهي الأسماء المعدودة.

تأتي هذه الأسماء في صيغة المفرد مثل boy وكذلك في صيغة الجمع (لأكثر من واحد منها) مثل boys.

يمكن استخدام a/an قبل صيغة المفرد. تستخدم a قبل الأسماء التي تبدأ بحرف صامت (a girl) ولكن لاحظ (an old table.

تستخدم an قبل الأسماء التي تبدأ بحرف صائت (an apple) ولكن لاحظ (a green olive).

قارن بين a hat و an hour . وتستخدم an عندما يكون حرف h صامتاً.

تستخدم a قبل الكلمات التي تبدأ بالحرف u حين ينطق هذا الحرف yoo مثل كلمة university.

لا يستخدم اسم مفرد من النوع المعدود بمفرده بل مع محدد. (انظر unit 52 لمزيد من المعلومات عن a و an و the).

تستخدم a/an للتعبير عن ماهية الاسم إن كان شيئاً أو شخصاً.

عند الحديث عن الأشخاص أو الأشياء في صيغة الجمع يستخدم الاسم وحده، أي بدون a/an.

يمكن استخدام صيغتي المفرد أو الجمع في جمل خبرية عامة: والحديث في المثلين التاليين، هو عن النوع كله.

غالباً ما نتحدث عن أكثر من شيء واحد، ولكننا لا نعرف عدده بالتحديد، ولذلك نستخدم some. (انظر unit 55 لمزيد من المعلومات عن some و any).

تجدر الاشارة إلى أن معنى كلمة fries يختلف عن معناها في some fries.

Exercises

1 Write *a* or *an*.

Examples: *a girl* *an apple*

1 ______ *orange*
2 ______ *exercise*
3 ______ *newspaper*
4 ______ *aeroplane*
5 ______ *letter*
6 ______ *easy test*
7 ______ *magazine*
8 ______ *old car*
9 ______ *Italian*
10 ______ *good book*
11 ______ *united team*
12 ______ *unfriendly man*

2 Write *a*, *an* or *some* and choose from these words.

book / books, desk / desks, egg / eggs, glass / glasses, letter / letters, paint / paints, taxi / taxis, umbrella / umbrellas

Examples: *I'm reading a book about Japan.*
Let's put some desks in that classroom.

1 *Did you write* ____________________ *to Ann?*
2 *It's going to rain. Take* ____________________ *with you.*
3 *Get* ____________________ *and we'll start a picture.*
4 *The children want a drink, so can you get* ____________________ *, please?*
5 *I usually have* ____________________ *, toast and coffee for breakfast.*
6 *We're late. Let's take* ____________________ *to the airport.*

3 Write the correct present forms of *be* or *do*.

Examples: *Look. Some boys are coming.*
Does a lesson take 45 or 50 minutes?

1 ________ *some students live in college?*
2 ________ *a new car very expensive?*
3 *Two girls* ________ *helping the teacher.*
4 ________ *a computer disk take long to copy?*
5 *A secretary* ________ *typing the report.*
6 *A good dictionary* ________ *really useful.*
7 ________ *the children in bed?*
8 *The students* ________ *having lunch.*

4 Write *some* or nothing (✗).

Examples: *Liz and Joe are ✗ teachers.*
We've got some new CDs. Look.

1 *Could you get* ________ *oranges, please?*
2 *I love* ________ *apples. I eat about five a day.*
3 *I'm going to buy* ________ *shoes in the sale.*
4 *Everybody studies* ________ *languages at school.*
5 *You look hungry. Have* ________ *biscuits.*
6 *We found* ________ *old gold coins under a rock.*

5 Write alternative general statements.

Example: *A tractor is a farm vehicle.*
Tractors are farm vehicles.

1 *A college is a place to study.*

____

2 *Large planes can carry very heavy loads.*

____

____

3 *Nowadays, a student needs to learn to use a computer.*

____

____

4 *Cars use more energy per person than trains or buses.*

____

____

6 Write *a*, *an*, *some* or nothing (✗).

At a jeweller's

● *Hello. Could I look at some rings, please? I want to buy a ring for my sister.*
❍ *Certainly, Madam. Here are* [1]________ *rings for ladies.*
● *These are all* [2]________ *diamond rings, aren't they?*
❍ *Yes, and they're* [3]________ *top quality pieces. Look at this one. It's* [4]________ *really lovely ring.*
● *Yes, but it's* [5]________ *expensive one too.*
❍ *Ah, but Madam,* [6]________ *things are never cheap.*
● *Perhaps you're right. But could I look at* [7]________ *other rings too? Could I see* [8]________ *different types of stone?*
❍ *Of course. Here's* [9]________ *very nice one. This green stone is* [10]________ *emerald.*

50 Irregular noun forms

clothes, scissors, news, team, sheep, etc

A few countable nouns are usually plural, so they take a plural verb. Learn these: *clothes, contents, thanks.*

*My **clothes** are in the cupboard.*
*He opened the bag and poured the **contents** on the floor.*
*I want to thank you. Many, many **thanks**!*

هناك مجموعة من الأسماء المعدودة التي غالباً ما تأتي في صيغة الجمع ويأتي معها الفعل في صيغة الجمع أيضاً وذلك مثل *clothes* و *contents* و *thanks*.

Some countable nouns are always plural because they have two parts. Learn these: *scissors, jeans, trousers, shorts, glasses, binoculars.* We can make them singular by using *a pair of.*

*Where are my **scissors**?* *Those are nice **jeans**!*
*There's **a pair of glasses** on the table.*

وهناك أسماء معدودة تأتي دائماً في حالة الجمع نظراً لأنها تتكون من شقين مثل *scissors*... الخ ويجري استخدامها في صيغة المفرد باستخدام *a pair of* معها.

A few countable nouns look singular because they have no *s*, but they are always plural and have no singular form. Learn these: *the police, cattle.* (Use these countable nouns for a singular form: *police officer, cow* or *bull.*)

***The police** are looking for three men.*
*Mr Giles has 200 **cattle** on his farm.*

وهناك مجموعة من الأسماء المعدودة التي تبدو وكأنها في صيغة المفرد لأنها لا تنتهي بـ *s* الجمع، ولكنها دائماً في حالة الجمع مثل *police* و *cattle*. وممكن استخدامها في صيغة المفرد بإضافات وتعديلات معينة مثل *police officer* و *cow*.

A few nouns look plural, but are not. Learn these: *athletics, news, mathematics, physics, gymnastics, the United States.*

*Here is the 9.00 **news**.*
***Mathematics** was the most difficult subject for me at school.*
***The United States** is 5,000 kilometres from east to west.*

وهناك مجموعة من الأسماء تبدو في حالة الجمع ولكنها ليست كذلك مثل *athletics* و *news* الخ.

Group nouns are singular, but we often think of members of the group and use a plural verb. Learn these: *family, team, club, class, school, staff, committee, government.*

*My **family** are all angry with me.*
*The **team** are very happy with the result of the match.*
*The **club** are looking for young members to join the team.*

تعامل أسماء المجموعات على أنها مفردة ولكنها عادة ما تعني الأفراد المكونين لها، وبالتالي نستخدم معها الفعل في حالة الجمع.

A few words are the same in the singular and the plural. Learn these: *sheep, fish, series, crossroads, species, headquarters, aircraft.*

*Mr Giles has 1,000 **sheep** on his farm.*
*You only caught one **fish**, but I caught three **fish**!*
*I saw three **aircraft** in five minutes.*

وهناك مجموعة من الأسماء تأتي في حالتي الإفراد والجمع على نحو سواء... منها الأمثلة المذكورة.

A few plurals are irregular. (See Appendix 2 for special spelling rules.) Learn these: *child → children, man → men, woman → women, person → people, foot → feet, tooth → teeth.*

*I've got one **child**. My brother has got two **children**.*
*One **man** was by the door, and there were three more **men** inside.*
*My dentist filled one **tooth** and took two **teeth** out.*

وهناك مجموعة من الأسماء التي تشذ عن قاعدة جمع المفرد العادية، منها ما هو مذكور.

Exercises

1 Complete the statements and questions with plural nouns.

Example: *Many* thanks *for all your help.*

1 *Somebody has taken all Mrs Bell's money.*
The ___________ *are on their way here now.*

2 *In the Old West in America, cowboys used to look after thousands of* ___________

3 *Open the can and empty the* ___________ *into a large bowl.*

4 *I'll cut your hair for you. Where are your* ___________

5 *It's very cold in the mountains, so take some warm* ___________ *with you.*

6 *Where are my* ___________ *? I can't see without them!*

7 *You can't play for our football in jeans. You need some proper* ___________

8 *We get meat, milk and wool from* ___________

2 Choose singular or plural present forms of *be* or *do*.

Examples: *Physics* is *my best subject.*
Do *fish feel anything when we catch them?*

1 *The news* ________ *very bad. Three people have died and hundreds have been injured.*

2 ________ *this pair of glasses belong to you?*

3 *Sheep* ________ *really stupid animals!*

4 ________ *mathematics interesting?*

5 *Your trousers* ________ *too long. I'd better shorten the legs.*

6 ● *Which* ________ *the biggest fish?*
❍ *This one, I think.*

7 *The new science series on TV* ________ *very good.*

8 *Gymnastics* ________ *dangerous if you don't train carefully.*

9 ________ *the United States have a prime minister or a president?*

10 *Aircraft today* ________ *often able to fly 10,000 miles or more.*

3 Complete the statements with singular or plural irregular nouns.

Examples: *Two* men *with beards came to the door.*
One man *spoke. The other said nothing.*

1 *We've got two* ___________ *. Pip is five and Lucy is four.*

2 *There's room for one more* ___________ *in the taxi.*

3 *My left* ___________ *hurts. I can't walk very well.*

4 *A normal adult human mouth contains 32* ___________

5 *This* ___________ *really hurts. The dentist will have to take it out.*

6 *This bus can carry 70* ___________

7 *In some countries* ___________ *do the same jobs as men.*

8 *That* ___________ *mustn't play in the road. It's dangerous. Let's stop her.*

4 Complete the statements with the plural forms of these nouns. (Before you start, study Appendix 2.)

battery, knife, life, loaf, match, photo, potato, roof, shelf, wife

Example: *Could you put the* shelves *up here, please?*

1 *The children shouldn't play with* ______________ *They might cut themselves.*

2 *The children shouldn't play with* ______________ *either. They might burn themselves.*

3 *We eat* ______________ *with every meal.*

4 *I've bought three* ______________ *of bread.*

5 *Look. These are our holiday* ______________ *This one shows our hotel.*

6 *The men played golf and their* ______________ *played a game of tennis.*

7 *This radio runs on four 1.5 volt* ______________

8 *When the ship sank, more than 1,500 people lost their* ______________

9 *The wind blew the* ______________ *off several houses last night.*

51 Countable and uncountable nouns

I'd like some olives. *I'd like some olive oil.*

FORMS

Countable nouns

● *I'd like some olives, please.*
❍ *How many would you like?*
● *Half a kilo, please.*

Uncountable nouns

● *And I'd like some olive oil, please.*
❍ *How much would you like?*
● *A litre, please.*

CROSSCHECK

Countable nouns

We can count a thing like *an olive* or *three olives*. It has a singular and a plural form and goes with singular and plural verb forms.

*These **olives are** very expensive.*

Uncountable nouns

We cannot count a thing like *olive oil*. We do NOT say *an olive oil* or *three olive oils*. We use a singular verb with an uncountable noun.

*This **olive oil is** very good.*

مكن عدّ الأشياء مثل an olive أو three olives ، فهذا
لاسم له صيغة مفرد وصيغة جمع، ويأتي مع الفعل في
التي الإفراد والجمع أيضاً.

يمكن عدّ بعض الأشياء مثل olive oil واستخدام a/an
مع عدد معها. بل صيغة المفرد من الفعل مع الاسم غير
لعدود.

Countable nouns can go with other words, eg *some, any, the, this/these, my, many* and *a few*.

*I'd like **some oranges**.*
*Are there **any bottles**?*
***The glasses** are in the cupboard.*
*Could I borrow **a few eggs**?*

Uncountable nouns can go with other words, eg *some, any, the, this, my, much* and *a little*.

*I'd like **some orange juice**.*
*Is there **any water**?*
***The salt** is in the cupboard.*
*Could I borrow **a little milk**?*

ستخدم الأسماء المعدودة مع كلمات اخرى مثل ...some
خ.

يمكن استخدام الأسماء التي لا تعد، مع كلمات أخرى
ثل much ...إلخ.

We can count amounts of uncountable things by using expressions such as *a litre of/kilo of/can of/loaf of/carton of/bag of/bottle of/box of/ packet of/piece of/roll of*.

***Three cans of** Pepsi, please.*
***Two loaves of** bread, please.*

These nouns are usually uncountable in English: *accommodation, advice, baggage, furniture, hair, health, information, knowledge, luggage, music, news, travel, trouble, work*.

*Excuse me. I need **some advice**.*
*I'd like to listen to **some music**.*

إمكاننا أن نعد كميات من الأسماء غير المعدودة وذلك
استخدام تعبيرات مثل a litre of ...إلخ.

هذه قائمة بأسماء غير معدودة عادة، في اللغة
لإنجليزية.

Some nouns can be countable or uncountable. The countable form is an example or a part. The uncountable form means something in general or a material. Compare the following.

*Football is a great **sport**!* (example)
*It's made of large and small **stones**.* (parts of the wall)

*I like **sport**.* (all sports)
*The wall is made of **stone**.* (material)

عض الاسماء يمكن أن تكون معدودة أو غير معدودة.
وتكون الصيغة المعدودة عبارة عن مثال أو جزء من
لدلالة. أما الصيغة غير المعدودة فتعني شيئاً عاماً أو
مادياً. لاحظ الأمثلة والفوارق فيها.

Some nouns can be countable or uncountable, but the meaning is different. Compare the following.

*Do you want a large **glass**?* (for drinking) OR *She wears **glasses**.* (for seeing)
*Rob has a small **business**.* (a small company)

*Windows are made of **glass**.* (material)
*They want to do **business**.* (work together)

عض الاسماء يمكن أن تكون معدودة او غير معدودة
ولكن المعنى يختلف كما في الأمثلة.

Exercises

1 Write the kitchen things in two lists – countable and uncountable. Write the countable nouns in the plural.

apple	*cheese*	*pea*
apple juice	*cooking oil*	*potato*
banana	*egg*	*rice*
bean	*milk*	*salt*
biscuit	*mineral water*	*soup*
bread	*olive*	*sugar*
butter	*onion*	*tea*
carrot	*orange*	*tomato*

	Countable nouns		**Uncountable nouns**
1	apples	13	apple juice
2	______	14	______
3	______	15	______
4	______	16	______
5	______	17	______
6	______	18	______
7	______	19	______
8	______	20	______
9	______	21	______
10	______	22	______
11	______	23	______
12	______	24	______

2 Write the nouns with or without *s*.

● *We need some* things *for dinner. (thing) For example, we haven't got any* [1]________ *(meat)*

❍ *Yes, and we've only got a few* [2]________ *(vegetable)*

● *You're right. We'd better get some* [3]________ *and* [4]________ *(bean) (onion)*

❍ *How much* [5]________ *have we got? (rice)*

● *Only a little. And look, this* [6]________ *is old. (bread) We should buy some more. And I'd like to get a few* [7]________ *too. (bread roll)*

❍ *These* [8]________ *are going bad too. (tomato)*

● *Yes, and we must remember to buy a bottle of* [9]________ *too. (olive oil)*

❍ *OK. Now I'm going to write a* [10]________, *so we don't forget anything. (list)*

3 Choose the correct words.

Examples: *I love this* music. *(music/musics)*
I want to buy a *newspaper. (a/some)*

1 *My father gave me* _____ *good advice. (a/some)*

2 *Can you give me some* ________ *about your company? (information/informations)*

3 *I've got some* ________ *for a new book. (idea/ideas)*

4 *Here* _____ *the 9.00 o'clock news. (is/are)*

5 *Put all the* ________ *in the corner, so we can clean the floor. (furniture/furnitures)*

6 *I must go. I have to do* _____ *work now. (a/some)*

7 *I've got* _____ *job to do at home tonight. (a/some)*

8 *Where did you leave your* ________ *(luggage/luggages)*

9 *Helen has got long, dark* ________ *(hair/hairs)*

10 *Have you got* _____ *writing paper, please? (a/any)*

4 Match the two halves.

1	*a packet of*	a	*kitchen paper*
2	*a carton of*	b	*cheese*
3	*a five-litre bottle of*	c	*matches*
4	*a roll of*	d	*cooking oil*
5	*three loaves of*	e	*tea*
6	*four cans of*	f	*bread*
7	*a box of*	g	*potatoes*
8	*a two-kilo bag of*	h	*Pepsi*
9	*a piece of*	i	*milk*

1 e *I'd like* a packet of tea.

2 ___ *I need* ________

3 ___ *I'd like* ________

4 ___ *I need* ________

5 ___ *I'd like* ________

6 ___ *I need* ________

7 ___ *I'd like* ________

8 ___ *I need* ________

9 ___ *I'd like* ________

52 Articles 1: *a, an, the* and *some*

Larry saw an old woman. *The woman smiled.*

FORMS

Yesterday, Larry saw ***an*** old woman in ***the*** park next to ***the*** bus station. She had ***an*** umbrella and ***a*** packet of sandwiches with her. ***The*** sun suddenly came out and ***the*** woman smiled. She sat down on ***a*** bench by ***the*** pond, and she put ***the*** umbrella on ***the*** bench beside her. She started to eat ***the*** sandwiches, and she threw ***some*** pieces of bread to ***the*** birds on the water. Half ***an*** hour later, she went, but she forgot ***the*** umbrella. Larry picked it up and went after her. He found her in ***the*** bus station. She was getting on ***the*** Number 26 bus to Old Town. She was really pleased. 'Stupid me!' she said. 'I nearly went home without it. Thank you for being such ***an*** honest person!'

a or *an*

Use *a* before a hard sound (consonant).

a bench, a packet, a sandwich, a woman

تستخدم a قبل الكلمة التي تبدأ بحرف صامت.

Use *an* before a soft sound (vowel).

an old woman, an umbrella, an ice-cream, an egg, an apple

تستخدم an قبل الكلمة التي تبدأ بحرف صائت.

But compare the following.

an umbrella BUT *a university* (Use *a* when the *u* sounds like *you*.)

a hat, a house BUT *an hour, an honest person* (Use *an* when the *h* is silent.)

عند مقارنة هاتين الكلمتين اللتين تبدآن بالحرف u نجد أننا نستخدم a عندما ينطق الحرف u وكأنه yoo ، وتستخدم an قبل الكلمات التي تبدأ بالحرف h ، وتستخدم a قبل الحرف h المنطوق.

a, an, some or *the*

Use *a* or *an* when you first mention something, eg *an old woman, an umbrella* and *a packet of sandwiches*.

*Larry saw **an old woman**. She had **a packet of sandwiches**.*

تستخدم a أو an عندما تبدأ بذكر اسمٍ ما كما هو مبين.

Use *some* for plural and uncountable nouns.

*She threw **some pieces of bread**.* *She threw **some bread**.*

وتستخدم some للأسماء في حالة جمع الاسماء غير المعدودة.

Use *the* when you mention something (singular, plural or uncountable) again. It is now old information. You already know, for example, about *the woman* and *the packet*.

***The old woman** smiled.* *She opened **the packet**.*

تستخدم أداة التعريف the عند إعادة ذكر الاسم بغض النظر عن كونه في حالة المفرد أو الجمع، وبغض النظر عن كونه من النوع المعدود أو من النوع غير المعدود.

We do not always use *a* or *an* when we mention something new. We use *the* when we all know the thing, eg *the sun* and *the sky*.

***The sun** suddenly came out.* ***The sky** was blue.*

لا نستخدم a أو an بشكل دائم عند ذكر شيء جديد، ونستخدم the عند ذكر شيء معروف لنا جميعاً مثل the sun.

More examples from nature: *the earth, the moon, the country(side), the air, the ground*.

More examples when you talk about a particular thing in a particular country: *the capital, the government, the army, the police*.

وكذلك الحال عند ذكر امثلة من الطبيعة. ايضاً عند الحديث عن شيء محدد في بلد محدد.

More examples when local people talk about particular local places.

... *in **the park** next to **the bus station***. (the only bus station in the local town)

وكذلك عندما يتحدث اناس محليون عن أماكن محلية محددة.

More examples when family members and friends talk about their things.

وكذلك عندما يتحدث أفراد العائلة والأصدقاء عن أشيائهم.

Let's do some work in ***the garden*** *today.* (our particular garden)
Did you hear ***the phone*** *ring?* (the only phone in our house)
I think ***the boss*** *has gone home.* (our boss, the boss that we both work for)
You should see ***the doctor****.* (your family doctor)

The speaker can point to something and use *the*. Compare the following.

ويمكن أن يشير المتحدث إلى شيء ما مستخدماً *the*... لاحظ الأمثلة.

She had ***an umbrella****.*
Look. Whose is ***the umbrella*** *on* ***the bench*** *over there?*

The speaker can give extra information to show which thing and use *the*.

ويمكن للمتحدث أن يعطي معلومات إضافية ليوضح ماهية الشيء مستخدماً *the*.

She was getting on ***the Number 26 bus****.*
She was getting on ***the bus to London****.*
She was getting on ***the bus outside the ticket office****.*

Special uses of *a*, *an* and *the*

Numbers: We usually use *a* with these numbers.

عادة ما تستخدم *a* مع الأرقام كما هو مبين.

a hundred, a hundred and ninety-nine
(I've got about ***a hundred****.* BUT *I've got exactly* ***one hundred****.)*
a thousand, a thousand and ninety-nine
(one thousand one hundred BUT *one thousand nine hundred and ninety-nine)*
a million, a billion, a trillion

Other quantities: We use *a* with other quantities such as *a month, a kilo, a litre, a dollar* and *a kilometre*.

وتستخدم *a* مع المدة الزمنية والكميات المبينة.

Rates: We can use *per* or *a/an* in the following.

وتستخدم كلمة *per* أو *an/a* كما هو مبين.

100 kilometres per hour OR *100 kilometres an hour*
three dollars per kilo OR *three dollars a kilo*

We use *the* to help talk about the position of things.

وتستخدم *the* لتساعد على تحديد مواقع الأشياء.

We live ***in the middle of London/on the edge of town****.*
The house is ***on the right/left****.*

Superlatives: A superlative adjective + noun needs *the* because there is only one (like *the sun* and *the moon*, etc).

وتستخدم *the* مع الدرجة الثالثة للصفة (أفعل التفضيل) لكونها الوحيدة من حيث درجة الصفة المستخدمة.

It's ***the fastest car*** *in the world.*
Question three was ***the most difficult*** *in the whole exam.*
Leaving school early was ***the worst mistake*** *he has ever made.*

We also use *the* to talk about correct information.

وتستخدم *the* أيضاً للحديث عن المعلومات الصحيحة والدقيقة.

What's ***the time****, please?* (the correct time now)
Can you tell me ***the way*** *to the cinema?* (the correct road)
The right answer *to Question 3 is ...* (We also say *the wrong answer.*)

Exercises

1 Write *a* or *an*.

Example: *I only had* an *apple for lunch.*

1 *Would you like ______ orange?*

2 *We planted about ______ hundred trees.*

3 *The car was travelling at 160 kilometres ______ hour.*

4 *Are we going to stop for ______ rest soon?*

5 *Slow down or we'll have ______ accident!*

6 *I've got ______ young son. He's only four.*

7 *When you work for ______ airline, you have to wear ______ uniform.*

8 *Alan was______ honest person. He never told ______ lie in his life.*

2 Write *a*, *an* or *the*.

Example: At a leather goods shop

● *I want to buy* a *red, leather bag. Can you help me?*

❍ *Yes, Madam. I think this is exactly* the *right bag for you.*

1 At a restaurant

● *I'd like* 1______ *table for three people, please.*

❍ *Yes, of course. Please take* 2______ *table over there by the window.*

2 After shopping

● *I've bought* 1______ *book and* 2______ *magazine.*

❍ *Is* 3______ *magazine for me?*

● *No.* 4______ *book is for you, but* 5______ *magazine. is for me.*

3 On the local radio news

● *Here's another piece of local news. There was* 1______ *bank robbery in central Oxford this afternoon. Police Inspector Ross, have you caught* 2______ *robbers yet?*

❍ *No. We're looking for two men in* 3______ *orange BMW.* 4______ *driver of* 5______ *car is wearing* 6______ *green anorak.* 7______ *passenger is wearing* 8______ *old leather jacket.*

4 In a garden near home

● *Excuse me. I'm looking for* 1______ *small, black cat. It's run away from home.*

❍ *Ah, yes. Look over there. Is that* 2______ *cat you mean?*

● *Yes, that's* 3______ *one. Thanks very much.*

5 In a street

● *Can you tell me* 1______ *way to Stanford Office Equipment?*

❍ *Go along Charles Street for* 2______ *kilometre, and you'll come to* 3______ *big crossroads. Turn left there, and you'll see three big buildings on* 4______ *left. Stanford Office Equipment is* 5______ *building in* 6______ *middle.*

3 Write *a*, *an* or *the*.

1 A holiday postcard

I wrote a postcard to my friends at work when I was on holiday last month. It was only 1______ *picture of* 2______ *hotel where I stayed, so it wasn't* 3______ *very special card, but I was angry. You see,* 4______ *card didn't reach* 5______ *office until* 6______ *week after I got back.*

2 Two accidents in one day

Harry has got 1______ *broken leg and* 2______ *broken arm. He got* 3______ *broken arm in* 4______ *car accident, but he got* 5______ *broken leg later. He was sitting in* 6______ *wheelchair and he was waiting for* 7______ *X-ray of* 8______ *broken bone. Unfortunately, he was waiting very near some stairs, and he moved* 9______ *wheelchair a little bit. One wheel went over* 10______ *edge of* 11______ *stairs, and that was how Harry's second accident happened.* 12______ *chair ran all* 13______ *way down* 14______ *stairs; Harry fell out of* 15______ *chair and into* 16______ *wall at* 17______ *bottom of* 18______ *stairs.* 19______ *doctors say Harry will have to stay in hospital for* 20______ *month!*

4 Complete the paragraph with *the* and these words.

beach, birds, fields, hill, sand, sea, sky, sun, trees, waves, wind, world

I remember a wonderful day when I was very young. We left our holiday home early, and we walked down the hill *for a swim at* 1________________ *It was a beautiful summer morning.* 2____________ *was shining, and* 3____________ *was blue.* 4________________ *were singing up in* 5______ *tall, green* 6____________ *In* 7______ *wide, green* 8____________ *to our left and right there were millions of flowers. They were all moving in* 9______ *gentle* 10____________ *Ahead of us, we could see* 11______ *blue and silver* 12____________ *and* 13______ *fast, white* 14____________ *as they crashed onto* 15______ *golden* 16____________ *For us,* 17__________________ *was a perfect place that day.*

5 Write *a* or *the*.

Examples: a) *The boys always stop at* the *park on their way home from school.*

b) *The Town Council are thinking of building* a *new park.*

1 a) *John,* ______ *phone is ringing. Could you answer it, please?*

b) *My brother has got* ______ *phone in every room.*

2 a) *We used to visit our grandparents every summer. We loved* ______ *old house.*

b) *Mr Brook is rich. He's got* ______ *very big house.*

3 a) *It's warm now. Let's eat lunch in* ______ *garden.*

b) *We're going to move house. We want somewhere with* ______ *big garden.*

4 a) *Susan is training to be* ______ *doctor.*

b) *Jimmy is feeling very ill. Quick. Call* ______ *doctor.*

5 a) *Is Mr Bradley* ______ *good boss?*

b) *Where's* ______ *manager, please? I need to see her.*

6 a) *I'm going to pay this money in at* ______ *bank today.*

b) *Excuse me. Is there* ______ *bank near here?*

7 a) *Your train is at 1.00, so I'll take you to* ______ *station now.*

b) *Our town used to have* ______ *station, but it's closed now.*

8 a) *I go to* ______ *dentist every six months.*

b) *I wouldn't like to be* ______ *dentist. I think it's a horrible job!*

9 a) *Every old town in England has* ______ *town square.*

b) *I'll meet you in* ______ *town square at midday.*

10 a) *Could you get some stamps at* ______ *post office for me, please?*

b) *There's* ______ *post office in King Street.*

6 Write *a* or *the* and these words instead of the underlined words.

long letter, mountain, phone, police officer, postman, present, reporter, ship, vase

Examples: *He brings our post every morning.*

The postman brings our post every morning.

The plane crashed into something.

The plane crashed into a mountain.

1 *Somebody answered when I phoned the newspaper.*

____

2 *Joe fell and knocked something over.*

____

3 *He stopped me for driving too fast.*

____

4 *It can travel from Britain to the USA in four days.*

____

5 *When I was away, I bought something for my parents.*

____

6 *I picked it up and called my sister.*

____

7 *Sarah wrote something to her father.*

____

53 Articles 2: general and specific

A plane is a beautiful thing.

FORMS

John is a pilot, and for him ***a plane*** is a beautiful thing – a man-made bird. '*The plane* has changed our world,' he says. '*Planes* allow us to travel anywhere in less than a day.' He flies a small jet, and he carries *people by air* from London to France, Germany and *the Netherlands*. But to John, flying is not just a job from *Monday to Friday*. *At home at the weekend*, he does not watch *TV* or read *the newspaper*. After *breakfast* on *Saturday morning*, he always goes straight to *the garage* and takes out his other plane – ***a microlite***!

General statements – singular

We can use a singular noun to make a general statement. *A plane* means 'any plane'. *The plane* means the type of thing called 'plane'.

***A plane** is a beautiful thing.* ***The plane** has changed our world.*

We can make general statements with plural nouns, eg *people*, and uncountable nouns, eg *life*. Compare the general statements (without *the*) and the specific statements (with *the*).

	General	Specific
Plural:	***People** fly every day.*	***The people** here are Dutch.*
	***Students** are usually poor.*	*Meet **the new students**.*
Uncountable:	*I like strong **curry**.*	*I enjoyed **the curry** last night.*
	*We need **water** to live.*	***The water** is hot now.*

يمكن استخدام اسم مفرد لتكوين جملة خبرية عامة. فاستخدام a plane يعني أي طائرة. ولكن استخدام the plane يعني الشيء المسمى «طائرة». ويمكن تكوين جملة خبرية عامة باستخدام أسماء في حالة الجمع مثل peo-ple، وكذلك أسماء غير معدودة مثل life.

ويتضح الأمر عند مقارنة الأمثلة العامة بدون استخدام أل التعريف the، مع الأخرى التي تتصف بالتحديد والتي تستخدم معها أل التعريف the.

Special expressions – *the* + things in groups

Groups in society: We often use *the* + adjective for groups in society, eg *the poor, the rich, the sick, the old* and *the young*.

*The gap between **the rich** and **the poor** is getting wider.*

تستخدم صفات مسبوقة بـ the غالباً للدلالة على فئات من المجتمع مثل the poor، the young....إلخ.

National groups: We use *the* with national and regional groups of people, eg *the Japanese, the French, the Germans, the Arabs* and *the Europeans*.

***The Japanese** and **the Germans** have worked hard to become rich.*

وتستخدم the أيضاً مع مجموعات من الناس وطنية واقليمية.

Geographical groups: Most country names do not take *the*, eg *Japan, France* and *Egypt*. But *the* is necessary for countries that are a group of smaller parts, eg *the Netherlands, the United Arab Emirates* and *the United States of America*.

لا تستخدم the مع غالبية أسماء البلدان، ولكنها ضرورية مع أسماء البلدان التي تتكون من عدة أجزاء.

Other groups of places also take *the* – islands, eg *the West Indies* and *the Seychelles*, but not single islands, eg *Madagascar*. Also mountains, eg *the Alps* and *the Himalayas*, but not single mountains, eg *Mount Everest*.

هناك مجموعات اخرى من الاماكن تقبل the ايضاً مثل الجزر، ولكن ليس الجزر المفردة، والجبال ولكن ليس الجبال المفردة.

Regions: We talk about regions in different ways. Some are names with *the*, eg *the Far East, the Middle East, the Rift Valley, the Sahara Desert* and *the Nile Delta*. But names with direction + noun do not take *the*, eg *North America* and *South Korea*.

وتسبق the أسماء المناطق الجغرافية مثل the Far east. ولكن أسماء المناطق الجغرافية المسبوقة بأحد الاتجاهات الجغرافية (North America) لا تسبقها the.

We can also talk about regions in this way.

northern/southern/eastern/western Australia OR *the north/the south/the east/the west of Australia*

ويمكن أيضاً، الحديث عن المناطق الجغرافية كما في الأمثلة المبينة.

Rivers, etc: Rivers, canals, seas, gulfs, oceans and deserts all need *the*.

The (River) Mississippi flows into the Gulf of Mexico.
The Panama Canal connects the Caribbean (Sea) and the Pacific (Ocean).

وتستخدم *the* مع أسماء الأنهار والقنوات والبحار والخلجان والصحارى.

Special expressions without and with articles

Places: We do not use *the* when we talk about normal activities that happen *at/to school, at/to work, at/to home*, and *in town, in bed, in hospital*, etc.

*Ann is **at school**. Bob's gone **to bed**.*

لا تستخدم *the* عند الحديث عن النشاطات العادية التي تحدث في المدرسة أو في العمل أو في المنزل أو في المدينة أو في الفراش أو في المستشفيات... الخ.

We use *the* when we talk about a specific building or place.

***The school** is opposite **the hospital**. Tom was on **the bed**.*

وتستخدم *the* عند الحديث عن مبنى معين أو عن مكان محدد.

Time: We do not usually use *a, an* or *the* with most time words and phrases. But we use an article when we add something extra about these times. Compare the following.

***New Year** was on a Sunday. We had **a fantastic New Year**.*
*I came last **week**. I came **the week** Tom was born.*

ولا تستخدم في العادة *a* أو *an* أو *the* مع أغلبية الكلمات أو أشباه الجمل التي تعبر عن الزمن. وتستخدم أحدها عند إضافة دلالات أخرى عن الزمن... لاحظ الأمثلة.

Remember these special expressions: *at night, during the night, on Saturday and Sunday, at the weekend, on Monday morning, in the morning*.

*I woke up **during the night**.*
*I was away **on Saturday and Sunday**.*
*I was away **at the weekend**.*
*I went out **on Monday morning**.*

من الأهمية تعلم التعبيرات المبينة وتذكرها بشكل جيد.

Meals: We do not usually use *a, an* or *the* with *breakfast, lunch, dinner* and *supper*. But we use an article when we add something extra about these meals. Compare the following.

*I have **breakfast** at 8.00.*
*I woke up at 9.00 and had **a late breakfast**.*
*We had steak for **dinner**. That was **the best meal** of my life!*

لا تستخدم *a* و *an* و *the* في الغالب مع أسماء الوجبات، ولكنها تستخدم عندما نضيف لأسماء الوجبات دلالات أخرى... لاحظ الأمثلة.

Transport: We do not use *a/an* or *the* when we talk about the method of transport. But we use an article when we talk about a specific plane, car, etc. Compare the following.

*I came by **plane**. I came on **the 5.00 plane** from Paris.*
*She likes travelling by **car**. It's **a very comfortable car**.*

لا تستخدم *a* و *an* و *the* عند الحديث عن وسائل المواصلات بشكل عام، ولكنها تستخدم عند الحديث عن واحدة محددة من الطائرات أو السيارات. لاحظ الأمثلة.

Entertainment: Note the use of articles in the following.

*I watch **TV** a lot, but I never listen to **the radio**.*
*We like going to **the cinema**, and we often go to **the theatre** too.*

لاحظ كيف تستخدم هذه الأدوات في الأمثلة المبينة.

Musical instruments: We use *the* to talk about playing instruments.

*He plays **the piano/the guitar/the drums**.*

تستخدم the عند الحديث عن العزف على الالات الموسيقية.

Exercises

1 Match the objects and their uses.

1	*A camera*		a	*picking up food.*
2	*A pen*		b	*holding papers.*
3	*A fork*	*is for*	c	*taking phone messages.*
4	*A file*		d	*taking pictures.*
5	*A diary*		e	*writing.*
6	*A fridge*		f	*keeping food cold.*
7	*An answering machine*		g	*noting dates of meetings, etc.*

1 d A camera is for taking pictures.

2 ___ ______________________

3 ___ ______________________

4 ___ ______________________

5 ___ ______________________

6 ___ ______________________

7 ___ ______________________

2 Match the people and their inventions.

1	*Bell*		a	*the electric lamp.*
2	*Otis*		b	*the radio.*
3	*Marconi*	*invented*	c	*the modern car tyre.*
4	*Biro*		d	*the lift* (or **elevator*).
5	*Edison*		e	*the sewing machine.*
6	*Dunlop*		f	*the ballpoint pen.*
7	*Singer*		g	*the telephone.*

*American English

1 g Bell invented the telephone.

2 ___ ______________________

3 ___ ______________________

4 ___ ______________________

5 ___ ______________________

6 ___ ______________________

7 ___ ______________________

3 Write true statements about these things. Use *I like*, *I don't like* or *I don't mind.*

black coffee, chocolate, fast cars, homework, long journeys, loud rock music, swimming, tennis

Examples: I like chocolate.
I don't like long journeys.

1 ______________________

2 ______________________

3 ______________________

4 ______________________

5 ______________________

6 ______________________

4 Choose the correct words.

Examples: *All children like* ice-cream. *(ice-cream/the ice-cream)*

Did you enjoy the film *last night? (film/the film)*

1 *Peter is riding* ____________ *which was ill last week. (horse/the horse)*

2 *My brother visits* ____________ *all over the world. (companies/the companies)*

3 *Could you pass* ____________ *, please? (salt/the salt)*

4 ____________ *aren't here. Where are they? (Books/The books)*

5 ____________ *isn't the most important thing in the world. (Money/The money)*

6 *People can't live for long without* ____________ *(water/the water)*

7 ____________ *live in Africa and India. (Elephants/The elephants)*

8 ____________ *is ringing. Could you answer it, please? (Phone/The phone)*

5 Complete the statements with *the* and these words.

old, poor, rich, unemployed, young

Example: The rich *have to pay high taxes.*

1 *In the old days the government did very little to help* ____________________

2 *These days* ____________________ *receive payments while they are unable to work.*

3 *Today,* ____________________ *are living for longer than ever before.*

4 ____________________ *have to learn from their parents and their teachers.*

5 ____________________ *often use a dog or a stick to help them find their way.*

6 Write the names of the people.

	Country	People
1	*Australia*	the Australians
2	*Britain*	____________
3	*China*	____________
4	*Denmark*	____________
5	*Egypt*	____________
6	*France*	____________
7	*Indonesia*	____________
8	*Japan*	____________
9	*Kuwait*	____________
10	*Netherlands*	____________
11	*Portugal*	____________
12	*Spain*	____________
13	*Russia*	____________
14	*Turkey*	____________
15	*the United States*	____________
16	*Venezuela*	____________

Now write the names of your country and your people.

____

____

7 Write *the* or nothing (✗).

Example: The *Netherlands is a small country in* ✗ *Europe.*

1 _____ *Mississippi is the longest river in* _____ *United States.*

2 _____ *Lake Victoria is a beautiful lake in* _____ *east Africa.*

3 _____ *Mount Everest is the highest mountain in* _____ *Himalayan Mountains to* _____ *north of India.*

4 _____ *Jamaica is a beautiful island in* _____ *West Indies, which are in* _____ *Caribbean Sea.*

5 _____ *Suez Canal lies along* _____ *western edge of* _____ *Sinai Desert in* _____ *Egypt. It connects* _____ *Mediterranean and* _____ *Red Sea.*

8 Write *the* or nothing (✗).

Paul Ross is an international rock star now, but life was not always so good. He grew up in the *north of England and went to* ✗ *school there. He did not enjoy his schooldays very much, but there was a very good music teacher at* [1]_____ *school, and she helped him a lot. He learned to sing well there, and he started to play* [2]_____ *guitar when he was 12. At the age of 18, he went to* [3]_____ *music college, and there he studied other instruments, including* [4]_____ *drums.*

When he left [5]_____ *college, he could not find* [6]_____ *work, so he started the rock band Magic Machine with some friends. Soon they were doing well and they went south to London. They went on* [7]_____ *TV for the first time on* [8]_____ *day Paul was 22.*

When they went to London, they drove there in Paul's old car, but now they travel everywhere by [9]_____ *air.*

Paul and the others work hard, but at the moment, they are on holiday. Paul wakes up late in [10]_____ *morning, and he eats* [11]_____ *breakfast late. He usually stays at* [12]_____ *home for most of the day, and he listens to new music on CDs or* [13]_____ *radio. Then in* [14]_____ *evening, he often goes to* [15]_____ *cinema.*

54 Demonstratives *this, that, these, those* — *one* and *ones* *one, ones*

FORMS

this, that, these* and *those

this/that vase
these/those tables

one* and *ones

the large/small *this/that*	*one*
the large/small *these/those*	*ones*

this, that, these and *those* as demonstrative adjectives

Use *this* and *these* for things which are near in place or time. Use *that* and *those* for things which are not near in place or time.

... *on **that** bookcase* ...
... *over there on **those** tables* ...

تستخدم أسماء الإشارة thisو these مع الأشياء القريبة من حيث المكان أو الزمان.

وتستخدم that و those للأشياء البعيدة من حيث المكان أو الزمان.

Use *this* or *that* with a singular or uncountable noun.

***This wallet** is mine.* ***That purse** is Sally's.*

Use *these* or *those* with a plural noun.

***These shoes** are cheap.* ***Those boots** are really nice!*

تستخدم this أو those مع الأسماء في حالة الجمع.

Use expressions with *that* to say something is right or wrong.

***That**'s right.* *No, **that**'s wrong.*

وتستخدم that مع التعبيرات التي تفيد الصواب أو الخطأ.

this, that, these and *those* as demonstrative pronouns

When the meaning is clear, we can leave out the noun and *one* or *ones*.

***This** is boring. Let's change channels.* (this programme)
*Look at **these**! They're my size.* (these shoes or clothes)

عندما يكون المعنى واضحاً فإننا نسقط استخدام الأسماء و الضمائر one أو ones.

one and *ones*

We use the pronouns *one* and *ones* instead of a noun. Use *one* or *ones* instead of repeating a noun.

*Which **vase**? → Which **one**?*
*Which **plants**? → Which **ones**?*

تستخدم الضمائر one و ones عوضاً عن الأسماء حتى لا نكرر الاسم.

Use *one* or *ones* when you can show what you are talking about.

- *Which is your jacket? Is it this **one**?* (pointing)
- *No, it's that **one** over there. Look!* (pointing)
  *It's the green **one** with red buttons.* (describing)
  *It's the **one** on the chair.* (saying where it is)

تستخدم one أو ones عندما تستطيع ان تبيّن ما تتحدث عنه.

Use *ones* just like *one* – for plural countable nouns.

- *What colour shirts would you like?*
- *A white **one**, please, and two red **ones**.*

وتستخدم ones بنفس الطريقة التي تستخدم فيها one ولكن للأسماء المعدودة في حالة الجمع.

Do not use *one* or *ones* with uncountable nouns. Use *some* instead.

*I'd like **some** white cloth, please, and **some** red cloth.*

لا تستخدم one أو ones مع الأسماء غير المعدودة، وتستخدم some عوضاً عنها.

Exercises

1 Write *this, that, these* or *those.*

Example: *I can't see. What are* those *things over there?*

1 *Could you put the bookcase over there between* ________ *two windows?*

2 ________ *curry last night was very good.*

3 *Look how* ________ *diamonds shine when I turn them in the light.*

4 *Look, you have to press* ________ *button here to start the machine.*

5 ● *Do you remember* ________ *people from Canada? We met them at* ________ *party in London last November.*

❍ *Do you mean* ________ *teachers – Bob and Lisa?*

● *Yes. Well, they're coming for dinner* ________ *evening.*

❍ *Great!*

2 Write *this, that, these* or *those.*

Example: ● *Is* this *your car here?*

❍ *No, mine is blue, not red.* That *'s it over there.*

1 ● *Alice,* ________ *is Tom Barnes, our new salesperson. Tom,* ________ *is Alice Parker, our Finance Director.*

❍ *Nice to meet you.*

● *Good to meet you too.*

2 ● *Could you look at my book, please Miss. Is* ________ *the right answer?*

❍ *Yes,* ________ *'s right. Well done!*

3 ● *Excuse me. Is* ________ *Hill Farm here?*

❍ *No,* ________ *is Lower Farm. Just keep going up the hill.* ________ *'s it, up there at the top.*

4 ● *Here you are, Susan.* ________ *is your desk, and* ________ *are your files. Enjoy your new job!*

❍ *Thanks very much.* ________ *is a nice office.*

5 ● *No, Tom. You've brought me the wrong books. I don't want* ________

❍ *Oh, so do you want* ________ *over there?*

● *Yes,* ________ *are the ones.*

3 Write *this/that (one)* or *these/those (ones).*

Example: ● *Look,* this *must be your bag.*

❍ *No,* this one *isn't my bag. Mine is* that one *over there.*

1 ● *Look. Are* ________ *Tom's shoes here?*

❍ *No.* ________ *over there are his.* ________ *here are Fred's.*

2 ● *After we turn on the computer, we need to put in a disk. Could you pass me* ________ *blue* ________ *on your desk, Bob?*

❍ *Do you mean* ________ *here?*

● *Yes,* ________, *please.*

3 ● *I need some lights for my bike, please.*

❍ *Yes, Sir. Have a look at* ________ *here.*

● *What about* ________ *over there?*

❍ *They're good too, but* ________ *are better.*

4 Write *one/ones* or *the one/the ones.*

Example: ● *Excuse me. I'm trying to find a house. It's Number 73.*

❍ *Do you see the three small* ones *there? Number 73 is* the one *on the left.*

1 ● *Go and say hello to Jim Baker.*

❍ *Which* ________ *is he?*

● *He's* ________ *over there with dark hair.*

2 ● *I'd like some shoes from the shop window, please.*

❍ *Of course. Which* ________ *would you like?*

● *They're* ________ *red* ________ *on the left.*

3 ● *Are David Frost and Roger West here?*

❍ *Yes, they're by the window. David is* ________ *on the right, and Roger is* ________ *on the left.*

4 ● *Could I borrow some plates for my dinner party?*

❍ *Of course. They're all in this cupboard. Which* ________ *would you like –* ________ *large* ________ *or* ________ *small* ________ ?

5 ● *Hello. You're from the band Magic Machine, aren't you? I'm Pete Price. I'm* ________ *who's interviewing you. Which of you is* ________ *who writes the songs?*

❍ *I'm Paul,* ________ *who writes wites the music. Ron and Bob are* ________ *who write the words.*

55 *some* or *any*

We've got some olives. *We haven't got anything.*

FORMS

- ● *Have we got any green olives?*
- ❍ *Yes, we've got some green olives, but we haven't got any black olives.*
- ● *Have we got any tomato juice?*
- ❍ *Yes, we've got some tomato juice, but we haven't got any orange juice.*
- ● *What about meat? Have we got anything for dinner?*
- ❍ *Yes, I think we've got something. Look, we've got some chicken.*

some or *any*

Use *some* in positive sentences with plural nouns and uncountable nouns.

*There are **some green olives**.* *There's **some tomato juice**.*

تستخدم some في الجمل المثبتة مع الأسماء في حالة الجمع وكذلك مع الأسماء غير المعدودة.

Use *any* in negative sentences with plural nouns and uncountable nouns.

*There aren't **any black olives**.* *There isn't **any orange juice**.*

تستخدم any في الجمل المنفية مع الأسماء في حالة الجمع وكذلك مع الأسماء غير المعدودة.

Use *any* with plural nouns and uncountable nouns in *Yes/No* questions. The answer can be *Yes* or *No*.

- ● *Have we got **any** green olives?* (❍ *Yes.*)
- ● *Have we got **any** orange juice?* (❍ *No.*)

تستخدم any مع الأسماء في حالة الجمع مع الأسماء غير المعدودة في الجمل الاستفهامية التي يجاب عنها بـ«نعم» أو «لا». ويمكن أن تقتصر الإجابة على «نعم» أو على «لا».

When we think the answer to our question is *Yes*, we use *some*.

*Are you going to buy **some** things in town today?*

تستخدم some في السؤال عندما نعتقد بان الرد بالايجاب.

We also use *some* to make requests and offers sound positive.

*Could I have **some** money, please?*
*Would you like **some** money?*

وتستخدم some أيضاً لجعل الطلبات والعروض تعطي انطباعاً ايجابياً.

We sometimes use *any* to talk about things that are possible, but uncertain.

*If there are **any** calls, please tell me.*
*Please send **any** letters to my new address.* (if there are any letters)

تستخدم any احياناً للحديث عن اشياء ممكنة ولكن غير اكيدة.

something or *anything*

We can use *some* and *any* to make these new words.

	thing	*body/one*	*where*
some	*something*	*somebody*	*somewhere*
any	*anything*	*anyone*	*anywhere*

تستخدم some و any لاشتقاق كلمات اخرى جديدة... كما هو مبين في الأمثلة.

We choose them as we choose *some* or *any*.

*He told her **something**.* (like *some news* – positive)
*We didn't see **anybody**.* (like *any people* – negative)
*Are you singing **anything** tonight?* (like *any songs* – uncertain)

(See Unit 63 for more information about *something*, *anybody*, etc.)

وتستخدم الكلمات المستحدثة بنفس طريقة استخدام some أو any.

We can use *any*, *anything* and *anybody* to mean 'it doesn't matter what'.

*You can buy these at **any** supermarket.*
*You can have **anything** you want. You choose.*
*It's easy to make. **Anybody** can do it.*

ويمكن أن يعني استخدام any و anything وanybody لتعني أن الأمرين سيّان.

Exercises

1 Write *some* or *any*.

Dear Aunt Lucy,
Well, here we are on holiday. We're having a good time, and there are some *great things about this place, but there are* [1]_____ *bad things too. The sea is great, but the hotel swimming pool isn't. There isn't* [2]_____ *water in the pool! There are* [3]_____ *interesting places to visit near here, but there aren't* [4]_____ *cars to hire. It's true, there are* [5]_____ *buses, but those are all in the middle of the day. There aren't* [6]_____ *in the morning or the evening.*

Must stop. See you soon.

Love, Sam

PS We'll bring you [7]_____ *local olives. They're really good!*

2 Write *some* or *any*.

Example: ● *Come and sit down. Now, have* some *coffee and biscuits.*
❍ *I'm sorry, but I don't drink coffee. Have you got* some/any *tea?*

1 ● *I'm looking for _____ cups, but I can't find _____*
❍ *Perhaps there are _____ in the dishwasher.*

2 ● *Rod, could you lend me _____ money?*
❍ *I'm sorry, Bob, but I haven't got _____. I wanted to ask you for _____ money!*

3 ● *I need _____ help with this work. Have you got _____ free time today?*
❍ *OK. I can give you _____ time tonight.*

4 ● *Ben, would you like to spend _____ time with your grandparents this summer?*
❍ *Well, they're very nice, but I haven't got _____ friends where they live.*

3 Write *some, any, somebody, anybody, something* or *anything*.

Example: ● *I'm getting* some *things at the market. Can I get you* anything/something?
❍ *No, I don't need* anything *thanks.*

1 ● *Is there ________ good on TV tonight?*
❍ *No, there isn't ________ really. There's just ________ about wildlife in India.*

2 ● *Listen! I think I heard a noise. Can you hear ________*
❍ *Do you mean that noise outside? I think ________ is coming to the front door.*

3 ● *Hello! Is ________ at home?*
❍ *Oh, hello, Richard. Come in. You're just in time for ________ tea.*

4 ● *Could ________ please open the door for me? My hands are full.*
❍ *Certainly. And would you like ________ help with carrying those things too?*

5 ● *You look hungry. I'll get you ________ to eat.*
❍ *Thanks. I haven't had ________ to eat since yesterday.*

6 ● *Are there ________ people still living in the house?*
❍ *No, we looked round, but there wasn't ________ there.*

4 Complete the answers. Use *any* (plus a noun from the question), *anything, anybody* or *anywhere*.

Examples: ● *Which car can we hire?*
❍ *We can hire* any car *we like.*
● *I mustn't spend too much.*
❍ *Don't worry. You can buy* anything *you want.*

1 ● *I like this car, but I don't like the colour.*
❍ *You can have ________ you want, Sir.*

2 ● *I'm from Channel 5 TV, and I'd like to interview some members of the team.*
❍ *You're welcome to interview ________ you want.*

3 ● *Are you sure you don't want to keep any of these things?*
❍ *Yes, you can take ________ you want.*

4 ● *Are many people coming to the meeting?*
❍ *I don't know, but we'll welcome ________ who comes.*

5 ● *Where shall we go on holiday this year, Tom?*
❍ *You can go ________ you want to go, Penny.*

56 *There, It* and *They*

There's a hotel in the village.   *It's in the square.*

FORMS

There is* and *There are

Driver: *Is there a place to stay near here?*
Man: *Yes, there's a small hotel in the next village.*

It* and *They

Man: *It's in the village square.*

***It* for time, weather and distance**

Driver: *Good – because it's getting late and it's getting cold. Is it far?*
Man: *No. It's only five kilometres.*

***It* as a dummy subject**

Driver: *All right. It'll be best to stop there for tonight.*

There is and *There are*

We can use *There is* and *There are* when we talk about something for the first time.

● ***Is there*** *a bakery in the town?* ❍ *Yes,* ***there's*** *one near the bank.*

يمكن استخدام there is و there are عند الحديث عن شيءٍ ما للمرة الأولى.

Use *There are* to talk about quantity with, eg *any, some, a lot (of), several, a few, many.*

● ***Are there any*** *other shops?* ❍ *Not* ***many****, but* ***there are a few****.*

تستخدم there are للحديث عن الكم وذلك مع أي من الكلمات المذكورة.

Use *There* with different forms of *be – will be, was/were, has/have been.*

Will there be *time to buy some things?*
There was *no time to do any shopping in the last village.*

تستخدم there مع تصاريف فعل be المختلفة كما هو مبين.

It and *They*

We often use *It* and *They* after *There* to introduce something. *It* and *They* refer back to that thing. We often use *It* like this for people (and other living things).

There was *a hotel in the last village, but* ***it wasn't*** *very nice.*
There were *some shops too, but* ***they were*** *closing.*

نستخدم they و it غالباً بعد استخدام there لتقديم شيء لأن it و they يدلان عليه. وغالباً ما تستخدم it في هذا المقام للدلالة على الأشخاص والأشياء الحية الأخرى.

It for time, weather and distance

Use *It* in expressions about time, weather and distance.

It*'s getting late.* ***It****'s time to go.*

● *What time is* ***it****?* ❍ ***It****'s 5.00.*

It*'s cold.* ***It****'s going to rain.* ***It*** *was a hot day.* ***It*** *was very sunny.*

● *Is* ***it*** *far to the village?* ❍ ***It****'s two miles.*

● *How far is* ***it*** *to London?* ❍ ***It****'s a long way.*

تستخدم it في التعابير التي تتعلق بالزمن والطقس والمسافة.

It as a dummy subject

Use *It ... to* and *It ... that* in expressions like these.

It*'s a good/bad idea* ***to*** *stop.* ***It*** *was good/lovely* ***to*** *see her.*
It*'s sad/a pity* ***that*** *you can't stay.* ***It****'s true* ***that*** *he's leaving.*

استخدم it...to و it...that في التعبيرات التي توضحها الأمثلة.

Use *It* ... verb + *ing* in these expressions.

It*'s (not) worth* ***buying*** *that old car.*
It*'s no use* ***talking****. He never listens.*

تستخدم it مع فعل مضاف له ing في التعبيرات المبينة.

Exercises

1 Write questions and answers. Use *there* + the correct form of *be*.

Examples: *(sugar?) (Yes/over there)*

● Is there any sugar?

❍ Yes, there's some over there.

(onions?) (No/buy some)

● Are there any onions?

❍ No, there aren't. I'll buy some.

1 *(potatoes?) (Yes/in the bag)*

● ______

❍ ______

2 *(coffee?) (No/buy some)*

● ______

❍ ______

3 *(large pan?) (No/buy one)*

● ______

❍ ______

4 *(carrots?) (No/buy some)*

● ______

❍ ______

5 *(butter?) (Yes/in the fridge)*

● ______

❍ ______

6 *(teapot?) (Yes/on the shelf)*

● ______

❍ ______

2 Write *There was, There were, There wasn't* or *There weren't.*

Example: There weren't *many people at the party.*

1 ______ *much food in the house.*

2 ______ *no time to talk.*

3 ______ *many shops open after 9.00.*

4 ______ *a lot of strange noises outside in the forest.*

5 ______ *no bank in the village.*

6 ______ *only a few days left before the exams.*

7 ______ *very little time to do anything.*

3 Write *There* + the correct form of *be* and pronouns.

Examples: There was *a dog in our garden yesterday.* It *came from next door.* There isn't *any butter. We finished* it *yesterday.*

1 ______ *some flowers for Ann.* ______ *'re from Tom.*

2 ______ *much sugar last night. Mum used most of* ______ *to make a cake.*

3 ______ *many people at the concert last night, but I think* ______ *enjoyed it.*

4 ______ *somebody on the phone for you. His name is Peter. Do you know* ______

5 ______ *any matches. Have you used* ______ *all?*

6 ______ *much water, so we'll have to use* ______ *very carefully.*

4 Complete the statements. Choose from these expressions.

It's	*a good/bad idea to ...*
It was	*good/lovely/sad to ...*
	sad that ...
	a pity that ...
	not worth ...
	no use ...

Example: It was a bad idea to *go camping in the middle of winter.*

1 ______ *see all the family together again today.*

2 ______ *walking ten kilometres yesterday just to see that boring view.*

3 ______ *shouting at the children. It doesn't do any good.*

4 ______ *we lost the match after we had done so much training.*

5 ______ *he died so young. He was only 32.*

57 Quantity

a lot of, many, much, a few, a little

FORMS

- ● *Have you got many cassettes?*
- ❍ *Yes, I've got a lot.*
- ● *What about CDs?*
- ❍ *I've only got a few.*

- ● *Have you got much pop music?*
- ❍ *Yes, I've got a lot.*
- ● *What about classical music?*
- ❍ *I've only got a little.*

With countable nouns use *a lot of, many* and *a few*. Use *a lot of* and *many* for a large number of things. The noun has an *s*, eg *a lot of cassettes* and *many videos*

With uncountable nouns use *a lot of, much* and *a little*. Use *a lot of* and *much* for a large amount of something. The noun has no *s*, eg *a lot of pop music* and *much time.*

Use *a lot of* with both countable and uncountable nouns. We use it in positive sentences more than in questions and negative sentences.

*She's got **a lot of cassettes**.* *She's got **a lot of pop music**.*

We can use the informal *lots of* instead of *a lot of.*

*He's got **lots of cassettes**.* *He's got **lots of pop music**.*

We can use short forms in answers to questions.

● *Are there many songs on the CD?* ❍ *Yes, there are **a lot/lots**.*

We usually use *many* and *much* in questions and negative sentences (but sometimes in formal positive sentences too). We can use *much* and *many* by themselves in answers to questions.

- ● ***Are there many** songs on the cassette?*
- ❍ *No, **there aren't many**.* OR *Yes, **lots**.*
- ● ***Is there much** music on the cassette?*
- ❍ *No, **not much**.* OR *Yes, **a lot**.*

We usually use *a few* and *a little* in positive statements, and also in requests and offers.

*There were **a few** people in the room.*
*There was **a little** food on the table.*
*Could I borrow **a few** stamps?* *Would you like **a little** money?*

a few is for a small number of something, but positive. *few* is also for a small number of something, but negative. The noun is plural.

*I'm going to see **a few friends** this evening.* (positive)
***Few people** live to 100.* (negative)

a little and *little* are similar and are for a small amount of something. The noun has no *s*.

*We've got **a little time**, so let's have tea.* (positive)
*Hurry! There's very **little time**.* (negative)

تستخدم a lot of و many و a few مع الأسماء المعدودة. وتستخدم a lot of و many عند الحديث عن عدد كبير من الاشياء. وتلحق الاسم علامة الجمع s.

تستخدم a lot of و much و a little مع الأسماء غير المعدودة. وتستخدم much و a lot of مع الكميات الكبيرة، ولا تضاف علامة الجمع s إلى الاسم.

تستخدم a lot of مع الأسماء المعدودة وغير المعدودة وتستخدم في الجمل المثبتة أكثرمما تستخدم في الجمل الاستفهامية والجمل المنفية.

ويمكن استخدام صيغة lots of غير الرسمية عوضاً عن a lot of.

ويمكن استخدام الصيغ المختصرة عند الإجابة على الأسئلة.

تستخدم many وmuch عادةً في الجمل الاستفهامية وفي الجمل المنفية (وأحياناً في الجمل الرسمية المثبتة أيضاً). ويمكن استخدام much و many بمفردهما عند الإجابة عن الأسئلة.

تستخدم a few و a little عادةً في الجمل الخبرية المثبتة وكذلك في الطلبات والعروض.

تستخدم a few لأعداد قليلة من الأشياء ولكن ايجاباً. أما few فتعبر عن عدد صغير من الأشياء ولكن سلباً. ويكون الاسم في حالة الجمع.

وينطبق الشيء نفسه على a little و little ويستخدمان لكميات صغيرة، ولا تضاف علامة الجمعs إلى الاسم.

Exercises

1 Complete the statements and questions. Use *a lot (of)*, *lots (of)*, *many* or *much*.

Example: ● *Have we got* much *tea?*
❍ *No, we haven't, but we've got* a lot of/ lots of *coffee.*

1 *Let's hurry. There's* ________ *work to do, and there isn't* ________ *time.*

2 *Harry talks to* ________ *people in his work, but he hasn't got* ________ *close friends.*

3 *I haven't got* ________ *money. How* ________ *have you got?*

4 *Some people spend* ________ *time at the office, but they don't really do* ________ *work.*

5 ● *Are there* ________ *people in the shops today?*
❍ *No, not* ________ *, even though* ________ *the shops are having sales.*

6 ● *How* ________ *time do you spend travelling every week?*
❍ ________ *Probably about 20 hours.*

7 ● *How* ________ *times have you been to France?*
❍ *Not* ________ *Three times altogether.*

8 ● *How* ________ *do you weigh?*
❍ *Too* ________ *Nearly 85 kilos.*

2 Complete the statements and questions. Use *a few, few, a little* or *little*.

Examples: *You'd better go to the corner shop. We've only got* a few *eggs and* a little *milk.*
We'd better hurry. There's very little *time.*

1 *We'd better go to the supermarket. There's only* ________ *orange juice, and there are only* ________ *tomatoes.*

2 *My motor-bike is very cheap to run. It uses very* ________ *petrol, and very* ________ *ever goes wrong with it.*

3 *Smoking is going out of fashion.* ________ *still smoke at work, but* ________ *of them think it's a good thing to do.*

4 *The soup isn't ready yet. I think it needs* ________ *cream and* ________ *more chopped vegetables.*

5 *We can only afford* ________ *small presents this year. We've got very* ________ *money.*

6 *Could you lend me* ________ *money? I only need* ________ *pounds.*

7 *The generals of the First World War were men with* ________ *ideas and* ________ *imagination.*

8 ● *I put on* ________ *weight while I was on holiday.*
❍ *How much?*
● *Only* ________ *kilos.*

3 Complete the conversation. Choose from these forms.

a few, few, a little, little, a lot (of), lots (of), many, much

● *How's business, Fred?*
❍ *It's quite good. We're getting* a lot of *orders this year. Not like last year. Last year we had very* [1]________ *work, and* [2]________ *of our staff lost their jobs. How's your company doing?*
● *It's still not very good, I'm sorry to say. We've only got* [3]________ *new orders at the moment, and not* [4]________ *of those are big ones.*
❍ *I'm sorry to hear that.*
● *There's another big problem too. Some customers owe us* [5]________ *money from jobs that we did months ago.*
❍ *That's terrible. How* [6]________ *money do they owe you?*
● *About £50,000. That's* [7]________ *for a small company like mine.*
❍ *Can you do anything to make them pay?*
● *No, I can't really do very* [8]________ *If a company really decides not to pay me on time, there's very* [9]________ *that I can do about it.*
❍ *Perhaps you should get them to pay you* [10]________ *each month.*
● *That's a good idea. I might try it.*

58 Partitives

All of, Most of, None of, Both of, Neither of, etc *every, each*

FORMS

***All of, Both of*, etc**

All of us enjoyed the trip.
We had two instructors. Both of them helped us a lot.

every* and *each

The weather was good every day except Thursday.

All of, Both of, etc

All of means 100% of a group. *None of* means 0% of a group.

***All/None of** us enjoyed rock climbing.*

يفيد استخدام all of جميع المعنيين، ولا يفيد استخدام none of أحداً منهم.

Most of means nearly all. *A few of* means a small number. *Some of* is between *Most* and *A few*. (Other phrases: *A lot of, Half of, One or two of.*)

***Most/Some/A few of** us wanted to do more archery.*

ويفيد استخدام most of الغالبية العظمى في حين تعني a few of عدداً قليلاً. وتستخدم some of لتعبر عن حالة وسط بين most وa few، لاحظ العبارات الاخرى المستخدمة.

Both of means 100% of a pair. *Neither of* means 0% of a pair.

***Both/Neither of** the instructors taught us sandsurfing.*

ويعني استخدام both of كلا الاثنين في حين تفيد neither of الانتفاء عن الاثنين.

With *Both* and *All* + noun, you can leave out *of*. With *Both* + noun, you can also leave out *the*.

***Both (of) (the)** instructors helped **all** (**of**) the students.*

يمكن الاستغناء عن of عندما تأتي مع both وall + اسم. وكذلك يمكن الاستغناء عن الاداة the عند استخدام both + اسم.

But you must use *of* before object pronouns and after *Most, Some, A few* and *Neither*.

Both of them, All of us, Most of you, One of them
Most of the students, Neither of the instructors

One of is different from *either of* and *any of*.

*You can use **either of** the cars.* (It doesn't matter which of the pair you use.)
*You can book **any of** the 200 rooms in the hotel.* (It doesn't matter which of the rooms you book.)

يجب استخدام of قبل الضمير في موقع المفعول به، وكذلك بعد most وsome وa few وneither.
وتختلف of عن either of او any of.

Compare *None of* and *Neither of* above with *not ... any of* and *not ... either of*.

	Subject	**Object**
Group:	*None of*	*not ... any of*
Pair:	*Neither of*	*not ... either of*

***None of** us enjoyed it. They did**n't** help **any of** the students.*
***Neither of** them taught us. We did**n't** like **either of** them.*

قارن بين الاستخدام السابق لـ none of وneither of، اعلاه، وكيفية استخدام not... any of وnot... either of.

Compare talking about a group and talking in general.

***Most of** the students enjoyed it.* (most of the groups of students)
***Most** students work hard.* (most of the group of students)

قارن كيفية الحديث عن مجموعةٍ ما وكيفية الحديث بشكل يتصف بالعمومية.

Use *All, Some* and *No* to talk in general.

***All** cats like milk.* ***Some** trees grow fruit.* ***No** man can fly.*

تستخدم all وsome وno للحديث عن العموميات.

every and *each*

We use *every* and *each* to talk about all members of a group. Use a singular noun and verb.

***Every** day was fun.* (all group members together)
***Each** day was different.* (all group members one by one)

تستخدم every وeach للحديث عن جميع افراد مجموعة. استخدم فعلاً واسماً في صيغة المفرد.

Exercises

1 Complete the statements about the students. Use these words.

all, almost all, a few, most, one, some

A teacher checked her class register for the last 15 lessons.

NAME	PRESENT	ABSENT
John	14	1
Lisa	1	14
Lucy	4	11
David	15	0
Robin	8	7
Greg	12	3
Sally	6	9

Examples: *John came to* almost all of the lessons.
Lisa only came to one of them.

1 *Lucy only came to* ____________________
2 *David came to* ____________________
3 *Robin came to* ____________________
4 *Greg came to* ____________________
5 *Sally only came to* ____________________

2 Complete the second statement in each pair. Use these words.

all of, both of, most of, half of, a few of, us, you, them

Example: *Rob and I don't always get to work on time.* Both of us *were late again today.*

1 *You and your brother look ill.* ____________ *need to see the doctor.*

2 *The teacher put the class in two groups.* ____________ *prepared questions, and the other half prepared their answers.*

3 *Well, everybody, you did very badly in the test.* ____________ *got less than 50%. That's really not good enough!*

4 *The senior and the junior basketball teams are doing very well.* ____________ *reached the national championships.*

5 *About 60 supporters went to the championships. The team coach took* ____________ *in his car, but* ____________ *went by bus. We had a great time.*

3 Complete the negative statements. Use these words.

any of, either of, neither of, none of

Examples: *The couple next door are strange. I don't like* either of *them much.*
None of *the children wanted to go home at the end of the party.*

1 *I asked Wayne and Brian, but* ____________ *them could lend me any money.*

2 *I offered all the old people a trip to London, but* ____________ *them wanted to go.*

3 *We looked at several restaurants, but we didn't like* ____________ *them.*

4 *Peter tried two different hotel jobs, but he wasn't very good at* ____________ *them.*

5 ____________ *Joe's clothes fitted him any more because he was growing so fast.*

6 ____________ *the teams scored, and the match ended at 0 – 0.*

7 *I test drove a number of new cars, but I didn't buy* ____________ *them.*

8 *I took two exams, but because I hadn't done enough work, I didn't pass* ____________ *them.*

9 *I've read both of these books and I didn't like* ____________ *them. They were very boring.*

10 *I asked the class if* ____________ *them would help me move the tables, but* ____________ *them did. So I did it myself.*

4 Complete the paragraph. Use these words.

all, both, each, every

Jamie and his friends, Bob and Pete, go to judo classes every *week. He and* [1]______ *his friends love judo, and they never miss their class* [2]______ *Friday evening. There are about 20 people in the class, and* [3]______ *of them train very hard. To start with, they* [4]______ *do exercises together. Then the teacher works with* [5]______ *member of the class, one by one.* [6]______ *student trains at his or her own standard.* [7]______ *three months, they take a test. If they pass, they go up to the next grade.*

59 Pronouns: subject and object

You can give it to me.

FORMS

	1st person	2nd person	3rd person
Singular			
Subject	*I*	*you*	*he she it*
Object	*me*	*you*	*him her it*
Plural			
Subject	*we*	*you*	*they*
Object	*us*	*you*	*them*

Personal pronouns refer to people and things. We use pronouns instead of nouns, eg for people's names, when the meaning is clear.

تشير الضمائر الشخصية الى الاشخاص والاشياء. وتستخدم الضمائر عوضاً عن الاسماء عندما تكون المعاني قد اتضحت.

First person pronouns refer to the speaker, or to the speaker and one or more other people.

We must get ... (the two speakers)
Give it to ***me***. (the speaker)

ويشير الضمير المفرد الاول الى المتحدث كشخص فرد، في حين يشير الضمير we الى متحدثين اثنين او اكثر.

Second person pronouns refer to the person or people listening.

You *can give* ... (the listener)

ويشير الضمير الثاني you الى المخاطب كفرد أو إلى مخاطبين اثنين أو أكثر.

Third person pronouns refer to either a person or people or a thing or things. These are outside the 1st and 2nd persons' conversation.

Give ***it*** *to* ***them***. (the package and some other people)

وتشير ضمائر الغائب (3rd person) الى فرد او الى افراد، او الى شيء واحد، أو اشياء، خارج حدود المحادثة بين المتحدث او المتحدثين.

A personal pronoun can be the subject or the object of a sentence.

Subject	**Object**
I*'m going home now.*	*Peter doesn't know* ***me***.
Is ***she*** *working tomorrow?*	*Sally called* ***her*** *three times.*
They *don't like loud music.*	*We answered* ***them***.

يمكن ان يأتي الضمير الشخصي في موقع الفاعل، أو المبتدأ في الجملة، أو في موقع المفعول به.

An object pronoun can be either a direct object or an indirect object. (See Unit 62 for more information about direct and indirect objects.)

Joe sent ***it***. (direct object)
Joe sent it ***to her***. (indirect object)

عندما يأتي الضمير في موقع المفعول به، يمكن ان يكون مفعولاً به مباشراً او غير مباشر. (انظر unit 62 للمزيد من المعلومات عن المفعول به المباشر وغير المباشر)

You can use pronouns in short answers to questions. The other way of doing this – with object pronouns – is informal.

- *Who broke this dish?* ❍ ***I*** *did./****I*** *didn't.* OR ***Me****./Not* ***me***.
- *Who'll wash the car for me?* ❍ ***We*** *will./****We*** *won't.* OR ***Us****./Not* ***us***.

يمكن استخدام الضمائر في الاجابات القصيرة عن الاسئلة. لاحظ كيف تستخدم الضمائر في صيغة المفعول به بطريقة غير رسمية.

There are ways of talking about people in general. The pronoun *you* is informal.

You *never know what's going to happen.*

يستخدم الضمير you للحديث عن الناس بشكل عام. ويعتبر استخدام الضمير you هنا استخداماً غير رسمي.

The pronoun *one* is very formal.

One *cannot judge people by the way they look.*

يعتبر استخدام الضمير one في هذا المقام صيغة رسمية جداً.

The pronoun *they* refers to other people in general, or to people who are in charge.

They *say some people hardly ever sleep.*
They *don't let foreigners visit without a visa.*

ويشير الضمير they الى الآخرين بشكل عام او الى اشخاص بعينهم من المسؤولين.

Exercises

1 Read the conversation. Then write the meanings of the underlined pronouns.

Paul: *What are* [1]*you doing tomorrow?*

Bill: [2]*I'm going to a football practice in the morning.*

Paul: [3]*I'd like to go to that too. I love football. What time does* [4]*it start?*

Bill: *At 10.00. Why don't* [5]*you come with* [6]*me? Then after that, we can meet Neil in town.* [7]*He wants to see the new Batman film.*

Paul: *Oh, yes. People say* [8]*it's good.*

Bill: *Yes,* [9]*they say it's the best Batman film yet. So I think* [10]*we should all go and see it together. What do you think?*

1 *you* = Bill
2 *I* = ______
3 *I* = ______
4 *it* = ______
5 *you* = ______
6 *me* = ______
7 *He* = ______
8 *it* = ______
9 *they* = ______
10 *we* = ______

2 Write the correct subject pronouns and short forms of *be*.

Example: ● *What are* you *doing, Sally?*
❍ I'm *making a cake.*

1 ● *Where are Tom and Bill going?*
❍ ______ *going to the cinema.*

2 ● *Susan looks great in that dress.*
❍ *Yes,* ______ *a beautiful girl.*

3 ● *What are* ______ *and the boys doing?*
❍ ______ *going to the swimming pool.*

4 ● *What's that dog doing in our kitchen?*
❍ ______ *taking our lunch!*

5 ● *Do you know Peter Wells?*
❍ *Yes,* ______ *the man with the big house at the end of our street.*

6 ● *How are* ______ *travelling round France, Fred?*
❍ ______ *travelling by bike.*

7 ● ______ *looking very happy today, Sally.*
❍ *Yes,* ______ *my birthday and* ______ *18 today.* ______ *having a party tonight. Please come.*

3 Write the correct object pronouns.

Example: ● *Where did you put my hat?*
❍ *I put* it *on the table.*

1 ● *Do you know where Ann is?*
❍ *Yes. I can see* ______ *over there.*

2 ● *I'll be at home this evening.*
❍ *All right. I'll call* ______ *at 7.00.*

3 ● *I need to see Mr Brice, please.*
❍ *Certainly. You can see* ______ *at 3.00.*

4 ● *Do you like these shoes?*
❍ *Yes. I'm going to buy* ______

5 ● *Why does Peter always call* ______ *in the evening, Tony?*
❍ *Because he always wants* ______ *to help* ______ *with his homework.*

6 ● *Were there any calls for* ______ *while we were out?*
❍ *There weren't any calls for Bill, but there was a call for* ______ *. Mrs Tucker phoned and she wants* ______ *to call* ______ *back.*

4 Write the correct subject and object pronouns and short froms of *be*.

It's Tom's first day at the office.

Jim: *Tom, come and meet Ann Scott.* She's *our Finance Director. Ann, this is Tom Blake.* [1]______ *our new sales assistant.*

Ann: *It's nice to meet* [2]______ *, Tom.*

Tom: [3]______ *good to meet* [4]______ *too, Mrs Scott.*

Ann: *Oh, please call* [5]______ *Ann.* [6]______ *all use our first names here.*

Later the same day

Jim: *Tom, could* [7]______ *help* [8]______ *please?*

Tom: *Yes, of course. What can* [9]______ *do?*

Jim: *Take this report to Finance and give* [10]______ *to Ann. And give* [11]______ *these papers too.* [12]______ *very important.* [13]______ *needs* [14]______ *for a meeting.* [15]______ *starting in a few minutes from now.*

Tom: *Right.* [16]______ *'ll go immediately.*

60 Pronouns: possessive

Is this your jacket? It's mine. It's Tim's.

FORMS

	Possessive determiners	Possessive pronouns
Singular		
1st person	*my*	*mine*
2nd person	*your*	*yours*
3rd person	*her/his/its*	*hers/his/its*
Plural		
1st person	*our*	*ours*
2nd person	*your*	*yours*
3rd person	*their*	*theirs*

Possessive with *'s*

This shirt belongs to Tim. →
This is Tim's shirt./This shirt is Tim's.
These shirts belong to the boys.→
These shirts are the boys' shirts.

Possessive determiners and possessive pronouns

my, your, their, etc, come before a noun. They are determiners. They are also posssessive – they show who or what owns something.

*Is this **your** jacket?*
*Where are **my** shoes? I can't see them.*

تأتي الضمائر my وyour وtheir... الخ قبل الاسم، وتعمل هنا كمحددات، كما انها تفيد الملكية اذ تبين لنا من يملك ماذا.

We can use *mine, yours, theirs*, etc, instead of a possessive determiner + noun. They are pronouns.

*This jacket isn't **mine**. Is it **yours**?*
*That car isn't **ours**. It's **theirs**.*

ويمكن استخدام صيغ الملكية mine... الخ عوضاً عن محددات الملكية مضافاً لها الاسم... وتعتبر هنا ضمائر.

Note that *his* and *its* are determiners and also pronouns. (But *its* as a pronoun is rare.)

● *Perhaps this is **his** bag.*
❍ *No, it isn't **his**. **It's** mine.*

تعمل his وits عمل المحددات وعمل الضمائر ايضاً. ولكن استخدام its كضمير امر نادر.

its is different from *it's*. *its* is a possessive determiner. *it's* is short for *it is* or *it has*.

*Here's the camera, and this is **its** case.* (possessive)
*Look. Now **it's** raining.* (***it's*** = *it is*)
*There's the bus! At last **it's** arrived.* (***it's*** = *it has*)

تختلف its التي تفيد تحديد الملكية عن it's التي تأتي اختصاراً it is او it has.

Possessive with *'s*

Use noun + *'s* like a possessive determiner.

*This is **her** coat.* → *This is Sally**'s** coat.*

عندما يضاف للاسم s' فانها تكون محددة للملكية.

Use noun + *'s* like a possessive pronoun.

*This hat is **hers**.* → *This hat is Sally**'s**.*

تعمل صيغة استخدام الاسم مع s' عمل ضمير الملكية.

After a plural noun with *s*, write noun + *s'*.

*These are the **girls'** coats.*
*These coats are the **girls'**, not the **boys'**.*

توضع s' بعد الاسم في حالة الجمع + s.

Exercises

1 Write possessive adjectives.

Example: *Hello. My name is Bob.*

1 *Could you write ________ address here, please?*
2 *The boy fell down and hurt ________ arm.*
3 *Let's take ________ holidays at the same time and go away together.*
4 *Could you call at Mr and Mrs Hill's house and give back ________ books?*
5 *Is Sally Barrett here? This is ________ bag.*
6 *That's ________ pen! Give it back to me!*
7 *The cat wants ________ dinner. Look, it's waiting outside.*

2 Write the answers.

Example: ● *Are these shoes Sally's? (No/bigger)*
❍ *No, they aren't hers. Hers are bigger.*

1 ● *Is that coat John's? (No/older)*
❍ ________________________________

2 ● *Are those magazines Julie's? (No/newer)*
❍ ________________________________
____

3 ● *Is that car Tom's and Lucy's? (No/smaller)*
❍ ________________________________
____

4 ● *Is that coat mine? (No/nicer)*
❍ ________________________________

5 ● *Are these reports ours? (No/longer)*
❍ ________________________________
____

6 ● *Is this umbrella yours?*
❍ *Yes, it is _____! Thank you very much!*

3 Write the answers.

Example: ● *Is this bag his or hers? (hers)*
❍ *It's hers. Look, it's got her name inside.*

1 ● *Are these boots yours or mine? (yours)*
❍ ________________________________
____

2 ● *Is this briefcase his or hers? (his)*
❍ ________________________________
____

3 ● *Are these shoes ours or theirs? (theirs)*
❍ ________________________________
____

4 ● *Is that jacket hers or yours? (mine)*
❍ ________________________________
____

5 ● *Are those T-shirts hers or mine? (hers)*
❍ ________________________________
____

6 ● *Is this book yours or his? (ours)*
❍ ________________________________
____

4 Write *its* or *it's*.

Examples: *The dog ate its food in less that a minute.*
It's 1.00 and this is the News.

1 *The sky has gone dark and ______ started to rain.*
2 *Here's the cassette, but I've lost ______ case.*
3 *Let's stay indoors. ______ too cold to go out.*
4 *I know ______ hard for you, but you must finish the work.*
5 *This is our cat. ______ name is Fluffy.*
6 *Don't try to move your leg. I think ______ broken.*

5 Complete the words with *'s* or *s'*.

Examples: *Look at Tony's pictures. They're lovely.*
The two boys' bikes are in the garage.

1 *My parent___ phone number is 345-321. You can call them any time.*
2 *My brother Peter___ phone number is 345-789.*
3 *Please, can you tell me Sally West___ room number?*
4 *A policeman___ job is often difficult.*
5 *The government has refused to raise hospital worker___ pay again this year.*
6 *Why did you laugh at Tony___ suggestions? I don't understand why you can't accept other people___ ideas.*

61 Pronouns: reflexive

You'll hurt yourself.

FORMS

Singular

1st person	*I'll hurt myself.*
2nd person	*You'll hurt yourself.*
3rd person	*He'll hurt himself.*
	She'll hurt herself.
	It'll hurt itself.

Plural

1st person	*We'll hurt ourselves.*
2nd person	*You'll hurt yourselves.*
3rd person	*They'll hurt themselves.*

Use a reflexive pronoun when the subject (S) of a verb (V) is also the direct object (DO) of the action. Compare the following.

S	V	DO	S	V	DO
You'll	*hurt*	*him.*	*You'll*	*hurt*	***yourself.***
He's	*cut*	*her.*	*He's*	*cut*	***himself.***

يستخدم الضمير المنعكس عندما يكون الفاعل هو المفعول به المباشر في الوقت نفسه، ويتضح ذلك من خلال مقارنة الجمل التالية.

Use a reflexive pronoun when the subject of an action is also the indirect object (IO) of an action. Compare the following.

S	V	IO	S	V	IO
She	*talked*	*to me.*	*She*	*talked*	*to **herself.***
He	*works*	*for us.*	*He*	*works*	*for **himself.***

يستخدم الضمير المنعكس عندما يكون فاعل الفعل هو نفسه المفعول به غير المباشر للعمل. ويتضح الامر من خلال مقارنة الجمل التالية:

Use a reflexive pronoun as an indirect object with a direct object. (See Unit 62 for more information about direct and indirect objects.) Compare the following.

S	V	IO	DO	S	V	IO	DO
She	*bought*	*me*	*a book.*	*She*	*bought*	***herself***	*a book.*
We	*taught*	*them*	*Arabic.*	*We*	*taught*	***ourselves***	*Arabic.*

يستخدم الضمير الانعكاسي كمفعول به غير مباشر مع مفعول به مباشر. (انظر unit 62 للمزيد من المعلومات حول المفعول به المباشر وغير المباشر) وقارن ما يلي:

Note the singular → plural change in *self* → *selves.*

*I enjoyed **myself** at the party.*
*We enjoyed **ourselves** at the party.*

تجدر ملاحظة التغييرات التي تطرأ على الضمير الانعكاسي self في حالة المفرد والذي يصبح selves في حالة الجمع.

Also use a reflexive pronoun to emphasize the subject of an action. This type of reflexive comes after the object of the verb.

● *Let me buy the ticket for you.*
❍ *No, thanks. I'll buy **it myself**.* (I want to do it – not you.)
*Jamie's five now, so he can put on **his clothes himself/by himself**.* (He doesn't need his parents' help.)

ويستخدم الضمير المنعكس للتأكيد على الفاعل.

ويأتي هذا النوع من الضمائر الانعكاسية بعد المفعول به مباشرة.

Also use *by* + a reflexive pronoun to emphasize that the subject of an action does the action alone.

*John climbed the mountain **by himself**.*
*The teacher made Ann sit **by herself**, away from the other girls.*

وتستخدم by + ضمير منعكس لتأكيد ان الفاعل هو الذي يقوم بالفعل منفرداً.

Exercises

1 Write the correct reflexive pronouns.

Example: *Stop shouting. Control* yourself.

1 *Tell the children to dry* ____________ *or they'll catch cold.*

2 *The light turns* ____________ *off automatically.*

3 *Her real name is Monica, but she calls* ____________ *Mo.*

4 *I was tired, so I gave* ____________ *a day off work.*

5 *Dan injured* ____________ *badly at work.*

6 *We need to protect* ____________ *from the sun. We'd better wear hats.*

7 *Don't play with knives or you'll cut* ____________

8 *Children, while I'm out I want you to behave* ____________

2 Write the correct verbs and reflexive pronouns. Use these verbs.

bought, burn, kill, look after, looked at, made, push, save, wash

Example: *Be careful with the pan. It's hot. Don't* burn yourself.

1 *The boat crashed into the rocks, but Fred managed to* ____________

2 *Drive more slowly in future, or you'll* ____________ *one day.*

3 *Tina tried on the hat, and then she* ____________ *in the mirror.*

4 *I was tired when I got home, so I* ____________ *a cup of tea.*

5 *Everybody in the team went to the sports shop and they* ____________ *the same kind of baseball cap.*

6 *We're not doing enough training. We've got to* ____________ *even harder if we want to win the championship.*

7 *Our cat is a very clean animal. It likes to sit in the sun and* ____________

8 *I shall miss you both while you're away. Be careful and* ____________

3 Write the correct types of pronoun.

Examples: *Then I saw Bob. He was quite near, so I called* him.
Sue bought some books, and she taught herself *to cook.*

1 *I looked at Sam. He looked back at* ____________

2 *Look at* ____________ *in the mirror! You're all in a terrible mess.*

3 *Sue doesn't think about other people. She only thinks about* ____________

4 *Your house is very near ours. You must come and visit* ____________ *soon.*

5 *Let's put on the cassette recorder, and then we can record* ____________

6 *They never help us, so I don't want to help* ____________

7 *My son is going to university soon. I shall miss* ____________ *very much.*

4 Write the answers. Use reflexive pronouns for emphasis.

Example: ● *Did Alan's assistant send the letters?*
❍ No, he sent them himself.

1 ● *Did your dad pay for your car?*
❍ ____________

2 ● *Does Sue's secretary prepare the reports?*
❍ ____________

3 ● *Is Steve's brother bringing the equipment?*
❍ ____________

4 ● *Will I have to tidy the children's room?*
❍ ____________

5 ● *Are the boys going to clean our car?*
❍ ____________

6 ● *I'm hungry! Are you going to make dinner now?*
❍ ____________

62 Direct and indirect objects

She sent them a card.

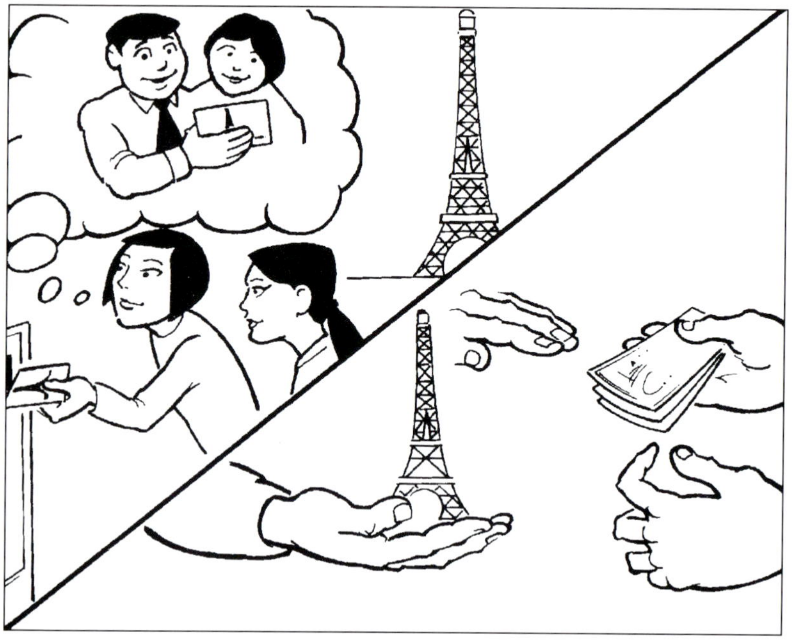

FORMS

S	V	(DO)	
Susan	*laughed.*		
Susan	*studies*	*(French).*	
Susan	*sent*	*a card.*	

Form 1 Indirect objects

S	V	DO	IO
Susan	*sent*	*a card*	*to her parents.*

Form 2 Indirect objects

S	V	IO	DO
Susan	*sent*	*her parents*	*a card.*

Form 3 Indirect objects

S	V	IO
Susan	*laughed*	*at us.*

Some verbs (V) do not take a direct object (DO).

*Susan **laughed**.* *We **talked**.*

بعض الافعال لا تتعدى إلى مفعول به مباشر.

Some verbs can be with or without a direct object.

*Susan **studies**.* *Susan **studies French**.*

وبعض الافعال يمكن ان تتعدى إلى مفعول به مباشر، أو لا تتعدى.

Most verbs must take a direct object.

*Susan **sent a card**.* *She **bought a souvenir**.*

معظم الافعال يجب ان تتعدى إلى مفعول به مباشر.

Some verbs take a direct object and an indirect object (IO) too. After these verbs we introduce the indirect object with *to*: *bring, give, lend, pass, pay, sell, show, take, teach, tell, throw.*

S	V	DO	IO
He	***paid***	***the money***	***to her**.*
Bob	***gave***	***his old car***	***to his brother**.*

وبعض الافعال تتعدى إلى مفعول به مباشر وآخر غير مباشر، ايضاً. وهنا نقدم على المفعول به غير المباشر اداة الجر to. وفيما يلي قائمة بهذه الافعال.

After these verbs we introduce the indirect object with *for*: *bring, buy, cook, do, get, make, order, take.*

S	V	DO	IO
I've	***brought***	*some books*	***for you**. Here you are.*
I'm	***doing***	*a letter*	***for the boss**.*

بعد هذه الافعال التالية ندخل المفعول به غير المباشر مع for.

We can use *bring* and *take* with both *to* + indirect object and *for* + indirect object.

S	V	DO	IO
I	***took***	*the books*	***to the teacher**.*
I	***brought***	*some flowers*	***for Mary**.*

يمكن ان نستخدم الفعلين bring وtake مع to + مفعول به غير مباشر، وكذلك مع for + مفعول به غير مباشر.

We often use Form 1 (see FORMS above) for emphasis.

*Don't pass **the ball to him**! Pass **it to me**.*

غالباً ما تستخدم الصيغة الاولى + to لتفيد التأكيد (لاحظ forms اعلاه)

But we usually use Form 2.

*He paid **her money**.* *I've bought **you a book**.*

ولكن تستخدم الصيغة الثانية (form 2) عادة.

In Form 3 there is no direct object, only an indirect object.

*Sue laughed **at us**.* *We smiled **at each other**.*

لا تحتوي الصيغة الثالثة (form 3) على مفعول به مباشر ولكنها تحوي مفعولاً به غير مباشر فقط.

Exercises

1 Write statements with the indirect objects in the correct position.

Examples: *I'm writing a letter. (to my sister)*
I'm writing a letter to my sister.
I'm writing a card. (my brother)
I'm writing my brother a card.

1 *Ann gave a present. (her parents)*
______

2 *Nick sent a book. (to his niece)*
______

3 *Did you really buy it? (for me)*
______

4 *Could you lend some money? (Harry)*
______

5 *Susie's grandmother made a lovely dress. (her)*
______

6 *I'll take some magazines next time I visit her in hospital. (Celia)*
______

7 *Could you pass the report when he arrives? (to the boss)*
______

8 *I offered a place to stay as he had nowhere else to go. (Rob)*
______

2 Write replies. Use Form 1 indirect objects for emphasis.

Example: ● *Could you give Bob this magazine? (Kim)*
❍ *No, don't give it to Bob. Give it to Kim.*

1 ● *I'm going to sell my pictures to Sally. (me)*
❍ ______

2 ● *I'd better take the car to the garage in town. (one near my house)*
❍ ______

3 ● *I think I'll buy a computer game for Sally. (her brother)*
❍ ______

4 ● *I'm going to show this information about Mr Blake to him. (the police)*
❍ ______

5 ● *I think I'll cook the steak for the children. (the adults)*
❍ ______

6 ● *Do I have to pay the money to Tom's teacher? (the school secretary)*
❍ ______

7 ● *I'll buy a present for you while I'm in Paris. (the children)*
❍ ______

3 Complete the memo with *to* or *for*.

Memo

From: JJ
To: KL *Date: 3rd March*

Ken,
Could you do a few things for me while I'm away in Rome? Could you finish the report on my desk [1] ______ *me? I've been writing it specially* [2] ______ *the Head of Sales, so could you please give it* [3] ______ *him personally by midday on Thursday? Please explain the special items* [4] ______ *him. I've made some notes* [5] ______ *you, so you'll know what to write.*

We've ordered some new computer equipment [6] ______ *the Sales Department. Could you ask the men from Compu-Tech to take the equipment* [7] ______ *Room 508? Please give the cheque on my desk* [8] ______ *the men when they come.*

Thanks. I'll get some really good Italian olive oil [9] ______ *you while I'm in Rome.*

See you next week.
Jack

63 *something, anybody, everyone,* etc

There's something for everyone.

FORMS

	thing	*body*	*one*	*where*
some	*something* (a thing)	*somebody* (a person)	*someone* (a person)	*somewhere* (in a place)
any	*anything* (a thing)	*anybody* (a person)	*anyone* (a person)	*anywhere* (in a place)
every	*everything* (all the things)	*everybody* (all the people)	*everyone* (all the people)	*everywhere* (in all the places)
no	*nothing* (no things)	*nobody* (no person)	*no one* (no person)	*nowhere* (in no place)

We can put *some, any, every* and *no* together with *thing, body, one* and *where* to form new words.

*My book is **somewhere** in this room.*
*Has **anyone** seen my book?*
***Everybody**! Please help me find it!*
*I looked, but I found **nothing**.*

يمكن تكوين كلمات جديدة عند اضافة الكلمات some وany وevery وno للكلمات thing وbody وone وwhere.

The words *something* and *anything*, etc, are like *some* and *any*.
Positive statements: *He told her **something**.*
Negative statements: *We didn't see **anybody**.*
Yes/No questions: *Did you go **anywhere**?*
Positive questions: *Did you find **something**?*
Offers: *Can I help **anyone**?*
Requests: *May I see **someone** in the office?*
Things that are possible, but not certain: *If **anybody** calls, tell me.*
(See Unit 43 for more information.)

وتعامل الكلمات something وanything ... الخ نفس معاملة some وany.. ويتضح ذلك من خلال الامثلة. (انظر unit 43 للمزيد من المعلومات).

All the words in this group are singular, including the words with *every*.

*Is **everyone** here now?*   ***Everything** takes a long time.*

تعتبر جميع الكلمات في هذه المجموعة في حالة المفرد بما في ذلك الكلمات التي تأتي مع every.

The words with *no* are negatives, so use the 3rd person singular positive forms of verbs.

***Nobody** is happy with the plan.*   ***No one** wants to go out.*

تكون الكلمات التي تأتي مع no في صيغة النفي، الأمر الذي يتطلب وضع الفعل المضارع مع الضمير المفرد الغائب في صيغة الاثبات.

We can use an adjective, eg *strange, funny* and *boring*, after words with *some, any* and *no*, (but not usually after words with *every*).

***Somebody** came to the door.*   *Is there **anything** funny on TV?*

يمكن استخدام صفة بعد الكلمات التي تضاف لـsome وany وno، ولكن ذلك ليس شائعاً بعد الكلمات التي تضاف لـ every.

We can use *else* after all these words.

*We haven't got **anything else** to eat.*
*There's **nowhere else** to go.*

يمكن استخدام كلمة else بعد كل هذه الكلمات.

We can use the possessive *'s* form with the words that end with *body* or *one*.

*Is this **anybody's** jacket?*   *The accident was **no one's** fault.*
***Somebody's** car is in our parking space!*

يمكن استخدام صيغة الملكية 's مع الكلمات التي تنتهي بـ body او one.

Exercises

1 Write *some, any, something, anybody, somewhere*, etc.

Examples: *I met* some *old friends yesterday.*
Yesterday I met somebody *who knows you.*

1 *I've got ______________ free time tomorrow.*
2 *I can't think of ______________ to do.*
3 *Have you got ______________ money?*
4 *Tony must be ______________ in the park.*
5 *Does ______________ here know how to work this machine?*
6 *Could I take ______________ paper, please?*
7 *If ______________ asks for me, just say I'm busy.*
8 *Would you like ______________ coffee?*
9 *She can't find her glasses ______________*
10 *I've got ______________ for you to do this afternoon.*

2 Complete the statements with the correct words beginning with *some-, any-, every-,* and *no-*.

Examples: *I don't know* anybody *as clever as Tom. (any-)*

1 *If ______________ is here now, the meeting can begin. (every-)*
2 *______________ we went in Africa, we found the people very friendly. (every-)*
3 *Excuse me. I've got ______________ important to say. (some-)*
4 *______________ in the world can run as fast as Steve. (no-)*
5 *If there's ______________ still in the building, tell them to come out quickly. (any-)*
6 *Is there ______________ quiet near here for us to talk? (any-)*
7 *Is there ______________ I can do to help you? (any-)*

3 Write *something, anybody, everyone, nowhere*, etc.

● *Has* anybody *seen my new Bruce Springsteen cassette? I've been looking for it* [1] ______________ *– all over the house.*
❍ *I don't think it's* [2] ______________ *in this room.*
● *Well, it must be* [3] ______________ *round here. It can't have disappeared.* [4] ______________ *must have seen it.*
❍ *Did you lend it to* [5] ______________ *Or did you take it* [6] ______________ *with you – into town, for example?*
● *No, I've been absolutely* [7] ______________ *since yesterday morning. I've just been at home. And* [8] ______________*'s borrowed it either.*
❍ *Wait. Look! There's* [9] ______________ *under that chair. Is that it?*
● *Where? I can't see* [10] ______________ *Oh, I see it now. You're right. That's it! Thanks very much!*

4 Complete the statements. Use the words in brackets.

Examples: *There's* something good *on TV tonight. (a good thing)*
We're all here now. There's nobody else *to come. (not another person)*

1 *There's ______________ on TV tonight. (no interesting thing)*
2 *I haven't told you the whole story. I've got ______________ to tell. (another thing)*
3 *This beach is too crowded. Isn't there ______________ we can go? (another place)*
4 *I've looked for the money ______________ ______________ (all possible places)*
5 *Is ______________ coming to dinner this evening? (a nice person)*
6 *There's ______________ to look for the money. (no other place)*

64 Relative clauses 1

He's the person who caused the accident.

FORMS

He's the person	*who* *that*	*caused the accident.*
That's the car	*which* *that*	*he was driving.*

A clause is a group of words with a subject and a verb. It can be a complete, simple sentence, or it can be a part of a larger sentence. A relative clause is only a part of a sentence. It adds meaning to the main clause of a sentence.

تعني كلمة "clause" عبارة تتكون من مجموعة من الكلمات تحوي فاعلاً وفعلاً، ويمكن ان تكون جملة كاملة، بسيطة، او جزءاً من جملة اكبر. اما العبارة الموصولية فتكون فقط جزءاً من جملة تضيف معنى للجزء الرئيسي في الجملة.

who, *which* and *that* introduce relative clauses. They refer back to a noun and stand instead of the noun.

*He's **the person who** ...*

*That's **the car which** ...*

They introduce a new idea about the noun.

*... **who caused the accident**.*
*... **which he was driving**.*

تقدم العبارات الموصولية بالكلمات who وwhich وthat، وهي تشير الى اسم سبق ذكره، وتأتي عوضاً عنه. وتضيف هذه الكلمات فكرة جديدة عن الاسم.

Below, idea 2 shows which bus and which friends the speaker means. Idea 1 is the main clause. Idea 2 supports it and completes the meaning of the sentence. It is a defining relative clause.

1 *The bus is going to London.*
2 *~~The bus~~ (which) has just left.* → *The bus **which has just left** is going to London.*

1 *I often see some old friends.*
2 *~~Some old friends~~ (who) live in Oxford.* → *I often see some old friends **who live in Oxford**.*

توضح الفكرة 2 أدناه، اي حافلة وأي اصدقاء يعنيهم المتحدث. وتشكل الفكرة 1 الجزء الرئيسي في الجملة، تدعمها الفكرة 2 وتُكمّل معنى الجملة. وبالتالي فهي العبارة الموصولية المعرّفة.

Use *who* or *that* for people.

***The man who/that** bought the coat is standing over there.*

تستخدم who او that للأشخاص.

Use *which* or *that* for things and animals.

*Those are **the cars which/that** crashed.*

وتستخدم which وthat للأشياء والحيوانات.

Use defining relative clauses in general statements.

*People **who do dangerous jobs** are usually paid well.*
*A nice car is something **which most people want**.*

تستخدم العبارات الموصولية المعرّفة في الجمل الخبرية العامة.

Use defining relative clauses to define and identify.

*Gold is a heavy metal **which is very valuable**.*
*Bell was the man **who invented the telephone**.*

وتستخدم العبارات الموصولية المعرّفة للتعريف والتحديد.

We usually use *who* or *which* in more formal writing, eg in business letters and reports.

Dear Sir,
*Thank you for the catalogue and price list **which** I recently requested. The person **who** spoke to me on the phone also promised to send some samples, but these ...*

تستخدم who او which عادة في الاسلوب الكتابي الرسمي مثل الرسائل التجارية ورسال الاعمال والتقارير.

Exercises

1 Write *who, which* or *that.*

Arthur Penn is an old farm worker who/that *lives in our village. He lives in a small house* [1]________ *his family have had for 100 years. Recently, he was outside, moving a pile of stones and bricks* [2]________ *used to be an old garden shed. Suddenly his spade hit something* [3]________ *wasn't stone or brick. It sounded like metal. He dug a little more, and he found it was a very old box. He called to a friend* [4]________ *was passing the garden gate. They worked together until they were able to pull the heavy box out. 'Perhaps it's something valuable* [5]________ *somebody wanted to hide years ago,' Arthur said. 'Let's open it and see,' his friend said. 'Come on. You're the one* [6]________ *should do that.' Arthur broke open the box, but there was no gold or silver – just a set of old-fashioned garden tools! 'They're the tools* [7]________ *my grandfather used,' Arthur said. 'He was the one* [8]________ *built the shed 100 years ago.'*

2 Join each pair of statements to make one statement with a relative clause.

Example: *A girl won the prize. She wrote the best essay.*
The girl who/that wrote the best essay won the prize.

1 *A pilot escaped without injury. He crashed his plane in the lake.*

____

2 *A student has got a place in the national team. He broke the 10,000-metre record.*

____

3 *A bus broke down. It takes people to the airport.*

____

4 *A file is on the top shelf. It has all the information.*

____

5 *A policeman has recevied an award. He rescued 15 people from a fire.*

____

6 *A woman wanted to speak to you. She phoned last night.*

____

3 Write relative clauses with *who, which* or *that*. Use these endings.

It teaches Japanese.
She painted that picture.
They built the first aeroplane.
It will pay a better salary.
She was lost for five days.
They are warm and friendly.
He scored all the goals.
He discovered America.
He can repair my old car.

Example: *Were the Wright brothers the ones* who/that built the first aeroplane?

1 *What was the name of the player* ______________________________

2 *I want to get a new job* ______________________________

3 *Where can we find a mechanic* ______________________________

4 *Ann wants to find a book* ______________________________

5 *I like people* ______________________________

6 *Do you know the artist* ______________________________

7 *Mountain rescuers have found the climber* ______________________________

8 *Columbus was the man* ______________________________

65 Relative clauses 2

The man they want is wearing a coat.

FORMS

Reduced relative clauses with objects

The man who we want is coming now.
The man we want is coming now.

***ing* and *ed* participles with relative clauses**

His case is the one which is coming now.
His case is the one coming now.
His case is the one that is marked with a cross.
His case is the one marked with a cross.

Reduced relative clauses with objects

who, *which* and *that* can be the subject of a clause, or they can be the object. If they are the object, we can leave them out.

> ***The man who wants us*** *is coming now.* (subject – no change)
> ***The man who we want*** *is coming now.* (object – change possible) → ***The man we want*** *is coming now.*
> *Did you see* ***the dress which she bought****?* (object – change possible) → *Did you see* ***the dress she bought****?*

يمكن ان تكون الكلمات who و which و that في موقع الفاعل من العبارة الموصولية، كما يمكن ان تكون في موقع المفعول به. وعندما تأتي في موقع المفعول به يمكن ان نغفل ذكرها.

ing and *ed* participles with relative clauses

The verb in a relative clause can be in a continuous tense. If it is, we can leave out *who*, *which* or *that* and then just use the *ing* (present) participle.

> *His case is the one* ***which is coming now****. → His case is the one* ***coming now****.*
> *I was angry with the people* ***who were shouting last night****. → I was angry with the people* ***shouting last night****.*

يمكن ان يكون الفعل في العبارة الموصولية في أحد الازمنة المستمرة... عندها يكون بالإمكان إغفال ذكر الكلمات who وwhich وthat، والاكتفاء بذكر الفعل مضافاً له ing فقط.

The *ed* (past) participle can be part of a passive tense. If it is, we can leave out *who*, *which* or *that* and then use the *ed* participle.

> *His case is the one* ***that is marked*** *with a cross. → His case is the one* ***marked*** *with a cross.*
> *He's the man* ***who was followed*** *by the police. → He's the man* ***followed*** *by the police.*

يمكن ان يكون الفعل المنتهي بـ ed جزءاً من الفعل في حالة المبني للمجهول، عندها يمكن إغفال ذكر who وwhich وthat، والاكتفاء بذكر ed التصريف الثالث.

With a continuous passive tense use *being* + *ed* participle.

> *He's the man* ***who is being watched*** *by the police. → He's the man* ***being watched*** *by the police.*
> *Those were the cases* ***which were being checked*** *by Customs. → Those were the cases* ***being checked*** *by Customs.*

تُستخدم مع الازمنة المستمرة في حالة المبني للمجهول، being + ed التصريف الثالث.

Exercises

1 Join each pair of statements to make one statement. Use *who, which* or *that* as the subject of the relative clause.

Example: *The person wasn't there. She had sold the watch.*
The person who/that had sold the watch wasn't there.

1 *The book has disappeared. It has all the answers.*

____

____

2 *We climbed over the fence. It separates the fields.*

____

____

3 *The old man can't see well. He crashed his car.*

____

____

4 *I'm going to give the boy some money. He found my camera.*

____

____

2 Join each pair of statements to make one statement. Use *who, which* or *that* as the object of the relative clause.

Example: *The house stood by the river. We bought it.*
The house which/that we bought stood by the river.

1 *The girls seemed sad. We met them at the wedding.*

____

____

2 *I want to go to the museum. You told me about it.*

____

____

3 *The taxi finally arrived. I'd ordered it.*

____

____

4 *The flowers are dying. She gave us them.*

____

____

3 Write *who, which, that* or nothing (✗)

Example: *The house* ✗ *we bought stood by the river.*
The person who/that *had sold the watch wasn't there.*

1 *The bus* ________ *we caught got to town early.*

2 *The man* ________ *will meet you is my brother.*

3 *Here's the money* ________ *I owe you.*

4 *Rob is the player* ________ *won the game.*

5 *This goes in the file* ________ *I put on the shelf.*

4 Write the active participle form of these verbs.

enter, finish, go, show, stand, wear

Example: *The police stopped a car* going *at 220 kph.*

1 *We listened to the guide* ______________ *us round the palace.*

2 *Did you see anybody* ______________ *the house?*

3 *I took photos of people* ______________ *the race.*

4 *Can you pass me the vase* ______________ *on the cupboard?*

5 *I didn't like that man* ______________ *a red jacket.*

5 Write the passive participle form of these verbs.

build, find, make, mend, paint, prepare, use, write

Examples: *This is the gun* found *in the car.*
The houses being built *in London Street will soon be ready.*

1 *This was the plane* ______________ *by the President on his trip to Australia.*

2 *I'm now going to show you a pot* ______________ *by hand. Watch carefully.*

3 *As we watched, there were two ships* ______________ *to go to sea.*

4 *This is a story* ______________ *for young people.*

5 *That's the bridge* ______________ *after the storm. It'll be closed for another week.*

6 *I prefer shoes* ______________ *of real leather.*

66 Relative clauses 3

There was a time when you could live well.

FISHERMEN FACE HARD TIMES

The fishing industry is going from bad to worse. There are now fishermen whose debts are rising and pushing them out of business.

Tom Billings, aged 58, says, 'There was a time when you could live well from the sea. But not any more. All the best areas where we used to fish are dead now.'

The main reason why this has happened is the fishing industry itself. With too many boats and efficient modern methods, the fishermen have fished the sea to death.

FORMS

Relative clauses with *whose*

There are fishermen whose debts are rising.

Relative clauses with *when, where* and *why*

There was a time when you could live well.
All the best areas where we used to fish are dead now.
The main reason why this has happened is the industry itself.

Relative clauses with *whose*

whose is a relative pronoun like *who*, but it is also possessive like *his, her, its, their*, etc.

1 *There are many fishermen with debts.*
2 *~~Their~~ (whose) debts are rising.* → *There are many **fishermen whose debts are rising**.*

تعتبر whose أحد ضمائر الوصل، مَثَلُها مَثَلُ who ولكنها تفيد الملكية ايضاً، مثل his وher... الخ.

We usually use *whose* with people. We sometimes also use it with things and animals too.

*Mary Owen was **the girl whose** story won first prize.*
*Japan is **a country whose** economy is very successful.*
*The boys found **a bird whose** wing was broken.*

تستخدم whose عادة مع الاشخاص، واحياناً تستخدم مع الاشياء والحيوانات ايضاً.

Relative clauses with *whose* are formal. We often use them in more formal writing. We do not use them much in conversation.

Dear Sir,
*I wish to complain about a member of your sales staff **whose behaviour towards my wife was very unpleasant**.*

تعتبر العبارات الموصولية بـ whose ذات طابع رسمي وتستخدم غالباً في الكتابة الرسمية، ولا تستخدم في المحادثة كثيراً.

Relative clauses with *when, where* and *why*

We can use several sorts of relative clauses about a 'time' noun.

*There was **a time when** you could live well.*
*There was **a time that** you could live well.*
*There was **a time** you could live well.*

يمكن استخدام العديد من العبارت الموصولية في جمل تنعت كلمة time عندما ترد كاسم.

'Time' nouns include words like *summer, year, week, day,* and *moment.*

*Do you remember that **summer when** we went to France?*
*I shall never forget the **day when** my sister was born.*

وهذه العبارات التي تتعلق بالزمن تضم كلمات مثل year, summer... الخ.

We can also use *where* to refer to a 'place' noun such as *house, street, town* and *city*.

*I remember the **house where** I grew up.*
*That's the **street where** John lives.*

ويمكن ايضاً استخدام where للاشارة الى اسم مكان وتحديده.

We can use *why* to refer to the noun *reason* in the same way.

*He's lazy! That's the **reason why** he failed.*

كذلك يمكن استخدام why التي تشير الى السببية وبالطريقة نفسها.

Exercises

1 Complete the questions with *whose, who, which* or *that*. Answer the questions.

Examples: ● *What was the name of the man* who *first reached America from Europe in 1492?*

❍ Christopher Columbus.

● *What is the name of the country* whose *capital is Kuala Lumpur?*

❍ Malaysia.

1 ● *What is the English name for the three ancient man-made structures* ________ *stand near Cairo?*

❍ ________________________________

2 ● *What was the man* ________ *first flew in space called?*

❍ ________________________________

3 ● *Name the woman scientist* ________ *most important work was the discovery of radium.*

❍ ________________________________

4 ● *What was the name of the Italian* ________ *travelled to China and home again 700 years ago?*

❍ ________________________________

5 ● *What is the country* ________ *flag is a red circle on a white square?*

❍ ________________________________

6 ● *Name the US state* ________ *is famous for cowboys and* ________ *symbol is a yellow rose?*

❍ ________________________________

2 Answer the questions. Use *whose* as the subject of the relative clause.

Your friend is looking at a wedding party guest list and trying to remember people.

Example: ● *Who was Yvonne Laroche? (Her husband had a large beard.)*

❍ She was the one whose husband had a large beard.

1 ● *Which one was George Barret? (His wife had a wonderful diamond necklace.)*

❍ ________________________________

____

____

2 ● *Do you remember the Schmidts? (Their children fell in the pool.)*

❍ ________________________________

____

3 ● *Who was Lucy Rosser? (Her hat flew off in the wind.)*

❍ ________________________________

____

4 ● *Do you remember the Lewis family? (Their car refused to start after the party.)*

❍ ________________________________

____

____

5 ● *And which ones were Mario and Maria di Stefano? (Their daughters wore lovely blue dresses.)*

❍ ________________________________

____

____

3 Write statements about the underlined parts of the conversation. Use *when, where* or *why* as the subject of the relative clause.

Example: ● *Do you remember that time on the river?*

❍ *Oh, yes. Our boat nearly sank!*

They talked about the time when their boat nearly sank.

1 ● *Our boat nearly turned over because you turned it in front of that big river cruiser.*

❍ *Yes, that was the reason.*

They talked about the ________________________________

____

____

2 ● *And then we stayed at that old hotel.*

❍ *Yes. We dried out our clothes there.*

They talked about the ________________________________

____

____

3 ● *And what about the night of the storm?*

❍ *Yes. The rain almost washed our tent away.*

They talked about the ________________________________

____

____

67 Relative clauses 4

He's the driver who won. *Alan Brant, who won in France, is ...*

NEW WORLD NUMBER ONE

Alan Brant, who yesterday won in France, is now Number One in the world. The race, which was watched by 100 million people world-wide, took place in temperatures of up to 40°C.

FORMS

Defining relative clauses

Anna: *Who's that in the picture?*
Jean: *Alan Brant. He's the driver who won the big race yesterday.*
Anna: *What race was that?*
Jean: *The race which they showed on TV yesterday.*

Adding clauses

Alan Brant, who won in France yesterday, is now Number One in the world. The race, which was watched by 30 million people world-wide, took place ...

Compare defining relative clauses with another type – adding clauses.

CROSSCHECK

Defining relative clauses

These clauses explain which driver and which race. The sentences are not complete without these clauses.

He's the driver ***who/that won the big race***.
The race ***which/that they showed on TV***.

Adding clauses

These clauses add extra information to the basic sentences. The basic sentences are complete without these clauses.

Alan Brant, ***who yesterday won in France***, *is now ...*
The race, ***which was watched by 30 million***, *took place ...*

تحدد العبارات الموصولية التعريفية ماهية السائق والسباق ولا تكتمل الجمل بدونها. ولا تستخدم في هذه الجمل الفواصل حيث تكون العبارات الموصولية هنا جزءاً أساسياً فيها. هذه العبارات تضيف معلومات الى الجمل الاساسية التي تعتبر كاملة في حد ذاتها من دون هذه العبارات. ويتم فصل هذا النوع من العبارات الموصولية عن الجملة الاساسية بفواصل او قواطع او اقواس.

These clauses do not have commas. They are a main part of the sentence.

We separate this type of clause from the basic sentence with commas (,), dashes (–) or brackets ( ).

We can use *that* instead of *who* or *which*. We can often use reduced forms. (See Unit 65.)

We mended the window ***which/that was broken.***
They'll only give jobs to pilots ***who/that are very experienced***.
Visitors should come on a day ***when the castle is open***.

We cannot use *that* instead of *who* or *which*. But we can use *whose*, *when* and *where*.

We mended the kitchen window, ***which was broken***.
The pilots – ***who are very experienced*** *– will be given jobs.*
*Visitors should come on Sunday (****when the castle is open****).*

يمكن في العبارات الموصولية التعريفية استخدام that بدلاً من who او which، كما يمكن استخدام الصيغ المختصرة في أغلب الاحيان. (انظر unit 65). اما في العبارات الموصولية الاضافية فلا يمكن استخدام that بدلاً من who او which، ولكن يمكن استخدام whose و which و where.

which can refer to a noun phrase or a whole sentence.

I mended ***the doll***, ***which*** *was broken.*
They worked on the car all night, ***which*** *helped Alan win.*

يمكن في العبارات الموصولية التعريفية استخدام which، للاشارة الى شبه جملة اسمية، او الى جملة كاملة.

Most relative clauses are defining relative clauses. (See Units 64, 65 and 66.) We use them in speaking and in writing.

We use non-defining relative clauses mainly in writing. Newspaper reports use them a lot because they give a lot of information quickly.

تعتبر معظم العبارات الموصولية تعريفية وتستخدم في الحديث وكذلك في الكتابة (انظر units 64,65,66) وتستخدم العبارات الموصولية غير التعريفية في الكتابة اساساً، كما تستخدم كثيراً في كتابة التقارير الصحفية لانها توفّر معلومات وافية بشكل سريع.

Exercises

1 Are the clauses in *italics* defining or adding? Write commas if necessary.

Example: *Beethoven, whose music is loved by millions, was born in 1770 and died in 1827.* adding

1 Dover Castle *which is a very impressive building* was built by the Normans. ____________

2 The girl *who found the wallet* handed it in to the police. ____________

3 The programme *that we watched last night* was awful. ____________

4 The writer Pete Holmes *whose most famous book is 'Glory'* has died today. He was 75. ____________

2 Join each pair of statements to make one statement with an adding clause with *who* or *which*.

Examples: *Harry Lane is a rich man now. He was at college with me.*
Harry Lane, who was at college with me, is a rich man now.

1 *Old Professor Jones is going to stop work soon. He's nearly 70.*

____

2 *To the north of India are the Himalayas. They include the highest mountains in the world.*

____

3 *I bought myself some good, new clothes. I needed them for my new job.*

____

4 *Barry Stone has built his own house. He works as a computer programmer.*

____

3 Match the statements 1–7 and a–g. Join each pair changing a–g into adding clauses with *which*.

1 *The baby cried all night.*
2 *The old ship stayed in port.*
3 *I was out when Peter called.*
4 *The company has won the contract.*
5 *They've started doing road repairs.*
6 *They sun has come out at last.*
7 *The school is building a new gymnasium.*

a *That saved it from the storm.*
b *It's causing bad traffic delays.*
c *That was why I didn't hear the news.*
d *It meant I was tired all next day.*
e *That means we can go to the beach.*
f *It's going to help their basketball teams a lot.*
g *That's good news.*

1 – d 2 – ___ 3 – ___ 4 – ___ 5 – ___ 6 – ___ 7 – ___

1 The baby cried all night, which meant I was tired all next day.

2 ____________________

3 ____________________

4 ____________________

5 ____________________

6 ____________________

7 ____________________

68 Adjectives 1

It's large. *It's a large suitcase.*

FORMS

Word order 1

It is a large suitcase.

The suitcase is large.

Word order 2

It's a large, brown suitcase.

Adjective + *to* + infinitive

It was stupid to lose it.

Adjectives describe nouns and pronouns. They give us more information about things. Their form is the same with singular and plural nouns. They do not add *s*.

red, green, blue *dark, light, bright* *large, small* *beautiful, ugly*
Japanese, English *my, your, her* *this, that, these, those* + noun

تصف النعوت الاسماء والضمائر، فهي تعطي مزيداً من المعلومات عن الاشياء، وهي لا تتغير تبعاً لإفراد او جمع الاسماء التي تصفها، ولا يضاف لها s الجمع.

Word order 1

Most adjectives can go in two places. They can go before a noun and the pronouns *one* and *ones*.

*I've got a **blue bag**.* ***That one** is **my bag**.*

تأتي معظم النعوت من حيث موقعها في احد مكانين: قبل الاسم وقبل الضمائر one و ones.

They can also go after a noun. Link verbs include *be, become, get* (become), *stay, feel, smell, sound, taste, look, seem* and *appear*.

*The **bag** is **blue**.* *I'm getting **tired**.* ***He** seems **nice** – but is he?*

وتأتي ايضاً بعد الاسم... وهذه قائمة بأفعال الوصل.

Word order 2

When you use two or more adjectives, put them in the right order. Put a 'feeling' adjective, eg *beautiful* and *terrible*, before an 'information' adjective, eg *red* and *dark*.

*Ann bought a **beautiful red** dress.* *It was a **terrible dark** night.*

عند استخدام النعوت، فإن النعوت المستخدمة توضع حسب ترتيب خاص بحيث تأتي النعوت التي تتعلق بالمشاعر (مثل beautiful) قبل تلك التي تزود بالمعلومات (مثل red).

Adjectives can give different types of information. We sometimes put different 'information' adjectives together. They go in the following order. We often put commas between several adjectives together.

تزودنا نعوت بأنواع مختلفة من المعلومات. ونضع احياناً نعوتاً مختلفة «مزودة بالمعلومات» معاً، في جملة واحدة، وتكون بالترتيب التالي، ادناه. وغالباً ما توضع فواصل بين النعوت التي يجتمع استخدامها في الجملة.

1 **Feeling**		2 **Size**	3 **Age**	4 **Shape**	5 **Colour**	6 **Origin**	7 **Material**	
	+							+ **Noun**
ugly		*big*	*old*	*square*	*red*	*French*	*metal*	
beautiful		*little*	*new*	*round*	*blue*	*German*	*wooden*	

*I bought a **beautiful, old, round, French** clock.*
*He saw an **ugly, little, blue, wooden** box.*

Adjective + *to* + infinitive

'Feeling' adjectives can take *to* + infinitive. The adjective usually follows *It*. Some common 'feeling' adjectives are *dangerous, delighted, difficult, easy, funny, important, pleased, safe, sorry* and *stupid*.

*It's **dangerous to play** in the road.* *I'm **pleased to meet** you.*

يمكن ان تأتي النعوت المشاعر مع to + المصدر. ويوضع النعت عادة، بعد it. وهذه قائمة بالشائع من نعوت هذا النوع.

Exercises

1 Complete the statements. Use these link verbs and adjectives.

Link verbs

feel, get, look, seem, smell, sound

Adjectives

angry, delicious, happy, right, terrible, tired

Example: *I'll have to check the sales figures again. They don't* look right.

1 ● *Dinner's ready.*
❍ *Mmm! It* ____________

2 *I didn't get enough sleep last night. I still* ____________

3 *Don't try to take a dog's food away, or it'll* ____________

4 ● *The children are all laughing.*
❍ *Yes, they* ________ *really* ________

5 *Oh, no! Annie's doing her music practice again. It* ____________

2 Write the words in the correct order.

Example: *(beautiful/a/flower/red)*
a beautiful red flower

1 *(book/old/a/boring)*

2 *(blue/an/diamond/unusual)*

3 *(film/exciting/new/an)*

4 *(yellow/light/a/strange)*

5 *(an/clock/German/interesting)*

6 *(little/a/lovely/baby)*

7 *(green/a/valley/pleasant)*

8 *(a/man/tall/young)*

9 *(round/box/a/plastic)*

3 Report the answers. Use commas between the adjectives.

Example: ● *What was the snake like?*
❍ *It was big! It was green! It was horrible!*
It was a horrible, big, green snake.

1 ● *What was the man like?*
❍ *He was little. He was old. He was funny.*

2 ● *What was the box like?*
❍ *It was ugly. It was brown. It was metal.*

3 ● *What were the jackets like?*
❍ *They were silk. They were new. They were Italian. They were beautiful.*

4 ● *What were the vases like?*
❍ *They were tall. They were wonderful. They were Chinese. They were round.*

4 Complete the statements. Use these endings.

to go home. *to drive when you're tired.*
to have you with us.
to meet you. *to play with matches.*
to remember to post them. *to understand.*

Example: *Goodbye for now. It was nice* to meet you.

1 *Put them down. It's dangerous* ____________

2 *I've really enjoyed this holiday. I'll be sorry* ____________

3 *Please don't forget these letters. It's very important* ____________

4 *Of course you can come too. We'll be delighted* ____________

5 *They were speaking very fast, so it was difficult* ____________

6 *You should have a sleep before you go. It isn't safe* ____________

69 Adjectives 2

The programme is interesting. *Alan is interested.*

FORMS

Adjectives with *ing* endings

The programme is interesting.
(interesting, boring, exciting, surprising, worrying)

Adjectives with *ed* endings

Alan is interested.
(interested, bored, excited, surprised, worried)

There are some pairs of important adjectives with the endings *ing* and *ed*.

هناك ازواج من بعض النعوت المهمة تنتهي بـ ing وكذلك بـ ed.

CROSSCHECK

Adjectives with *ing* endings

These describe something, eg a TV programme, a film, a book or a person.

Compare these examples.

*Ann thinks computer games are **boring**.*
*The football match was **exciting**.*
*Rod works at an **amazing** speed.*
*A bad school report is very **depressing**.*

Adjectives with *ed* endings

These describe your feelings about something, eg a TV programme, a film, a book or a person.

Compare these examples.

*Ann gets **bored** when her brother plays computer games.*
*Everybody at the match was **excited**.*
*We are **amazed** at the speed Rod works.*
*Mum will be very **depressed** when she reads my school report.*

تصف النعوت التي تنتهي بـ ing شيئاً ما كبرنامج تليفزيوني او فيلم او كتاب او شخص.

وتصف النعوت التي تنتهي بـ ed مشاعر الشخص تجاه شيء ما مثل برنامج او فيلم او كتاب او شخص.

ويتضح الامر من خلال مقارنة الامثلة من النوعين من النعوت.

Be careful about the difference between these sentences. You will be embarrassed if you say the wrong one!

*I'm **boring**!* *I'm **bored**!*

(*I'm **boring**!* means that other people are not interested in me.)

يجب الانتباه الى الفارق بين هذه الجمل لانك ستصاب بالحرج اذا استخدمت العبارة الخاطئة.

This is a list of common pairs of adjectives with *ing* and *ed* endings.

وهذه قائمة بازواج النعوت الاكثر شيوعاً والتي تنتهي بـ ing و ed.

amazing/amazed
amusing/amused
annoying/annoyed
astonishing/astonished
boring/bored
confusing/confused
depressing/depressed
disappointing/disappointed
disgusting/disgusted
embarrassing/embarrassed
exciting/excited
exhausting/exhausted
fascinating/fascinated
frightening/frightened
horrifying/horrified
infuriating/infuriated
interesting/interested
irritating/irritated
puzzling/puzzled
relaxing/relaxed
satisfying/satisfied
shocking/shocked
surprising/surprised
terrifying/terrified
thrilling/thrilled
tiring/tired
worrying/worried

Exercises

1 Write the correct adjectives.

Example: *Thunderstar 2 is the most* exciting *film of the year. (exciting/excited)*

1 *Everybody was* ________________ *when we reached the huge waterfall. (exciting/excited)*

2 *The map of the city was out of date, and I was soon* ________________ *(confusing/confused)*

3 *One of the* ________________ *things about Steve is his stupid laugh. (annoying/annoyed)*

4 *I was* ________________ *by the engines in the Science Museum. (fascinating/fascinated)*

5 *We were all* ________________ *after walking round town all day. (exhausting/exhausted)*

6 *The police have found the facts of this crime very* ________________ *(puzzling/puzzled)*

7 *It's* ________________ *that Tina is late. She's usually on time. (surprising/surprised)*

8 *The story of the Earth's development is* ________________ *(amazing/amazed)*

2 Write the correct adjectives.

Example: *(bore)*

● *This programme is* boring.

❍ *Yes, I'm* bored *with it too. Let's turn it off.*

1 *(astonish)*

● *I was* ________________ *that Tim passed the exam.*

❍ *Yes, he found it* ________________ *too!*

2 *(shock)*

● *The way Sam talks to people is* ________________

❍ *I know. I was* ________________ *when I heard him being so rude.*

3 *(embarrass)*

● *It was really* ________________ *to ask for my money.*

❍ *Why? You shouldn't be* ________________ *to ask for the money they owed you.*

4 *(depress)*

● *I've failed my driving test again. I'm very* ________________ *about it.*

❍ *I remember the feeling. It certainly is* ________________

5 *(interest)*

● *Here is an* ________________ *job advert in the paper. Look.*

❍ *Are you* ________________ *in applying for it?*

6 *(disappoint)*

● *The team were very* ________________ *that they only came fifth in the competition.*

❍ *The trouble is, the way they played was so* ________________

7 *(irritate)*

● *Don't you get* ________________ *when you see the same TV commercial all the time?*

❍ *Yes, there are some really* ________________ *ones on TV at the moment.*

8 *(tire)*

● *I've been working all day, but I don't feel* ________________ *at all.*

❍ *Well, you're lucky. I find this job very* ________________

3 Complete the statements. Use these words with the correct endings.

amuse, disgust, frighten, horrify, infuriate, relax, satisfy, terrify, worry

Example: *I don't like being high up. It's really* frightening.

1 *That boy always wants more to eat! He's never* ________________

2 *The assistant manager lost his job because everybody was* ________________ *by his lies.*

3 *Susan keeps refusing to eat and is losing weight. It's very* ________________

4 *When we got back to town, we saw the* ________________ *damage done by the storm.*

5 *The President is feeling* ________________ *after a good holiday.*

6 *The film isn't very funny, but it's quite* ________________

7 *Oh, no! The train is going to be late again. It's really* ________________

8 *We thought the plane was going to crash. We were all* ________________

70 Adjectives and adverbs

He's a slow worker.   *He always works slowly.*

FORMS

Adjective or adverb

Noun + adjective   Verb + adverb

Adjective → regular adverb

slow → *slowly*

Irregular forms

1 *good/well*
2 *hard, fast*, etc
3 *hard/hardly*, etc
4 *friendly, lively, likely*, etc

CROSSCHECK

Adjectives

Adjectives say more about nouns.

That boy is | ***slow***. / ***quick***. / ***bad***.

Adverbs

Adverbs say more about verbs.

He works | ***slowly***. / ***quickly***. / ***badly***.

النعوت تقول المزيد عن الاسماء. اما الظرف فيقول المزيد عن الفعل .

This sentence uses a link verb, *is*. Other link verbs include *become, get* (become), *stay, feel, smell, sound, taste, look, seem* and *appear*.

That boy	***is*** / ***looks*** / ***seems***	***slow***.

This sentence uses an action verb, *works*. Other action verbs include *run, talk, drive* and *write*. Adverbs go with action verbs, not link verbs.

That boy	***works*** / ***moves*** / ***runs***	***slowly***.

يستخدم في هذه الجملة الفعل be كاحد افعال الوصل المبينة.

وتحوي هذه الجملة (الثانية) فعلاً حركياً. ويأتي الظرف مع الافعال الحركية وليس مع افعال الوصل.

Some verbs are both link and action verbs, but with different meanings.

*Ann **looked** happy.*	*Peter **looked** quickly in the cupboards.*
*I **felt** awful, so I went to bed.*	*The chef **felt** the vegetables carefully and bought the best ones.*
*The milk **tasted** bad.*	*I **tasted** the food nervously. It was OK.*

بعض الافعال هي افعال وصل وافعال حركية ولكن بمعانٍ مختلفة.

Adjective → regular adverb

We form most adverbs from adjective + *ly*, eg *slow* + *ly* → *slowly*.

beautifully, carefully (note ... *l* + *ly*), *coldly, freely, quickly, quietly, sadly, safely, warmly*

تتشكل معظم الظروف (adverbs) من النعوت وذلك بإضافة ly لها.

We form other adverbs according to special spelling rules. (See Appendix 2.)

angry → *angrily, easy* → *easily, lucky* → *luckily*
comfortable → *comfortably, gentle* → *gently, possible* → *possibly*
true → *truly, whole* → *wholly*

وتتشكل ظروف (adverbs) اخرى وفق قواعد هجائية خاصة (انظر الملحق 2).

Irregular forms

good* → *well

Note this irregular form – *good* → *well*. *well* is also an adjective.

يجب ملاحظة أن *good* ← *well* تشكلان صيغة غير قياسية ولا تسيران حسب القاعدة.

*The car goes **well**.*

● *Is she **well**?* ❍ *No, she's ill.*

***hard, fast*, etc**

These are both adjectives and adverbs: *deep, direct, early, far, fast, free, hard, high, late, long, low, near, right, short, straight, wrong.*

تأتي القائمة التالية من الكلمات كصفات وكذلك كظروف.

*It's a **deep** swimming pool.* *He dived **deep** into the water.*

*It's a **fast** car.* *He climbed the tree **fast**.*

*We must catch the **late** bus.* *He didn't want to arrive **late**.*

***hard/hardly*, etc**

A few words have two adverb forms – one form is like the adjective and one form ends in *ly*. They have different meanings. Compare the sentences in CROSSCHECK below.

تأتي بعض الكلمات كظروف في صيغتين إحداهما كالصفة وتنتهي الأخرى بـ *ly*. وتعطي كلتا الصيغتين معنىً مختلفاً... لاحظ ذلك من خلال مقارنة الأمثلة.

direct/directly, free/freely, hard/hardly, high/highly, late/lately, near/nearly, short/shortly

CROSSCHECK

Adjective/adverb form	*ly* form
*I went **direct** from the station to the wedding.* (straight)	*I'll phone you **directly** I hear anything.* (immediately after)
*Airline staff can fly **free**.* (without paying)	*The animals can move round **freely**.* (without control)
*We worked **hard** all night.* (with a lot of energy)	*We had **hardly** any sleep that night.* (almost no)
*John works **high** above the city, on the 183rd floor.* (above)	*This snake is **highly** poisonous. Don't touch it!* (very)
*I have to work **late** this evening.* (a long time after normal)	*What's Sue doing these days? I haven't seen her **lately**.* (recently)
● *Is the hotel far?* ❍ *No, it's quite **near** now.* (close)	*We've **nearly** run out of bread. I'll buy some more.* (almost)
*My brother was very ill, so we cut **short** our holiday and went home.* (reduced)	*The bus will be here **shortly**.* (soon)

ly adjectives

These adjectives end in *ly: deadly, friendly, likely, lively, lonely, lovely, silly, ugly.*

تنتهي القائمة التالية من الصفات بـ *ly*.

*They're a very **friendly** family.* *That poor girl is **lonely**.*

We cannot use them as adverbs. We have to say something like *in a* + adjective + *way*.

لا يمكن استخدام الصفات التي تنتهي بـ ly كظروف بل كما يلي (in a + صفة + way).

*He spoke **in a lively, friendly sort of way**.*

*He always speaks **in that silly way of his**.*

Exercises

1 Write an adjective after a link verb or an adverb after an action verb.

Examples: *The old man looked* sad. *(sad)*
The old man spoke sadly *to us. (sad)*

1 *We finished the work* ____________ *so we could go home early. (quick)*

2 *Ann looks very* ____________ *in that dress. (nice)*

3 *This soup tastes* ____________ *What's in it? (wonderful)*

4 *Have a good trip home. It's a little foggy so drive* ____________ *(safe)*

5 *Spring is coming and the weather is getting* ____________ *(warm)*

6 *Mrs Pearce greeted the new neighbours* ____________ *and she invited them for coffee* ____________ *(warm) (immediate)*

7 *Old Tom seems very* ____________ *, but he's really very* ____________ *(hard) (kind)*

8 *The back of the ship rose* ____________ *high into the air, and then the whole ship slid* ____________ *into the cold, black sea. (slow) (quiet)*

2 Write the correct adjectives or adverbs.

Example: *(slow/slowly)*
● *Arthur is a* slow *worker.*
❍ *Yes, he's very* slow. *He does everything very* slowly.

1 *(proper/properly)*
● *Is this the* ____________ *tool for the job?*
❍ *No, I'm afraid this one won't do the job* ____________

2 *(quiet/quietly)*
● *Lucy is a very* ____________ *person, isn't she?*
❍ *Yes, she talks so* ____________ *that it's sometimes difficult to hear her.*

3 *(smooth/smoothly)*
● *I drove the new Mitsui Tiara the other day. It was a very* ____________ *drive.*
❍ *I agree. And it handles extremely* ____________ *in wet road conditions too.*

4 *(pleasant/pleasantly)*
● *The weather is very* ____________ *at this time of year.*
❍ *And the garden looks really* ____________ *now, with all the flowers coming out.*

5 *(intelligent/intelligently)*
● *Sally dealt with the problem very* ____________*, I thought.*
❍ *Yes, she's a very* ____________ *woman.*

6 *(bad/badly)*
● *Look, the builders have built this wall really* ____________
❍ *You're right. They've done a very* ____________ *job. They'll have to do it again.*

7 *(effective/effectively)*
● *Which of these cleaning chemicals is more* ____________*, do you think?*
❍ *Well, Clean-ezy works more* ____________ *with really heavy dirt, but Clean-up seems just as* ____________ *as Clean-ezy for most jobs.*

3 Write the correct adverbs.

Examples: *Ann sang that song* beautifully. *(beautiful)*

1 *Ellen didn't panic after the accident. She acted very* ____________ *(sensible)*

2 *We were able to cut through the dead wood* ____________ *(easy)*

3 *The pilot is looking for somewhere to land* ____________ *(safe)*

4 *The astronauts completed all their tasks* ____________ *(successful)*

5 *I had forgotten to take any cash.* ____________*, I had my cheque book with me. (lucky)*

6 *We don't usually think* ____________*, but this time I agree* ____________ *with you. (similar) (whole)*

7 ____________*, everything went wrong with my plan and now I'm* ____________ *and* ____________ *sorry for the problems I've caused you all. (unfortunate) (real) (true)*

4 Complete the statements. Use these irregular adverbs.

direct, early, far, hard, high, late, low, short, straight, well, wrong

Example: *The horse jumped* high. *It got over every fence.*

1 *We got home very* ___________ *that night.*

2 *They'll have to leave* ___________ *in the morning, or they'll miss the train.*

3 *The bus goes* ___________ *from Oxford to London without stopping.*

4 *They worked* ___________ *all night to get the car working again.*

5 *The plan seemed to be working, but then everything went* ___________ *at the last minute.*

6 *I tried to throw a rope up to the girl, but it fell* ___________

7 *The Clark family don't live* ___________ *from here – just five minutes on foot.*

8 *The children sang* ___________ *in the concert.*

9 *You don't need to ask the hotel telephone operator. You can call any outside number* ___________

10 *The helicopter flew* ___________ *over the trees and then landed near them.*

5 Write the correct forms of the adverbs.

Example: *(late/lately)*

a) *Have you seen Peter* lately?

b) *He'll be in trouble if he goes back to college* late.

1 *(hard/hardly)*

a) *The people in this part of Africa have got* ___________ *any food left to eat.*

b) *The UN are fighting* ___________ *to get help to the people soon.*

2 *(high/highly)*

a) *Our pilots are all* ___________ *aware of the need for safety in the air.*

b) *They watch the plane's control systems at all times as they fly* ___________ *above the ground.*

3 *(near/nearly)*

a) *The ball landed on the ground* ___________ *the house.*

b) *It very* ___________ *hit the kitchen window.*

4 *(free/freely)*

a) *After the borders were opened, people like us were able to move much more* ___________ *round Europe.*

b) *As we were students, we couldn't afford to pay much for our travel, but we often travelled* ___________ *by hitchhiking.*

5 *(short/shortly)*

a) *Unfortunately, we have fallen* ___________ *of our sales target for this year.*

b) *However, the economy is getting better, and we expect better sales* ___________

6 *(direct/directly)*

a) *Please call me* ___________ *you get any more news.*

b) *You can call me* ___________ *on this number.*

6 Write the correct adverbs or adjectives. Choose from these changing the form where necessary.

early, easy, hard, late, quick, serious, tired

Ann: *Hi, Tom. I haven't seen you for ages. What have you been doing* lately?

Tom: *Good to see you, Ann. I've been working really* [1]___________ *to pass my exams.*

Ann: *Oh, I'm sure you'll pass them* [2]___________ *No problem. You should relax more. Why not finish work* [3]___________ *this evening and come out with us for an hour or two? You don't need to stay out very* [4]___________

Tom: *No, sorry, I don't think I should. I'm feeling really* [5]___________ *and I'd like to finish as* [6]___________ *as possible and then just go to bed.*

Ann: *Well, all right, but I think you should take life a bit less* [7]___________

71 Adverb positions

He drove slowly. *He slowly drove.*

FORMS

Adverbs in front, middle and end positions

It's a quiet road, and Brian *usually* drives *quite fast there. Luckily* he was *only* driving *slowly that day. Suddenly* he saw the tree. He hit it, but he wasn't hurt.

Questions

Have you ever been to Rome?
Who was working quickly?

Front position

We often use an adverb in front position to show a feeling or for special emphasis. The adverb adds its meaning to the whole sentence.

> ***Luckily*** *he was only driving slowly.* (speaker's feeling)
> ***Slowly*** *the car began to move.* (special emphasis)
> ***Finally*** *we all decided to go.* (special emphasis)

يستخدم الظرف غالباً في بداية الجملة، وذلك بقصد تبيان مشاعر المتحدث او بقصد وضع تشديد خاص ويضفي الظرف معناه على الجملة برمتها.

Middle position

Main verb only – put the adverb before the main verb.

> *He **usually** drives a long way.*
> *We **quickly** finished dinner.*

عندما تحوي الجملة فعلاً أساسياً واحداً يأتي الظرف قبل الفعل مباشرة.

Auxiliary verb only – put the adverb after a positive auxiliary verb.

> *He **is certainly** the best player.*

عندما تحتوي الجملة على فعل مساعد واحد فقط يأتي الظرف بعد الفعل في حالة صيغة الاثبات.

We often put the adverb before a negative auxiliary verb.

> *You **certainly weren't** very good today.*

وغالباً ما يأتي الظرف قبل الفعل في حالة النفي.

Auxiliary + main verb – put the adverb between the auxiliary and the main verb.

> *He was **only** driving a short distance.*
> *Ron has **always** lived in London.*

عندما تحوي الجملة فعلاً مساعداً بالإضافة الى فعل اساسي يأتي الظرف بينهما.

End position

We often put the adverb after the verb, at the end of a sentence. An adverb of time goes after any other adverb or an adverbial phrase.

> *He was driving **slowly today**.*
> *I'll be working **over there tomorrow**.*
> *We're living **in London now**.*

غالباً ما يأتي الظرف بعد الفعل في نهاية الجملة، ويأتي الظرف الذي يعبر عن الزمن بعد اي ظرف آخر في الجملة وبعد عبارة ظرفية.

Questions

We do not usually put the adverb in front position in questions. The adverb usually goes in middle or end position.

> *Has Ron **always** lived in London?*
> *Where has Ron **always** lived?*
> *Was he driving **slowly**?*
> *Who was driving **slowly**?*

لا يأتي الظرف عادة، في الموقع المتقدم في الجملة الاستفهامية، ولكنه يأتي في منتصف الجملة او في آخرها.

Exercises

1 Write these adverbs in front position.

Speaker's feeling
amazingly, frighteningly, hopefully, luckily, sadly

Special emphasis
angrily, finally, quietly, stupidly

Example: Amazingly, *John learned French in a month.* (Speaker's feeling)

1 ________________ *we'll be able to finish work in time to go to the cinema.* (Speaker's feeling)

2 ________________ *I forgot to take my passport with me to the airport.* (Special emphasis)

3 ________________ *the boss banged his desk and shouted, 'Get out!'* (Special emphasis)

4 ________________ *pieces from the ceiling started to fall around us.* (Speaker's feeling)

5 ________________ *the bus arrived – 45 minutes late!* (Special emphasis)

6 ________________ *Bob moved past the sleeping dogs and escaped.* (Special emphasis)

7 ________________ *the great painter died before finishing the picture.* (Speaker's feeling)

8 ________________ *the burning plane managed to land without crashing.* (Speaker's feeling)

2 Write the adverbs in middle position.

Example: *(is flying) (probably)*
John is probably flying *home now.*

1 *(get) (always)*
I ________________ *to work at 8.30.*

2 *(only) (was trying)*
Everybody was angry with Sam, but he ________________ *to help them.*

3 *(sometimes) (can see)*
You ________________ *France from England.*

4 *(will be) (only)*
Peter ________________ *here for two days.*

5 *(don't work) (usually)*
We ________________ *on Saturdays.*

6 *(clearly) (has been failing)*
Alan ________________ *to do this job properly.*

7 *(have you been) (ever)*
________________ *to Japan before?*

8 *(must talk) (never)*
You ________________ *like that again.*

3 Write the adverbs in end position.

Example: *(all day) (very hard)*
I've been working very hard all day.

1 *(very soon) (there)*
Don't worry. We'll be ________________

2 *(in America) (for five years)*
Brian lived ________________

3 *(yesterday) (very heavily)*
It snowed ________________

4 *(since last September) (much harder)*
Lisa has been studying ________________
____

5 *(as soon as possible) (over here)*
Please get ________________
____

6 *(wrong) (all the time)*
Poor old Paul. He gets things ________________
____

4 Write these adverbs in the letter.

over here, usually, last week, sadly, last year, definitely, this time, soon

Dear Chris,
It was good to hear from you [1]__________ . *We were pleased to hear you'll be travelling* [2]__________ .
[3]__________, *we were away when you visited Miami* [4]__________ . *So you* [5]_____ *must stay with us* [6]__________ *We're* [7]__________ *at home in the evening, so call us* [8]__________ .

72 Adverb types

fast, there, today, usually, luckily, very, etc

FORMS

A breakdown truck *soon* got there from a local garage. *Fortunately* the garage was able to repair Brian's car *quite quickly. Now* he *always* drives *extremely carefully.*

Adverb type	Explains	Examples
Manner	how	*fast, slowly, wrongly*
Place	where	*there, here, outside*
Time	when	*today, now, then*
Frequency	how often	*usually, always*
Degree	how much	*very, only, quite*
Sentence	the speaker's feeling	*luckily, certainly*

Adverbs of manner (*fast, quickly*, etc)

These usually go in end position and sometimes middle position. Irregular adverbs, eg *fast*, *well*, etc, go in end position. Use front position for emphasis.

*Peter **quickly** stopped.*
*Peter stopped **quickly**.*
***Quickly** Peter stopped.*

يأتي ظرف الحال عادة في نهاية الجملة واحياناً يأتي في وسطها. وظروف الحال اللاقياسية مثل fast وwell تأتي في نهاية الجملة. وعندما يأتي ظرف الحال في بداية الجملة فانه يفيد التوكيد.

Adverbs of place (*there, outside*, etc)

These usually go in end position. They do not go in middle position. Use front position for emphasis. An adverb of place usually goes after an adverb of manner.

*The children are playing **outside**.*
*I know I'll find her **somewhere**.*
***Somewhere** I know I'll find her.*

يأتي ظرف المكان في نهاية الجملة ولا يأتي في منتصفها، وعندما يأتي في بداية الجملة فإنه يفيد التوكيد.. ويأتي ظرف المكان عادة، بعد ظرف الحال.

Adverbs of time (*today, tomorrow*, etc)

These usually go in front position or end position. In end position, a time adverb goes after any other adverb.

***Tomorrow** we're all going to the beach.*
*We're all going to the beach **tomorrow**.*

يأتي ظرف الزمان في بداية الجملة او في نهايتها. ويأتي ظرف الزمان في نهاية الجملة بعد اي ظرف آخر.

Adverbs of frequency (*usually, always*, etc)

These usually go in middle position. Adverbs of frequency include *always, almost always, usually, generally, normally, often, frequently, sometimes, occasionally, hardly ever, rarely* and *never*. (See the diagrams on the facing page for more information.)

*I **always** go to bed at 10.30.*
*Pete **usually** plays football on Sundays.*
*It's sad, but I **hardly ever** see my brother because he lives in Australia.*
*They **never** ate sweets when they were children.*

تأتي ظروف التكرار في وسط الجملة. وتشمل ظروف التكرار ما يلي:

always

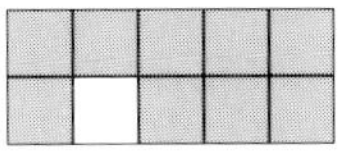

almost always

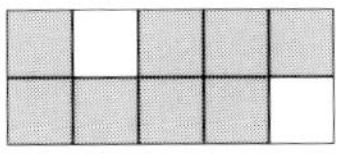

usually, generally, normally

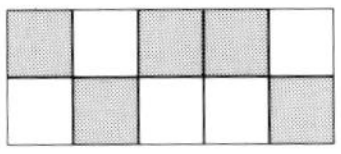

often, frequently

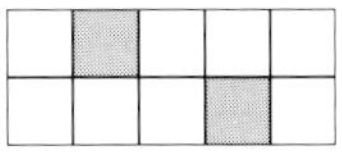

sometimes, occasionally

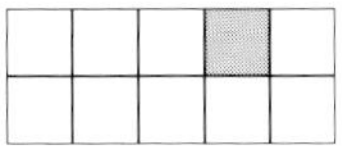

hardly ever, rarely

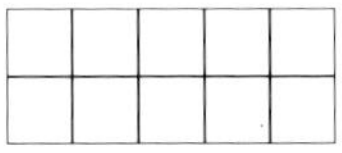

never

We often use *ever* in questions about frequency.

● *Have you **ever** visited London?* ❍ *Yes, I've often been there.*

غالباً ما تستخدم كلمة ever عند السؤال عن التكرار .

You can show frequency with adverbial phrases like these. They usually go in end position.

once	*a*	*day*
twice		*week*
three times		*month*
several times		*year*

*Most people eat **three times a day**.*
*I take the medicine **once a day**.*

ويمكن تبيان التكرار باستخدام عبارات ظرفية تأتي عادة، في نهاية الجملة.

Adverbs of degree (*very, quite*, etc)

Use these adverbs to make an adjective or another adverb weaker or stronger.

تستخدم الظروف التي تبين درجة القوة لجعل صفة من الصفات، او ظرف آخر، اضعف او اقوى.

Weak: *slightly, a little, a bit* (informal)
*I felt **slightly** ill, but I didn't stop.*

Stronger: *quite, fairly, rather, pretty* (informal)
*It isn't snowing, but it's **quite** cold. Bring some warm clothes!*

Strongest: *very, extremely*
*Eddy is **extremely** good at tennis. In fact, he's Number 10 in the world.*

Be careful. *very* and *too* are different. *too* means more than a certain amount. (See Unit 75.)
*I was **very** tired, but I went on walking.*
*I was **too** tired to walk. I had to stop.*

تجدر ملاحظة اختلاف very وtoo. too تعني اكثر من كمية او حدّ معين. (انظر unit 75).

Sentence adverbs (*luckily, probably*, etc)

Sentence adverbs often go in front position. They give their meaning to the whole sentence. They show the speaker's feeling about the information in the sentence. Sentence adverbs include *luckily, sadly, surprisingly, disappointingly, obviously, certainly, probably* and *perhaps*.

الظروف التي تعطي معناها للجملة بكاملها غالباً ما تأتي في مقدمة الجملة.

فهي تبين مشاعر المتحدث تجاه ما تحويه الجملة من معلومات. وهي تشمل ما يلي:

*Then we ran out of petrol. **Luckily** there was a petrol station 300 metres along the road.*
***Sadly** Alan is ill and can't be with us.*
*The train will **probably** be late, and then we **obviously** won't get to the meeting.*

Exercises

1 Find and write the adverbs.

Example: *My brother arrived yesterday.* yesterday

1 *The boys are working upstairs.* ___________

2 *The train is definitely late.* ___________

3 *Time passed slowly as we waited.* ___________

4 *I'm tired, so I'm going to bed now.* ___________

5 *This book is very hard to understand.* ___________

6 *John always does what he promises.* ___________

7 *Luckily the tree fell just behind our car.* ___________

2 Name the types of adverb and adverbial phrase in *italics*. Choose from these.

degree, frequency, manner, place, sentence, time

I remember one Japanese national holiday [1]*well.* Some friends and I decided to go to the mountains 100 kilometres from Tokyo in two cars. The problem was that everybody else in Tokyo seemed to be going [2]*there* too. The road was [3]*very* busy and we moved [4]*extremely* [5]*slowly.* We travelled [6]*all night* and we [7]*finally* got to the house [8]*at 6.00.* We were [9]*terribly* tired, and we went to sleep [10]*immediately.*

We enjoyed the next three days [11]*a lot.* We walked through the woods to the village [12]*once a day* to buy food. And [13]*every day* we cooked our meals [14]*outside* on a barbecue. Time went [15]*quickly*, and the last day came. We [16]*certainly* didn't want to return to Tokyo but, [17]*sadly*, we had to go.

'Let's leave [18]*late*,' somebody said. 'That way the roads will be quieter.' [19]*Unfortunately* everybody else had the same idea. The journey home was just as slow as the trip from Tokyo. We seemed to get [20]*nowhere* in the long, long line of cars. At 2.00 the people in the first car [21]*suddenly* left the main road to try a smaller road. We followed in the second car. Five more cars followed us, so we thought, 'This must be a good road. The Japanese are using it too.'

[22]*Strangely*, the road became narrower. At 2.45 it came to an end. We were back in the mountains again. The cars stopped, and everybody [23]*slowly* got out. The Japanese were embarrassed. 'We didn't know you were foreigners,' one of them said. 'You [24]*definitely* seemed to know the way, so we followed you.' Everybody laughed [25]*politely*, but we all felt [26]*really* tired.

We reached Tokyo [27]*early in the morning*, and [28]*then* we all had to go to work.

[29]*After that* I [30]*always* stayed at home during national holidays!

1 *well* – manner
2 *there* – ___________
3 *very* – ___________
4 *extremely* – ___________
5 *slowly* – ___________
6 *all night* – ___________
7 *finally* – ___________
8 *at 6.00* – ___________
9 *terribly* – ___________
10 *immediately* – ___________
11 *a lot* – ___________
12 *once a day* – ___________
13 *every day* – ___________
14 *outside* – ___________
15 *quickly* – ___________
16 *certainly* – ___________
17 *sadly* – ___________
18 *late* – ___________
19 *Unfortunately* – ___________
20 *nowhere* – ___________
21 *suddenly* – ___________
22 *Strangely* – ___________
23 *slowly* – ___________
24 *definitely* – ___________
25 *politely* – ___________
26 *really* – ___________
27 *early in the morning* – ___________
28 *then* – ___________
29 *After that* – ___________
30 *always* – ___________

3 Write the adverbs and phrases of manner, place and time in end position.

Example: *(soon) (somewhere)*
I'm tired of driving. Let's stop somewhere soon.

1 *(before midday) (there)*
Hurry up! We have to get ____________________

2 *(beautifully) (yesterday)*
The team played ____________________

3 *(for a year) (everywhere)*
The police looked for the two men ____________________

4 *(angrily) (last night) (at the meeting)*
A lot of people spoke ____________________

5 *(at college) (these days) (well)*
Harry is doing ____________________

4 Write the adverbs and phrases of frequency in the most usual position – middle or end.

Examples: *Jack goes into town. (sometimes)*
Jack sometimes goes into town.
A ship visits the island. (twice a month)
A ship visits the island twice a month.

1 *I do the washing on Monday. (usually)*
____

2 *Do you visit your old school? (ever)*
____

3 *Flights to New York leave. (once an hour)*
____

4 *You have to take the medicine. (twice a day)*
____

5 Emphasize the speaker's feeling. Change the adjective in the second sentence into an adverb in front position. Leave out unnecessary words.

Example: *I fell. It was lucky that I managed to catch a tree branch.*
I fell. Luckily, I managed to catch a tree branch.

1 *I called Ann at 7.00. It was sad that she'd already gone.*
I called Ann at 7.00. ____________________

2 *Bill is getting better. We're hopeful that he'll be well soon.*
Bill is getting better. ____________________

3 *My wife and I are scientists. We were surprised that our children were good at Art.*
My wife and I are scientists. ____________________

4 *The prize goes to Clint Starr. It's unfortunate that he isn't here to receive it.*
The prize goes to Clint Starr. ____________________

6 Write the words in the best order.

Example: *(will be) (probably)*
Ann will probably be *late home.*

1 *(has finished) (definitely)*
The football game ____________________ *now.*

2 *('ll visit) (never)*
I ____________________ *that place again!*

3 *(are delivered) (always)*
New books ____________________ *on Monday morning.*

4 *(hasn't understood) (clearly)*
She ____________________ *anything I've said.*

5 *('ll see) (hardly ever)*
If you move, I ____________________ *you again.*

73 Comparison 1: adjective and adverb forms

cheaper, cheapest *more expensive, most expensive* *more quickly, most quickly*

FORMS

Comparison with adjective + *er/est*

The Highlight is cheaper than the Gazelle. It's the cheapest of the three.

Comparison with *more/most, less/least* + adjective

The Rebel is more expensive than the Gazelle. It's the most expensive car.

Comparison with two-syllable adjectives

He wants the Rebel, but she is happier with the Gazelle.

Comparison with adverbs

The Rebel accelerates more quickly than the others. It accelerates the most quickly.

We use a comparative form of an adjective (adjective + *er* or *more* + adjective) to compare two things. We use a superlative form of an adjective (adjective + *est* or *most* + adjective) when one of a group is beyond the others, eg *the cheapest* and *the most expensive*. Compare the following comparative and superlative forms.

تستخدم صيغة التفضيل (صفة +er او more + صفة) للمقارنة بين شيئين. وتستخدم صيغة التفضيل العليا لصفة ما (صفة + est او most + صفة) عندما يفوق فرد ما غيره في المجموعة.

Comparative adjectives:	*cheaper (than)*	*more* / *less*	*expensive (than)*
Superlative adjectives:	*(the) cheapest*	*(the) most* / *(the) least*	*expensive*

ويتضح الفرق بين الصيغتين من خلال مقارنة الامثلة المبينة.

We usually use *than* after a comparative form. It connects the two things that we are comparing. We usually use *the* before a superlative form. It refers to the thing which we are describing.

تستخدم than عادة بعد صيغة التفضيل فهي التي تربط بين الشيئين اللذين تجري مقارنتهما. وتستخدم the عادة قبل صيغة التفضيل العليا فهي تشير الى الشيء موضع الوصف.

Comparison with adjectives + *er/est*

We use *er/est* with nearly all one-syllable adjectives. Note the spelling changes. (See Appendix 2 for more information on spelling rules.)

تستخدم er / est مع جميع الصفات التي تتكون من مقطع واحد تقريباً. وتجدر ملاحظة التغييرات التي تطرأ على الهجاء.

Adjective	**+ *er***	**+ *est***	**Adjective**	**+ *r***	**+ *st***
small	*smaller*	*smallest*	*nice*	*nicer*	*nicest*
slow	*slower*	*slowest*	*large*	*larger*	*largest*

Adjective + doubled consonant		**+ *er***	**+ *est***
big	*+g*	*bigger*	*biggest*
hot	*+t*	*hotter*	*hottest*

*His house is **smaller** than hers.*
*Mexico City is the **largest** city in the world.*
*Today is the **hottest** day of the year.*

Comparison with *more/most* or *less/least* + adjective

We use *more/most* or *less/least* for all adjectives with three syllables or more. We also use these forms for all adjectives ending in *ing* or *ed*, eg *pleasing/pleased, tiring/tired, worrying/worried* and *embarrassing/embarrassed*.

تستخدم more / most او less / least مع جميع الصفات التي تتكون من ثلاثة مقاطع او اكثر. وتستخدم ايضاً مع جميع الصفات التي تنتهي بـ ing او ed.

*Cars are **more reliable** now than they were 20 years ago.*
*She's the **most beautiful** girl in the world!*
*I'm **less tired** than I was yesterday.* *It's the **least tiring** job.*

We can also use these forms for all adjectives with two syllables.

*Jack is the **most lazy** boy I know.*

*John's work is **less careful** than it should be.*

We can also use *more/most* and *less/least* like *fewer/fewest* to talk about quantity.

ويمكن استخدام صيغ more و most و less و least مع جميع الصفات التي تتكون من مقطعين.

كما يمكن استخدامها مع الصفات التي تتعلق بالكميات. وبنفس الطريقة يمكن استخدام fewer و fewest.

Comparison with two-syllable adjectives

You can use *more/most* and *less/least* for all adjectives with two syllables. But we often use *er/est* with two-syllable adjectives.

*The road is **more narrow/narrower** here.*

*He's the **most lazy/laziest** boy in the class.*

يمكن استخدام most/more و least/less مع جميع الصفات التي تتكون من مقطعين، ولكن غالباً ما يتم استخدام صيغة est/er مع الصفات التي تتكون من مقطعين أيضاً.

We often use *er/est* with these very common two-syllable adjectives: *clever, cruel, gentle, narrow, pleasant, polite, quiet, simple, stupid, tired.*

*Ann is **politer** than her sister.*

*Tom is the **cleverest** boy in the class.*

غالباً ما تستخدم est/er مع الصفات الشائعة التالية والتي تتكون من مقطعين.

We also often use *er/est* with two-syllable adjectives ending in a consonant + *y*, eg *dirty, easy, funny, happy, lazy, lovely, pretty, silly, sunny* and *tidy*. They change like this: *dirty + ier/iest → dirtier/dirtiest.*

*Jack is the **laziest** boy I know.*

*Question 2 is **easier** than question 1.*

غالباً ما تستخدم est/er مع الصفات التي تتكون من مقطعين والتي تنتهي بحرف ثابت + y، ويتغير حرف y إلى iest/ier.

Comparison of adverbs

We use a comparative form of an adverb (adverb + *er* or *more* + adverb) to compare two actions. We use a superlative form of an adverb (adverb + *est* or *most* + adverb) when one of a group does something beyond the others, eg ... *accelerates the most quickly.*

تستخدم صيغة المقارنة للظرف (er أو more + ظرف) للمقارنة بين حدثين. وتستخدم صيغة التفضيل العليا (ظرف + est أو most + ظرف) عندما يقوم شخص بعمل يفوق قدرة الآخرين.

Many adverbs have the form adjective + *ly*, eg *quickly, slowly* and *nicely*. (See Unit 70 for more information on adjectives, adverbs and adverb formation.) Just like longer adjectives, these *ly* adverbs take the forms *more/most* and *less/least*.

*Rob works **more quickly** than Steve.*

*Jane sings the **most beautifully** in the class.*

تتكون كثير من الظروف بزيادة ly على الصفات، وبالتالي فإنها تعامل بصيغة most/more و least/less.

Some adverbs look like short adjectives which take *er/est*, eg *deep, early, fast, hard, high, late, long* and *near*. Just like these short adjectives, these adverbs usually take the forms *er/est*.

*The Rebel goes **faster** than the Gazelle.*

*I arrived the **earliest** at the meeting.*

هناك بعض الظروف التي تبدو وكأنها صفات قصيرة وتستخدم معها صيغة est/er.

Note the irregular forms.

كذلك يجب ملاحظة الحالات اللاقياسية المبينة.

Adjective	**Adverb**	**Comparative**	**Superlative**
good	*well*	*better*	*best*
bad	*badly*	*worse*	*worst*
far	*far*	*farther/further*	*farthest/furthest*

*This year's results are **better** than last year's.*

*My headache is getting **worse**.*

*We can't go any **farther** tonight.*

Exercises

1 Write the *er* and *est* forms.

	Adjective	*er* form	*est* form
1	*short*	shorter	shortest
2	*pretty*	prettier	prettiest
3	*long*	________	________
4	*ugly*	________	________
5	*large*	________	________
6	*big*	________	________
7	*small*	________	________
8	*nice*	________	________
9	*cool*	________	________
10	*easy*	________	________
11	*simple*	________	________
12	*fine*	________	________
13	*thin*	________	________
14	*hot*	________	________

2 Write the correct *er* forms of the underlined adjectives.

Example: *Bill has a large car. It's even* larger *than my brother's.*

1 *Yesterday's test was easy – much ________ than last month's.*

2 *Question 2 was simple. It was certainly ________ than question 1.*

3 *My cousin is nice – a lot ________ than my brother.*

4 *It's been hot today, and it'll be even ________ tomorrow.*

5 *The job took a long time. It took ________ than I thought.*

3 Write the *est* forms. Use these adjectives.

early, fit, funny, late, narrow, quick

Example: *There's a train at 5.30 am. That's the* earliest *one.*

1 *This is the ________ model. It's just come out.*

2 *Which is the ________ way to Paris, please?*

3 *We're coming to the ________ part of the river now. Here it's only five metres wide.*

4 *Rod is the ________ member of the team. He's been training very hard.*

5 *He was the ________ man I've ever heard. I couldn't stop laughing.*

4 Complete the radio adverts with regular *er* and *est* forms. Use these adjectives.

easy, fast, fine, fit, low, white

Example: *SPEED CLEAN was always the* fastest *home cleaner. Now it's* faster *than ever before. It does the job in seconds.*

1 *You'll be ________ in just three days with the HOME EXERCISER. And after a month you'll be the ________ you've ever been in your life.*

2 *There's no ________ watch in the world than the perfect TIME PERFECTA. Remember, we've been makers of the ________ watches in the world for 30 years.*

3 *You'll find the ________ prices in town at GOOD WAY SUPERMARKETS. And that's a promise. If you can find ________ prices anywhere else, we'll give you your money back.*

4 *GLEAM CREAM cleans your teeth ________ than white. For the ________, cleanest teeth of all, choose GLEAM CREAM.*

5 *Do you hate all those video controls? Well, now TELE-SELECT is here. It's the ________ thing in the world to use. Just talk to it. Tell it the time, the channel and the film to record, and TELE-SELECT does the rest. What could be ________ than that?*

5 Complete the conversations. Use *more/most, less/least* or *fewer/fewest.*

Example: ● *I've just moved to a bigger apartment in the same building.*
❍ *Do you have to pay* more *rent?*
● *Yes, it's the biggest in the building, so it costs the* most.

1 ● *Bob seems to get richer, but meaner every day. I can't stand him these days.*
❍ *Yes, he's got ________ money than ever before, but he's got ________ friends!*

2 ● *I'm still hungry. Is there any ___________*

❍ *But you've already had the ___________ out of everybody. Don't be so greedy!*

3 ● *This motor-bike is certainly quite cheap. It costs ___________ than all the other models we've looked at.*

❍ *I've read that it also costs the ___________ to run out of all the bikes this size. And I've also heard that it has the ___________ mechanical problems.*

● *But if there's a mechanical problem, spare parts are very expensive. In fact, they cost the ___________ out of all the models in the 750cc class.*

6 Write the comparative and superlative forms of the adjectives.

Example: *No language is easy to learn, but Italian is* less difficult *than I thought. In fact it's the* least difficult *language I've ever studied. (difficult)*

1 *Joe is doing well at art college. He isn't the ___________________ student in his year, but he's ___________________ than 90% of the other students. (talented)*

2 *Why do you always have to buy the ___________________ thing in the shop? Couldn't you choose something ___________________ (expensive)*

3 *I think rock climbing is even ___________________ than deep sea diving. In fact, I think it's one of the ___________________ outdoor activities you can do. (dangerous)*

4 *Uncut diamonds are ___________________ than diamonds that are cut. A diamond that was recently sold for $975,000 is the ___________________ one in the world at the moment. (valuable)*

5 *I don't like Robin Black's new book as much as his last one. It's ___________________ In fact, I think it's the ___________________ book he's ever written. (interesting)*

7 Complete the statements with a verb and comparative adverb.

Examples: *Ann is a quicker worker than Sue.*
Ann works more quickly *than Sue.*

1 *Grandad is a slower driver than his me.*
Grandad ___________________________ than me.

2 *Stephen Prince is a more exciting writer than Sid Shelley.*
Stephen Prince ___________________________ than Sid Shelley.

3 *Don is a lighter sleeper than his brother.*
Don ___________________________ than his brother.

4 *Ron is always an earlier arrival at work than Bob.*
Ron always ___________________________ at work than Bob.

5 *Joe is a less intelligent football player than Steve.*
Joe ___________________________ than Steve.

8 Write statements with superlative adverbs.

We tested three washing machines – the Crystal, the Wash-Tech and the Snowline. Here are the results.

Examples: *(Snowline/wash/+ good/Crystal/wash/ - effective)*
The Snowline washed the best, and the Crystal washed the least effectively.

1 *(Crystal/perform/+ reliable/Wash-Tech/perform/ - reliable)*

____

____

____

____

2 *(Wash-Tech/run/- economical/Crystal/run/+ cheap)*

____

____

____

____

3 *(Crystal/finish/+ fast/Snowline/finish/- quick)*

____

____

____

74 Comparison 2: sentence patterns

Hill finished faster than Rossi. *He's the fastest man in the world.*

FORMS

Sentence patterns with comparatives
Hill finished faster than Rossi.

Sentence patterns with superlatives
Hill is the fastest man in the world.

Sentence patterns with *(not) as ... as*
Rossi is good, but he is not as good as Hill.

Comparison and object pronouns
I drove faster than he did. → *than him.*

Sentence patterns with comparatives

A comparative sentence compares two things. When we mention both things, we link them with *than*.

*Hill is **faster than** Rossi.* *A CD lasts **longer than** a cassette.*

تقارن جمل التفضيل بين شيئين او بين شخصين. وعند ذكر الاثنين نربطهما بكلمة than.

When we compare with an adjective, we do not always mention both things.

● *Which is your jacket?* ❍ *The **bigger one**.*

وعند المقارنة مع صفة، لا نذكر كلا الشيئين دائماً.

Sentence patterns with superlatives

We usually use *the* before superlative adjectives.

*Paul is **the tallest** person here.*

تستخدم the عادة قبل صفة التفضيل العليا.

We do not often use *the* before superlative adverbs. Compare the following.

● *Which is **the best** song?* ❍ *I like Sad Heart **best**.*

لا تستخدم the غالباً، قبل ظروف التفضيل العليا. قارن ما يلي:

We can use *in* or *of* after a superlative. Use *in* to talk about places and groups. Use *of* to talk about other things, including numbers.

*I'm the **tallest boy in the class**.*
*July is the **warmest month of the year**.*

ويمكن استخدام in او of بعد صفة التفضيل العليا. وتستخدم in عند الحديث عن المكان والمجموعات في حين تستخدم of للحديث عن الاشياء الاخرى بما فيها الاعداد.

Sentence patterns with *(not) as ... as*

Use *as ... as* to say that two things or actions are equal.

*Paul is **as tall as** his father now.* *I drive **as well as** Tom.*

تستخدم صيغة as...as للقول بان شيئين او حدثين متساويان.

Use *not as ... as* (or *not so ... as*) to say that two things or actions are not equal.

*English **isn't as difficult as** Maths.* (Maths is harder than English.)
*He **can't work as quickly as** I can.* (I can work faster than he can.)

وتستخدم not as... as او (not so... as)، للقول بان شيئين او حدثين غير متساويين.

Comparison and object pronouns

After a comparative with *than* or *as ... as*, we often talk about another person. If we use a name we can do it in these two ways.

*I drove faster **than Carlo did**.* *I drove faster **than Carlo**.*

غالباً ما نتحدث بعد صفة التفضيل مع than او as... as عن شخص آخر. وعند ذكر الاسم يمكن استخدام اي من الصيغتين المبينتين.

If we use a pronoun, the subject pronoun + auxiliary verb change to an object pronoun.

*I drove faster **than he did**.* → *I drove faster **than him**.*
*He can't run as quickly **as I can**.* → *He can't run as quickly **as me**.*

اذا استخدمنا الضمير، فان صيغة ضمير الفاعل + الفعل المساعد تتغير الى صيغة ضمير المفعول به.

Exercises

1 Write statements with comparative adjectives.

Example: *Tom is 17. Sam is 19. (old)*
Sam is older than Tom.

1 *Sue is 10. Ann is 12. (young)*

___

2 *The Honda costs £10,000. The Toyota costs £12,000. (expensive)*

___

3 *Robin can do 100 metres in 10 seconds. Jack runs 100 metres in 10.5 seconds. (fast)*

___

4 *Five climbers have died on Mount George. Eleven climbers have been killed on Mount Egmont. (dangerous)*

___

5 *The journey by sea is an hour. The journey by tunnel is only half an hour. (short)*

___

2 Write statements with superlative adjectives and *be* in the correct form.

Example: *(the new Boeing/be/big/plane in the world)*
The new Boeing is the biggest plane in the world.

1 *(yesterday/be/hot/day of the year)*

___

2 *(the XL400/be/popular/car in Europe this year)*

___

3 *(Tom and Sam/be/good/players in last year's team)*

___

4 *(some people say Casa Blanca/be/fine/film ever)*

___

3 Correct the statements. Use *isn't nearly as … as …*

Example: ● *Kuwait is larger than Saudi Arabia.*
❍ *That's not right.* Kuwait isn't nearly as large as Saudi Arabia.

1 ● *A Jumbo 747 is faster than a Concord.*
❍ *That's wrong.* ___

2 ● *Britain is warmer than Egypt.*
❍ *I'm afraid that's not quite right.* ___

3 ● *Silver is more expensive than gold.*
❍ *I'm sorry, but that's wrong.* ___

4 ● *Rome is older than Athens.*
❍ *No, it's the opposite.* ___

5 ● *English food is better than French food.*
❍ *I'm afraid I don't agree.* ___

4 Write the correct pronouns.

Examples: *He's cleverer than* they *are. (they/them)*
He's cleverer than them. *(they/them)*

Tom: *Sue, why did you give the mailroom manager's job to Tim. Ann is twice as clever as* [1]___ *is. (he/him)*

Sue: *Yes, but he knows the work better than* [2]___ *(she/her) Remember, he's been with the company much longer than* [3]___ *has. (she/her)*

Tom: *Well, what about Alan and Emma? Tim hasn't been here any longer than* [4]___ *have. (they/them) And he certainly doesn't know the work any better than* [5]___ *(they/them)*

Sue: *Yes, but they're both cleverer than* [6]___, *and I'm going to give them better jobs. (he/him)*

Tom: *Well, I still don't agree about Tim.*

Sue: *Believe me, you don't know him as well as* [7]___ *do. (I/me) If you did, I'm sure you'd make the same decision as* [8]___ *(I/me)*

75 *too* and *enough*

He's too young. He isn't old enough.

FORMS

***too* + adjective/adverb**

Ron is too old.
Bob is not too old/young.

Adjective/adverb + *enough*

Bob is old/young enough.
Len is not old enough.

Further patterns

Len is too young | *to get the job.*
| *for the job.*

too and *enough*

We use *too* and *enough* when we talk about the right amount of something, eg *money, clothes size, exam marks* and *age*.

too and *enough* go with adjectives and adverbs. *too* goes before an adjective/adverb. *enough* goes after an adjective/adverb.

Adjectives	**Adverbs**
*Len is **too young** to get the job.*	*Slow down! We're going **too fast**.*
*Len isn't **old enough** to get the job.*	*Hurry! We aren't going **fast enough**.*

تستخدم too وenough عند الحديث عن الكمية الصحيحة
ن شيء ما مثل المال وقياس الملابس.. الخ.
تستخدم too وenough مع الصفات ومع الظروف. تأتي
too قبل الصفة او الظرف في حين تأتي enough بعد
الصفة او الظرف.

too + adjective/adverb

too means more than the right amount. *not too* means the right amount. Note that we often leave out the last part in brackets.

*Ron is 50, so he's **too old** (to get the job).*
*Bob is 25, so he **isn't too old** (to get the job).*
*The plane won't take off. It's going **too slowly** (to take off).*

too is not the same as *very*. Compare the following. (See also Unit 76.)

*Harry was **very old**, but he kept on working.*
*Harry was **too old** to work. He had to stop.*

تعطي too معنى الزيادة على الكمية الصحيحة، وتفيد not
too بأن الكمية صحيحة. ولاحظ باننا غالباً ما نحذف
الجزء الاخير من الجملة كما هو مبيّن.

too ليست مثل very. قارن ما يلي. (وانظر ايضاً unit
76)

Adjective/adverb + *enough*

enough means the right amount – not more, not less. *not enough* means less than the right amount. Note that we often leave out the last part in brackets.

*Bob is 25, so he's **old enough** (to get the job).*
*Len is only 20, so he **isn't old enough** (to get the job).*

تفيد enough ان الكمية صحيحة بلا زيادة ولا نقصان.
وتعني not enough ان الكمية اقل مما ينبغي. وتجدر
الملاحظة ان الجزء الأخير من الجملة غالباً ما يُحذف.

Further patterns

enough can go with a noun – before, not after. *too* needs *much* or *many* to go with a noun. (We sometimes also say *too little/too few*.)

*Is there **enough orange juice**? We haven't got **enough sandwiches**.*
*There's **too much orange juice**. Have we got **too few sandwiches**?*

After *too* and *enough* we can use *to* + infinitive + noun or *for* + noun.

*He's **too young to get the job**. He isn't **old enough for the job**.*

We can also use them together.

*This shirt is **good enough to wear** at home, but it's **too old-fashioned for the party** tonight.*

يمكن ان تأتي enough قبل الاسم ولكنها لا تأتي بعده.
وتحتاج too إلى استخدام much او many، واحياناً نقول
too little أو too few.

يمكن استخدام to + مصدر + اسم بعد too وenough،
وكذلك يمكن استخدام for + اسم.

Exercises

1 Write *too* + these adjectives or adverbs.

Adjectives	Adverbs
late, strong, young	*quickly, quietly, slowly*

Example: *Can't you work faster? You're working* too slowly.

1 *I'm only 15, so I can't drive yet. I'm* ______
2 *Time goes* ______ *when you're having fun.*
3 *I couldn't hold the thief. He was* ______
4 *I ran, but I missed the train. I was* ______
5 *Tell Ann to speak up. She's talking* ______

2 Write these adjectives or adverbs + *enough*.

Adjectives	Adverbs
big, good, soon	*carefully, hard, quickiy*

Example: *Can't you work faster? You aren't working* quickly enough.

1 *I can't climb through the window. It isn't* ______
2 *I can tell you the answer tomorrow. Is that* ______
3 *The engine broke down. The engineers hadn't checked it* ______
4 *Nick is going to lose the race. He hasn't trained* ______
5 *I'm going to buy the smaller sound system. It isn't the best, but it's* ______

3 Complete the dialogues. Use *too* + *little/few*, *enough* or *not/n't ... enough*.

Mr Simpson and his assistant are checking stock in his small stationery shop.

1 (*✓ A5 paper/✗ A4 paper/✗ brown envelopes*)
Mr S: *We've got* enough A5 paper, *but we have* n't *got* enough A4 paper.
Asst: *And we've got* too few brown envelopes.

2 (*✗ large paper clips/✗ medium clips/✓ small clips*)
Mr S: *We have* ___ *got* ______ ______ *and we have got* ______
Asst: *But we've got* ______

3 (*✗ brown sticky tape/✗ clear tape/✓ elastic bands*)
Mr S: *We've got* ______ ______ *and we have* ___ *got* ______ ______
Asst: *But we've got* ______ ______

4 (*✗ glue/✗ stapling machines/✗ staples*)
Mr S: *We've got* ______ *and we've got* ______ ______
Asst: *And we have* ___ *got* ______

4 Write statements.

Example: *The boys don't like the weather. It's too hot.*
The weather is too hot for the boys.

1 *I really want a holiday. I haven't got enough money.*
______
______

2 *Your mother won't like this coffee. It's too strong.*
______
______

3 *The family are all very happy with the new house. It's big enough.*
______
______

5 Write statements.

Example: *I don't want to go out. It's too hot.*
It's too hot to go out.

1 *We don't want to go out. It isn't warm enough.*
______

2 *They tried to catch the bird. It was too fast.*
______

3 *We wanted to catch the bus. We were too late.*
______
______

4 *The plane missed the mountain. It was flying just high enough.*
______
______

76 a bit, very — much, a lot — so, such

I felt a bit ill. — *I felt much better.* — *I felt so tired.*

FORMS

***a bit, very*, etc + adjective/adverb**

He felt a bit tired, but he did not stop.

***much, a lot*, etc + comparative adjective/adverb**

He was able to come down much more quickly. He felt a lot better.

***so* + adjective/adverb, *such* (+ adjective) + noun**

Back at home, he was so tired that he went straight to sleep.
It had been such a hard journey that he rested all next day.

a bit, very, etc + adjective/adverb

Use these words to give an adjective or an adverb a weaker or stronger feeling. *a bit, pretty* and *really* are informal. Use them in friendly conversation.

تستخدم هذه الكلمات لإضفاء احساس اقوى او اضعف، على صفة او ظرف. وتستخدم الكلمات a bit و pretty و really في المواقف غير الرسمية وفي الاحاديث الودية.

Weakest	Weak	Stronger	Strongest
not (+ verb) + *very*	*slightly, a little, a bit*	*quite, rather, fairly, pretty*	*very, extremely, really*

*He did**n't feel very well**. In fact, he felt **quite ill**.*
*Eddy is **extremely good** at tennis. He's Number 10 in the world.*

very and *too* are different. Compare the following. (See also Unit 75.)

*He was **very** tired, but he went on climbing.*
*He was **too** tired to walk. He had to stop.*

يتضح الفرق بين استخدام very و too من خلال مقارنة الامثلة المبينة. (انظر ايضاً، unit 75)

much, a lot, etc + comparative adjective/adverb

Use these words to give a comparative adjective or adverb a weaker or stronger feeling.

وتستخدم هذه الكلمات المبينة لتضفي، على صفة المقارنة، وعلى ظروف المقارنة، مشاعر اضعف او اقوى.

Weak	Strong	Strongest
slightly, a little, a bit	*much, a lot*	*far*

*Could you please talk **a little more quietly**?*
*I felt **a lot better** after a good night's sleep.*
*Susan can speak Japanese **far better** than she can write it.*

CROSSCHECK

***so* + adjective/adverb**

Use *so* to make an adjective or adverb very strong.

*The film was **so boring**!*
*What took you **so long** to get here?*
*I didn't see. It happened **so quickly**!*

We can add a *that* phrase to show the result of the *so* part of the sentence.

*The story was **so exciting that** I couldn't stop reading.*
*I was **so cold that** I wore two sweaters.*

***such* (+ adjective) + noun**

Use *such* (+ adjective) + noun in the same way.

*He always talks **such rubbish**!*
*What took you **such a long time**?*
*This is such **a beautiful house**.*

We can do exactly the same with a sentence containing *such*.

*It was **such an exciting story that** I couldn't stop reading.*
*It was **such a cold day that** I wore two sweaters.*

تستخدم so لتضفي على الصفة او على الظرف درجة عالية من القوة.

وتستخدم such (+ صفة) + اسم بنفس الطريقة.

يمكن اضافة العبارة التي تستخدم فيها that بغرض تبيين الأثر الناتج عن استخدام so في الجملة. ونستطيع فعل الشيء نفسه مع الجملة التي تحتوي على such.

Exercises

1 Complete the statements. Use these words.

a bit, not very, quite, very

Example: *The traffic was travelling at 5 kph. The journey was* very *slow.*

1 *Sally is doing much better at Maths now, but she's still* ________ *slow.*

2 *I like football, but I'm* ________ *good at it.*

3 *I'm* ________ *hungry. I need food now!*

4 *The new XR200 is* ________ *a good car, but it isn't my favourite.*

5 *Don't climb on that old fence. It's* ________ *strong.*

2 Complete the statements. Use these words.

a little, far, much

Example: *Tony is still very ill, but he's getting* a little *better every day.*

1 *These shoes look the same, but these are £50 more than those. They're* ________ *more expensive.*

2 *I failed my driving test badly the first time, but I did* ________ *better the second time, and I passed.*

3 *Sue is* ________ *older than Tim. She's 10 and he's 9.*

4 *Our new house is* ________ *bigger than our old one. It's got four bedrooms instead of two.*

5 *Tony drives* ________ *more carefully than he did a few years ago, but he still frightens me!*

3 Complete the conversation with *so* or *such*.

● *You're* so *quiet! Is anything wrong?*

❍ *It's my exams. They're* [1]______ *soon, and I've got* [2]______ *a lot of work. I've got to stay up all night.*

● *Don't be* [3]______ *an idiot! You're obviously* [4]______ *tired that you can't work properly. It would be* [5]______ *a waste of time if you stayed up all night! What's more, you'd be* [6]______ *exhausted tomorrow that you'd waste the whole day!*

❍ *But I'm* [7]______ *worried! If I don't pass, it'll be* [8]______ *a disaster!*

● *You'll pass. The trouble with you is that you're* [9]______ *a worrier, and you've really* [10]______ *little to worry about!*

4 Match statements 1–8 and a–h. Then join them using *so* or *such ...* (*that*).

1 *The weather was bad.*
2 *The students are making a noise.*
3 *The birds are friendly.*
4 *The children made a mess.*
5 *Everybody is busy.*
6 *I haven't driven for a long time.*
7 *After the trip we were all tired.*
8 *They took a long time to get ready.*

a *All the neighbours are complaining.*
b *They nearly missed their plane.*
c *We went straight to sleep.*
d *They even take food from your hand.*
e *We gave up our holiday and went home.*
f *Nobody is answering the phone.*
g *I feel quite nervous about going on the road.*
h *It took an hour to clean the room.*

1 – e 2 – ___ 3 – ___ 4 – ___ 5 – ___ 6 – ___
7 – ___ 8 – ___

1 The weather was so bad (that) we gave up our holiday and went home.

2 ______________________________

3 ______________________________

4 ______________________________

5 ______________________________

6 ______________________________

7 ______________________________

8 ______________________________

77 Prepositions 1: place and movement

on, onto, into, out of, across, by, down, from, in, through, under, etc

The prepositions in this unit express their place or movement. The preposition refers to the noun which always follows it. (See Unit 78 for differences between the prepositions of place *in, on* and *at.*)

تتعلق أدوات الجر في هذه الوحدة بالمكان والحركة. وهي ترتبط بشكل دائم بالاسم الذي يليها.

*The hotel is **down** the hill.* (place)
*The Wood family are walking **down** the hill.* (movement)

on, on top of

*There's a suitcase **on** the chair.*
*There's another suitcase **on top of** the cupboard.*

on, onto, off

*Nick Wood is putting a pile of clothes **onto/on** the bed.*
*His cap is falling **off** the pile.*

in, into, out of

*There are some clothes **in** the suitcase.*
*He's putting them **into/in** the case.*
*Nick is taking some more clothes **out of** the cupboard.*

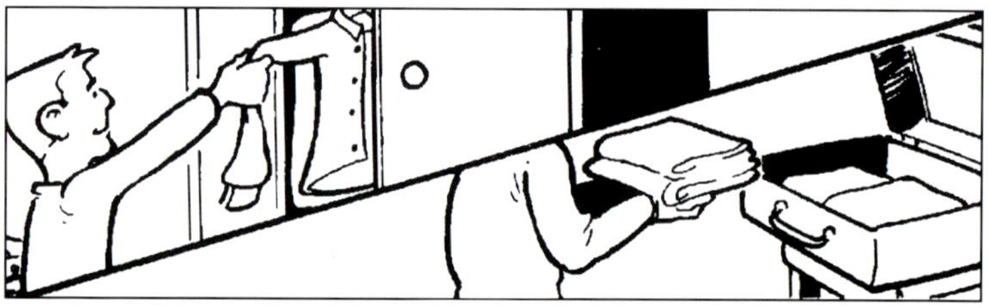

down, up

*Nick is taking his case **down** the stairs.*
*His sister is going **up** the stairs.*

inside, outside

*There are two sports bags **inside** the front door.*
*There are some beach things **outside** the front door.*

behind, in front of, around, round

*The car was in the garage **behind** the house.*
*Now it's **in front of** the house.*
*Mr Wood has brought it **around/round** the house.*

next to, by, beside

The car is ***next to/by/beside*** *the garden fence.*
There are some pieces of luggage ***next to/by/ beside*** *the car.*
Mr Wood is standing ***next to/by/beside*** *the car.*

across, along

Mrs Wood is going ***across*** *the road.*
A friend is coming ***along*** *the road.*

near, from, to

The Wood family live in Sandford ***near*** *Oxford.*
Today they're driving ***from*** *Sandford* ***to*** *Heathrow Airport.*

away from, towards, past

They're driving ***away from*** *Sandford.*
They're going ***towards*** *the motorway.*
They're driving ***past*** *the motorway sign.*

over, under, through

They've just driven ***over*** *a bridge.* (***across*** *a bridge* is also possible.)
There's a river ***under*** *the bridge.*
They're going to drive ***through*** *a tunnel.*

above, below

The Wood family catch their plane. Soon it's ***above*** *the clouds.*
Nick watches the clouds ***below*** *the plane.*

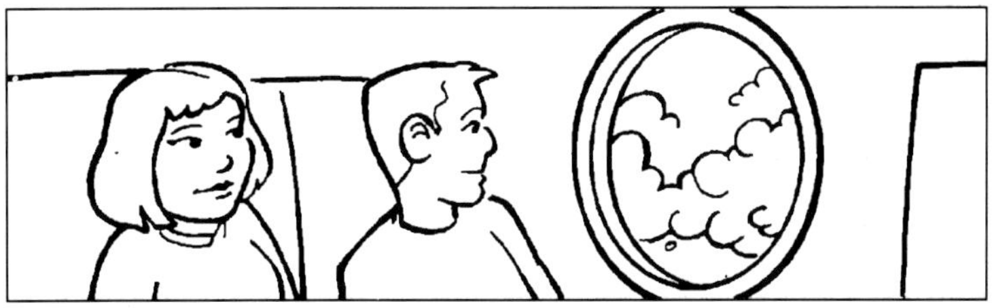

between, among, opposite

The Woods finally reach their hotel. It's ***between*** *the hills and the sea.*
It stands ***among*** *a lot of trees.*
It's ***opposite*** *a small island.*

Exercises

1 Look at the picture. Then complete the statements with these prepositions.

above, behind, between, in, in front of, near, next to, on, opposite, under

Example: *There is a light* near *the window.*

1 *There is a desk* ________ *the window too.*

2 *There is a light* ________ *the desk.*

3 *There is a chair* ________ *the desk.*

4 *There is a lamp* ________ *the desk.*

5 *There is a paper bin* ________ *the desk.*

6 *There is an empty box* ________ *the paper bin.*

7 *There is a phone* ________ *the desk.*

8 *There is a filing cabinet* ________ *the desk.*

9 *There is a large wall map* ________ *the window.*

10 *The desk is* ________ *the window and the wall map.*

2 Write the correct prepositions.

Example: *There were a lot of people* outside *the cinema before the doors opened. (inside/outside)*

1 *There's someone* ___ *the door. Could you answer it, please? (in/at)*

2 *Is Lucy* ___ *home today? (in/at)*

3 *Listen! I think I can hear somebody* ___ *the garden. (in/at)*

4 *I'm sorry. Mr Davis isn't* ___ *his office just now. He's seeing the Director. (in/at)*

5 *There's a newspaper shop on the other side of the road,* ________ *our house. (opposite/in front of)*

6 *Please don't stand* ________ *the children. They can't see what's happening. (opposite/in front of)*

7 *Look! Can't you see your glasses now? They're right* ________ *you. (opposite/in front of)*

8 *Swindon is a large town that stands on the road* ________ *London and Bristol. (between/among)*

9 ________ *all the white sheep in the field there were a few black ones. (between/among)*

10 *The woods are lovely there, and we camped* ________ *the trees by the stream. (between/among)*

3 Look at the picture. Then complete the statements with prepositions.

Example: *(across, along, into, past, through)*
The cat walked along *the road for a while.*

1 *It went* ___________ *the bus stop.*

2 *Then it suddenly ran* ___________ *the road.*

3 *It came* ___________ *our garden.*

4 *It came in* ___________ *the gate.*

(along, over, round, towards, up)

5 *It walked a little way* ___________ *the garden path.*

6 *Then it ran* ___________ *the tree.*

7 *Next it went* ___________ *our summer house.*

8 *It jumped* ___________ *the flower bed on the way.*

9 *It climbed* ___________ *one side of the summer house.*

(away from, down, inside, out of, under)

10 *And it climbed* ___________ *the other side.*

11 *It crawled* ___________ *the summer house.*

12 *Then it went* ___________ *the summer house for a moment.*

13 *But then it jumped* ___________ *the window.*

14 *Finally, it ran* ___________ *the summer house and left the garden.*

78 Prepositions 2: place

at, in, on

at

Use *at* to talk about an exact place.

تستخدم *at* عند الحديث عن مكان محدد.

He lives ***at Number 25, Park Road****.*
Where's Mary? She isn't ***at her desk****.*
I'll meet you ***at the cinema entrance****.*

Use *at* to talk about an event.

وتستخدم *at* عند الحديث عن حدث ما.

Were you ***at the football match****?*
Over 100 people were ***at the meeting****.*

in

Use *in* when there is something around, eg a person in a country or a pen in a pocket.

تستخدم *in* عند الحديث عن شيء في الجوار، مثل شخص في بلد ما أو قلم في الجيب.

He lives ***in Sandford****,* ***in England****.*
● *Is she* ***in the TV room****?* ○ *No, she's* ***in the garden****.*
Did you put the pen ***in your pocket****?*

Compare the use of *in* and *at*.

ويصبح الفرق أكثر وضوحاً عند مقارنة استخدام *in* و *at* فيما يلي.

The meeting was ***in Room 93****.* (the place)
Over 100 people were ***at the meeting****.* (the event in the place)

on

Use *on* for any surface.

تستخدم *on* عند الحديث عن شيء موجود على أي سطح.

Nick was standing ***on the chair****.* *Her name is* ***on the door****.*
There's a mark ***on the ceiling****.* *The answer is* ***on page 75****.*

Use *on* for a line that runs between two places.

وتستخدم *on* عند الحديث عن شيء أو عن خط يصل بين مكانين.

Sandford is ***on the River Thames****,* ***between Oxford and Abingdon****.*
The Wood family were ***on the road to the airport****.*
There were guards ***on the frontier between India and Pakistan****.*

Note these common expressions of place.

وتوضح الأمثلة المبينة الاستخدامات الشائعة لأدوات الجر التي تتصل بالمكان.

at	***in***	***on***
at school/work/home/college	*in hospital/town*	*on holiday/business*
at the library/bus station/cross roads	*in the country/shopping centre*	*on the beach/lake/island*
at the (third) turning	*in the middle of the road*	*on the right/left*
at the top/bottom of the hill	*in the middle/centre of the city/town/village*	*on the edge/outskirts of town/the city*
at a party/meeting/lesson	*in a group/queue/line*	*on the front/back of an envelope/a book*
at the front/back of a queue/hall/bus	*in the front/back of a car*	*on TV/cassette/disk*
at the end of a corridor/queue		

Exercises

1 Match statement halves 1–10 and a–j. Then write the complete statements.

1 *Tom lives at*
2 *There's a notice on*
3 *Ann is buying some things in*
4 *Dad is having a sleep in*
5 *My aunt lives in*
6 *Come and meet all the trainees in*
7 *I want you to introduce me to everyone at*
8 *There are two men working up on*
9 *Sally put the vase of flowers on*
10 *Both London and Oxford are on*

a *the shopping centre.*
b *Room 564.*
c *a small town outside London.*
d *the small bedroom.*
e *the roof.*
f *the party.*
g *Number 25, North Street.*
h *the River Thames.*
i *the wall outside my office.*
j *the table.*

1 – g 2 – ___ 3 – ___ 4 – ___ 5 – ___ 6 – ___
7 – ___ 8 – ___ 9 – ___ 10 – ___

1 Tom lives at Number 25, North Street.
2 ______________________________
3 ______________________________
4 ______________________________
5 ______________________________
6 ______________________________
7 ______________________________
8 ______________________________
9 ______________________________
10 ______________________________

2 Complete the statements. Use these phrases.

at that desk, at the entrance, at the meeting, in a village, in the garden, in the middle of, on that wall, on the way, on the bottle, on the edge of

Example: *Sally lives* on the edge of *London. She can see the country from her house.*

1 *I live* ______________ *London. It takes an hour to get out of the city.*
2 *We can stop for some petrol* ______________ *to the shops.*
3 *A lot of people spoke* ______________
4 *Let's put this picture* ______________
5 *What does the label* ______________ *say?*
6 *My brother usually works* ______________
7 *You can buy your ticket* ______________
8 *Mary is picking some flowers* ______________
9 *My sister lives* ______________ *near Oxford.*

3 Complete the dialogues. Use *in, on* or *at.*

● *Excuse me. Where can I find a photocopier?*
❍ *There's one* in *Room 303. Go upstairs and turn right* [1]___ *the top of the stairs. It's* [2]___ *the right* [3]___ *the end of the corridor.*

● *Look. There's a note* [4]___ *the front door.*
❍ *Oh, yes. It's written* [5]___ *the back of an envelope. It's from Jenny. She says she's* [6]___ *a meeting* [7]___ *college. She'll be back for dinner.*

● *Is Sue* [8]___ *home this afternoon?*
❍ *No, sorry. She's* [9]___ *the library.*
● *Is that the one* [10]___ *Bath Street* [11]___ *town?*
❍ *No, she always usees the one* [12]___ *the shopping centre* [13]___ *the edge of town.*

79 Prepositions 3: time

at, in, on *past, to*

FORMS

at, in* and *on

The Wood family had their holiday in July.
They left on Saturday.
They left on 7th July.
They left at 7.20.

past* and *to

They left at twenty past seven.
They arrived at twenty to one.

at

Use *at* for time.

*Lunch will be **at 1.00**.*
*Mum called us **at dinner time**.*

تستخدم at عند الحديث عن الزمن.

Use *at* for a known point in the past or the future.

*They married young. **At that time**, they were poor.*
*We will arrive at 10.00. **At that point**, you will open the main door.*

وتستخدم at عند الحديث عن نقطة زمنية محددة في الماضي او في المستقبل.

Use *at* for special days, short holidays and festivals.

*We always have a party **at New Year**.*

وتستخدم at عند الحديث عن أيام خاصة او عن العطلات القصيرة او عن الاعياد.

in

Use *in* for centuries, years, months and seasons.

*The car was invented **in the 19th century**.*
*We bought our house **in 1989**.*
*School started again **in September**.*
*We always go skiing **in (the) winter**.*

وتستخدم in مع القرون والسنوات والشهور والفصول.

Also use *in* for periods of time.

*We don't do much work **in the holidays**.*
*Are you going away **in the summer break**?*

وتستخد in مع الفترات الزمنية.

Compare these examples with *at* + short period of time.

*We always have a party **at New Year**.*
*What are you doing **at the weekend**?*

وتتضح الصورة عند مقارنة الامثلة المبينة، حيث تستخدم at + فترة زمنية قصيرة.

Use *in* for parts of the day (but not usually with the word *night*).

*I ate **in the morning/afternoon/evening**.*
*We arrived late **at night**.*

وتستخدم in مع اجزاء اليوم ولكنها لا تستخدم عادة، مع كلمة الليل.

Use *in* for a measured time.

*Tony finished the job **in three weeks**.*
*Your pizzas will be ready **in ten minutes**.*

وتستخدم in مع الوقت الذي يجري تحديده وقياسه.

on

Use *on* for days and dates.

They arrived ***on Saturday****.*
We left ***on 7th July****.*

تستخدم *on* مع الأيام ومع التواريخ.

Use *on* for special days.

I visited my parents ***on New Year's Day****.*
I didn't have a party ***on my birthday****!*
Did things go well ***on your wedding day****?*

وتستخدم *on* مع الأيام الخاصة والمعروفة.

Use *on* for parts of a particular day. Compare the following.

Did they go ***on Saturday morning****?*
Did they go ***in the morning****?*

وتستخدم *on* عند تحديد جزء من يوم معين. ويتضح الفرق من خلال مقارنة المثالين:

Do not use *in* or *on* with *this, last, next, yesterday, tomorrow, each* and *every.*

I came to work late ***this morning****.*
Did you go away ***last weekend****?*
Tom cleans his car ***every weekend****.*

لا تستخدم *in* أو *on* مع أي من الكلمات المبينة.

Note these common expressions of time with *at, in* and *on.*

He's usually happy, but ***at times*** *he feels sad.* (sometimes)
He's rich now, but ***at one time*** *he was very poor.* (for a time in the past)
The soldiers climbed the ropes three ***at a time****.* (three together)
We met ***in time*** *to talk before the film.* (with enough time)
The plane took off ***on time****.* (at the right time – not too early, not too late)
You must always get to work ***on time****.* (You must not be late for work.)

لاحظ التعبيرات الشائعة المبينة التي تعبر عن الزمن باستخدام *at* و *in* و *on*.

past **and** ***to***

We can tell these times in different ways.

12.15 → twelve fifteen OR *quarter past twelve*
12.30 → twelve thirty OR *half past twelve*
12.45 → twelve forty-five OR *quarter to one*
12.50 → twelve fifty OR *ten to one*

يمكن التعبير عن الوقت بطرق مختلفة توضحها الأمثلة المبينة.

We can also tell these times in different ways. If you use the second way, you must say *minutes.*

1.03 → one oh three OR *three minutes past one*
1.39 → one thirty-nine OR *twenty-one minutes to two*

ويمكن التعبير عن الأوقات المذكورة بعدة طرق. وفي حالة استخدام الطريقة الثانية، يجب ذكر كلمة *minutes* في الجملة.

Exercises

1 Complete the conversation. Use *at*, *in* and *on*.

Tony and his mother are talking on the phone.

Mum: *So can you come home* on *Saturday, Tony?*

Tony: *I'm sorry, Mum, but I can't come* [1]___ *the weekend this week or next week.*

Mum: *Well, are we going to see you* [2]___ *the holidays? Can you get away from London* [3]___ *the last week of December?*

Tony: *Well, I can get away* [4]___ *the 30th.*

Mum: *The 30th. That'll be a Thursday, won't it?*

Tony: *That's right. And I can stay for three days.*

Mum: *Good! So you'll be with us* [5]___ *New Year. It's good to be at home with your family* [6]___ *that time of the year.*

Tony: *Right. And we'll have a good time* [7]___ *New Year's Eve – just like the old days.*

Mum: *Wonderful! So what time can we expect you* [8]___ *Thursday? Will you be arriving late* [9]___ *night?*

Tony: *I'll probably leave London* [10]___ *lunchtime, so that means I'll get to you* [11]___ *about 6.00.*

Mum: *So you'll be with us* [12]___ *the evening. Dad and the children will be pleased.*

2 Complete the statements. Use *at*, *in* and *on*.

Example: *I'll be away* on *Thursday.*

1 *The meeting will start* ___ *10.00.*

2 *I took a short holiday* ___ *January.*

3 *Columbus sailed across the Atlantic* ___ *1492.*

4 *We flew to Malta late* ___ *Saturday.*

5 *Are you doing anything special* ___ *your birthday?*

6 *The telephone was invented* ___ *the nineteenth century.*

7 *I'll be in New York* ___ *this time next week.*

8 *We always go to France* ___ *the summer.*

9 *I won't be away for long. I'll be home* ___ *three days.*

10 *The President is arriving* ___ *midday.*

11 *Ann usually watches TV* ___ *the evening.*

12 *What are you doing* ___ *Wednesday evening?*

13 *We'll be at a party* ___ *New Year's Eve.*

14 *We'll be away for a week* ___ *New Year.*

15 *Hurry! We have to leave* ___ *an hour's time.*

16 *The climbers reached the top* ___ *the fifth day.*

17 *Tom left home* ___ *the age of 15.*

18 *We finished the job* ___ *less than a week.*

19 *I haven't got any money* ___ *the moment.*

3 Complete the conversation. Use *at*, *in* or *on* or nothing (✗).

● *Hello, Fred. I was trying to call you* ✗ *last weekend.*

❍ *Did you call* on *Saturday?*

● *Yes, that's right. I phoned* [1]___ *Saturday morning and again* [2]___ *lunchtime.*

❍ *I'm sorry, but I was out. I always go sailing* [3]___ *Saturdays.*

● *So I suppose that means you're going sailing again* [4]___ *Saturday* [5]___ *this weekend too.*

❍ *I'm afraid so. What's the problem?*

● *Well, I'd like your help with a new computer that I bought* [6]___ *last week.*

❍ *Sure. No problem. I can help you* [7]___ *Sunday night.*

● *Ah, but I'll be away all day until late. You see, I visit my parents* [8]___ *each Sunday.*

❍ *I see. Well, what about* [9]___ *the evening? I'm free after I finish work* [10]___ *5.30. In fact, I don't usually do much* [11]___ *the week these days, and I'm free* [12]___ *nearly every evening.*

● *Well, I have to go out* [13]___ *tonight, but could we get together* [14]___ *tomorrow evening?*

❍ *Fine. I'm free* [15]___ *the evening tomorrow too. I'll come round to your place* [16]___ *7.00.*

● *Thanks. That'll be really great!*

4 Complete the statements. Use these phrases.

at times, at a time, at one time, in time, on time

Example: *Don't be late. Make sure you're there* on time.

1 *The runners left in groups every two minutes. They left six* ____________

2 *I enjoy life most of the time, but* ____________ *I'd like to go back to the old days.*

3 *We arrived just* ________________ *The shop was just going to close.*

4 *There are factories everywhere here now, but* ________________ *there were just green fields.*

5 *The trains always leave* ________________ *They're never late.*

5 Write the times in words. Use *past* and *to*.

Examples: *12.15 – a quarter past one*
10.41 – nineteen minutes to eleven

1 *3.10 –* ________________

2 *7.50 –* ________________

3 *9.30 –* ________________

4 *2.45 –* ________________

5 *5.15 –* ________________

6 *1.13 –* ________________

7 *11.31–* ________________

8 *12.59 –* ________________

6 Rewrite the diary notes as full statements. Use the present continuous.

You work for a busy company director. Remind him of his activities in the next two weeks.

Example: *On Monday the 26th you're travelling to New York at 8.30 in the morning.*

1 ________________

2 ________________

3 ________________

4 ________________

5 ________________

6 ________________

7 ________________

8 ________________

Diary

May

Mon, 26th May
8.30 a.m. – travel to NY

Wed, 28th May
3.45 p.m. – return to London

Fri, 30th May
all day – meet Japanese visitors from the Subarashi Corporation

Sat, 31st May
evening – speak at the goodbye party for the Managing Director

June

Mon, 2nd June
p.m. – attend the sales conference

Tues, 3rd June
a.m. – talk at the sales conference

Thurs, 5th June
7.15 a.m. – fly to Rome

Fri, 6th June
11.45 a.m. – leave Rome for Madrid

Sat, 7th June
midday – travel back to London

80 Prepositions 4: time

for, since *ago, before* *during, while* *until/till, by*

FORMS

for* and *since

He has lived there for 50 years.
He has lived here since 1945.

ago* and *before

He moved there 50 years ago.
He had lived with his parents before that.

during* and *while

A lot has changed during those 50 years.
A lot has changed while he has been there.

until/till* and *by

He will be there until/till he dies.
By the year 2,000 he will be 75 years old.

CROSSCHECK

for

We use *for* to say how long in any tense, in the past, present or future.

It rained ***for three hours***.

We use *for* with the present perfect to say how long up the the present. *for* refers to the time between the start and now. (See also Unit 10.)

ago

We use *ago* to say when something happened in the past. Count back from the present.

Where's my book? It was here ***a minute ago***!

during

Use *during* + noun, eg *the day*, or + noun phrase, eg *the early afternoon*.

I'll call again ***during the week***.

until/till

until/till refers to a period continuing to a point in time.

I'll be busy ***until 5.00***. (I have no free time between now and 5.00. Therefore I can't call before 5.00, but I will be able to call at 5.00.)

since

We use *since* to say how long mainly in the present perfect.

He's lived here ***since 1945***.

We use *since* with the present perfect to say how long up to the present. *since* refers to the start. (See also Unit 10.)

before

We use *before* to say when something happened in the past. Count back from another event in the past.

I finished at 4.30, but the others had finished ***two hours before***.

while

Use *while* + verb, eg *I was training*, or + clause, eg *I was away on holiday*.

I'll visit you ***while I'm in town***.

by

by refers to a point in time.

Please reply ***by 5.00***. (Please call at or before 5.00. 5.00 is the latest possible time. Before 5.00 is better.)

تستخدم كلمة for للتعبير عن الفترة الزمنية في الماضي او في الحاضر او في المستقبل.

وتستخدم كلمة since للتعبير عن «منذ متى» وغالباً في زمن المضارع التام.

تستخدم for مع المضارع التام للتعبير عن مدة الفترة الزمنية حتى الوقت الحاضر. وهي تشير الى الزمن بين البداية والآن.

كما تستخدم since مع المضارع التام للتعبير عن مدة الفترة الزمنية حتى الوقت الحاضر ولكنها تشير الى البداية. (انظر ايضاً unit 10).

تستخدم ago للدلالة على وقت حدوث شيء ما في الماضي، والعدّ الرجعي يبدأ من الوقت الحاضر.

وتستخدم before للتعبير عن وقت حدوث الفعل في الماضي، والعدّ الرجعي يبدأ من حدث آخر في الماضي.

تستخدم كلمة during + اسم او عبارة اسمية.

وتستخدم كلمة while + فعل او جزء كامل من جملة، كما في المثال.

تعبر until و till عن فترة زمنية تستمر حتى نقطة زمنية محددة.

وتشير by الى نقطة زمنية محددة.

Exercises

1 Complete the story with *for* or *since*.

Oxford Lasers has not been in business for *very long. In fact, the company has only existed* since *1977. The five directors had done a lot of work on lasers at Oxford University* [1]________ *several years before that. They continued to work at the University* [2]________ *some time after 1977 too, so their new company developed very slowly. In fact,* [3]________ *a while it seemed likely to close down. But* [4]________ *the introduction of new products in 1982, Oxford Lasers has grown fast. There were financial problems in the early 1990s* [5]________ *a year or two, but the company has remained a top laser producer* [6]________ *the mid-1980s.* [7]________ *a number of years it has been developing sales world-wide. It has also owned a company in the USA* [8]________ *1985.*

2 Complete the dialogues with *ago* or *before*.

Examples: ● *Tim bought a BMW two days* ago.
❍ *He had an old Fiat* before, *didn't he?*

● *You went to Ibiza two years* [1]________, *didn't you?*
❍ *That's right. We'd never been there* [2]________

● *How long* [3]________ *did you try to call her?*
❍ *An hour* [4]________ *But she'd left ten minutes* [5]________

● *Lucy went away to college three years* [6]________ *, didn't she?*
❍ *Yes, and it was a hard time because she hadn't been away from home very much* [7]________

3 Complete the statements with *during* or *while*.

Examples: *Jim Brown called* while *you were out.*
There will be a fire practice during *the morning.*

1 *What's Tom going to do* ________ *he's in America?*

2 ________ *the meeting, we'll discuss the sales report.*

3 ________ *you're cleaning the car, could you clean the ashtrays too?*

4 *Are you going to visit Australia* ________ *your trip round the world?*

5 *Somebody got into the house* ________ *the night.*

6 *They'd never seen anything like that* ________ *their whole lives!*

7 *I worked out my travel plans* ________ *I was waiting for the train.*

4 Complete the dialogues with *by* or *until/till.*

Examples: ● *Do you think you'll be able to finish the picture* by *tomorrow morning?*
❍ *Yes, but I'll have to work* until *midnight to do it.*

● *Ann was already married* [1]________ *the age of 19.*
❍ *She lived at home* [2]________ *then, didn't she?*

● *I'm sorry, Sir. Your car won't be ready* [3]________ *early tomorrow afternoon.*
❍ *So, if I come at 4.30, will it be ready* [4]________ *then?*
● *Oh, yes. No problem, Sir.*

❍ [5]________ *this time tomorrow, I'll be in Tokyo.*
● *How long are you going to stay there?*
❍ [6]________ *this time next week.*

● *I'm sure Tony has left the office* [7]________ *now.*
❍ *I don't think so. He said he'd have to work* [8]________ *late this evening.*

5 Complete the story.

Arthur had worked in the same, large office for *30 years. 'I've worked here* [1]________ *I was 19,' he often thought. 'And* [2]________ *all those years I haven't done anything very exciting.'*

One day, [3]________ *he was at a very boring meeting, he suddenly decided to change his life completely. He thought, 'I'll go on working* [4]________ *another six months –* [5]________ *my 50th birthday – and then I'll stop. I'll sell the house, buy a boat and go sailing.'*

[6]________ *the middle of the following year he had done all these things. As he sailed among the Scottish islands on his first long trip, he thought, 'Why didn't I do this* [7]________ *? I should have left that office ten years* [8]________ *!'*

81 Preposition + noun, noun + preposition

by Shakespeare, for you, on TV, etc

Preposition + noun

Some expressions have the form preposition + noun. These are some of the most common.

تستخدم بعض التعبيرات اللغوية أداة جر + اسم وهذه أكثرها شيوعاً.

It's a picture ***by Rembrandt***.
I paid ***by cheque/credit card***. (but *in cash*)
They cut through the rock ***by hand***.

There's someone on the phone. It's ***for you***.
We're having fish ***for dinner***.
Let's go out ***for a walk/swim/run/meal.***
They've gone ***for a short holiday***. (but *go on holiday*)

I heard it ***on the radio***. (but *at the cinema/theatre*)
He hurt her ***on purpose***. (but *by accident/mistake/chance*)
The house is ***on fire***.
Sally is ***on a diet***. *She wants to lose six kilograms.*

The bus leaves at 12.00, so be there ***on time***.
We're going to stop for tea ***on the way*** *there.*
Bill is going to Africa ***on business/holiday/safari***.
They're going ***on a trip/bus tour***.

We're going ***by car/bike/plane/train/ship/road/air/rail/sea***, etc. (but *on foot/in his car/on his bike/the bus/the plane/the train/the ship*)

Noun + preposition

Some expressions have the form noun + preposition. These are some of the most common.

وتستخدم بعض التعبيرات اسماً + أداة جر، وهذه أكثرها شيوعاً.

Tom's teacher sent the theatre a ***request for*** *60 tickets.* (also *application for/need for/reason for*)
He was very pleased as the theatre reduced the ***price of*** *the tickets by 20%.* (also *cost of/hope of/way of*)
Unfortunately, there was a ***problem with*** *the bus company.* (also *trouble with/matter with*)
There was a ***rise in*** *the price of the bus.* (also *fall/increase/decrease in*)

Exercises

1 Complete the dialogues with *at, by, for, in* and *on*.

Example: ● *Did you go by bus?*
❍ *No, we went* in *Steve's car.*

1 ● *Let's go to the beach* ______ *foot.*
❍ *No, let's go* ______ *bike. It's quicker.*

2 ● *I saw you! You hit Sam* ______ *purpose!*
❍ *No, I didn't. I did it* ______ *accident!*

3 ● *Someone is* ______ *the phone. It's* ______ *Bob.*
❍ *He isn't here. He's gone out* ______ *a run.*

4 ● *I'm going to have some toast* ______ *breakfast.*
❍ *No, you aren't. It's* ______ *fire! Can't you smell it?*

5 ● *Are you here* ______ *holiday?*
❍ *No, I'm* ______ *a short business trip.*

6 ● *Can I pay* ________ *credit card?*
❍ *I'm sorry, Sir. We can only accept payment* ______ *cash or* ______ *cheque.*

7 ● *Is there anything good* ______ *TV tonight?*
❍ *No, and there's nothing interesting* ______ *the radio either.*

8 ● *What's the new play* ______ *the theatre this week?*
❍ *It's called 'Paris in the Spring'. It's* ______ *that new writer, Mark Ross.*

2 Complete the statements with these words. Put a preposition before each one.

a diet, air, an artist, a school trip, a tour, a walk, dinner, his bike, my car, plane, the cinema

Example: *I'm hungry. Let's stop at that restaurant* for dinner.

1 *My cousins from Australia are visiting Britain. They're* ____________ *of the country.*

2 *Their car is full. You'd better go* ____________

3 *Tony's class is going* ______________________ *to Italy.*

4 *Tony and his friends are travelling to Italy* ____________

5 *Can you see Rob? He's over there. He's* ____________

6 *It's a nice day. Let's go* ____________ *along the river.*

7 *They're showing a new film* ____________ *in George Street.*

8 *If you want to get this package to America fast, send it* ________

9 *We aren't eating very much at the moment. We're* ____________

10 *It's a wonderful picture. It's* ____________ *who lived about 600 years ago.*

3 Complete the statements with these words. Put a preposition after each one.

applications, call, difficulties, fall, hope, increase, interested, matter, need, problem, way

Example: *We've had a lot of* applications for *the job of Chief Engineer.*

1 *What's the* ____________ *you? You always seem angry about something.*

2 *Could you please keep quiet? There's no* ____________ *all this noise.*

3 *We'd better stop here for tonight. There's no* ____________ *reaching the village before dark.*

4 *Prices have gone up a little this year. There's been a small* ____________ *the cost of living.*

5 *Scientists have found a new* ____________ *producing electricity cheaply.*

6 *There's a* ____________ *your plan. I'm afraid it won't work.*

7 *The rescue team has had a* ____________ *help. They're on their way to the accident now.*

8 *There has been a* ____________ *the size of families. They're smaller nowadays.*

9 *I'm very* ____________ *photography.*

10 *Peter had* ______________________ *his homework.*

82 Adjective + preposition

He's good at Maths.

Some adjectives often take one or more prepositions. These are some of the most common.

تأتي مع بعض الصفات في الغالب أداة جر واحدة أو أكثر، وهذه أكثرها شيوعاً.

Sam is a junior accountant. He's ***excited about*** *his first business trip next month.*
He's ***worried/anxious about*** *his accountancy exams next week.*
He got ***angry/annoyed about*** *a noisy party next door last night.*
His neighbour was ***sorry about*** *the noise.*

He got ***angry/annoyed with*** *his neighbour last night.*
He sometimes gets ***bored/fed up with*** *his work.*

He's ***afraid/nervous of*** *failing his exams next week.*
His family will be ***proud of*** *him if he passes.*
He's ***tired of*** *studying late every night.*

He's not ***used/accustomed to*** *so much hard work.*
Luckily, he's very ***interested in*** *what he's doing.*

Sam was ***amazed/surprised/shocked at/by*** *the number of books he had to read for the exams.*

His boss is ***pleased/happy with/about*** *Sam's work now.*
He was ***disappointed with/about*** *Sam's work at first.*
Sam is very ***careful/careless with/about*** *his work.*

Sam is ***responsible for*** *the weekly sales figures.*
The figures are nearly ***ready for*** *printing.*
He's ***late/early for*** *a meeting.*
Sam's family feel ***sorry for*** *him when he works late.*
His mother thinks the work is ***bad for*** *his eyes.*
His father knows the work is ***good for*** *his future.*

He's ***good/brilliant at*** *figures and Maths.*
He's ***bad/terrible/hopeless at*** *languages.*

He sometimes thinks life is very ***similar to*** *school again.*
He sometimes thinks life is no ***different from/to*** *school.*

Exercises

1 Complete the statements with *about, at, for, of* and *with*.

Example: *I feel very sorry* for *Ann. The poor girl has been ill for so long.*

1 *Are you ready ________ a big surprise?*

2 *Tim is quite good ________ sport.*

3 *I'm very angry ________ Sam. He never answers my letters.*

4 *We really thought our team would win, so we were disappointed ________ the bad result.*

5 *I wish they'd be more careful ________ their work.*

6 *You must stop working day and night. It's very bad ________ you.*

7 *I'm fed up ________ eating at home all the time. Let's go out.*

8 *Tony and Lisa were so annoyed ________ the people next door that they called the police.*

2 Complete the statements with these words. Put a preposition after each one.

different, early, good, late, proud, responsible, shocked, terrible, worried

Example: ● *I was* shocked at *the bad sales figures.*
❍ *Me too. I'd expected much better sales.*

1 ● *I can't understand this Maths problem.*
❍ *But it's easy! You must be really ________________ Maths*

2 ● *People in Manchester are very ______________ their football team.*
❍ *Yes, especially as they've won the championship again.*

3 ● *The men have done the job again, but it still looks bad.*
❍ *I agree. It's no ______________________ last time.*

4 ● *It isn't ______________ small children to stay up late at night.*
❍ *That's right. It means they're very tired the next day.*

5 ● *Calm down! Why are you running around like that?*
❍ *Because I'm ______________ a very important meeting.*

6 ● *Have you heard? Joe's a senior manager now.*
❍ *Yes, I hear he's ________________________ the whole factory now.*

7 ● *I hope you got to the interview on time.*
❍ *Yes, I did. In fact, I was twenty minutes ______________ it.*

8 ● *Have Robin and Steve reached Australia in their little boat yet?*
❍ *No. They're two weeks late, and we're very ______________________ them.*

3 Write a statement using the underlined words and the words in brackets.

Example: *Ann reads a lot about sailing. (interested)*
She's interested in sailing.

1 *Bob is going to give away his old computer games. (tired)*
He's ____

2 *Working at night was strange at first, but it's all right now. (used)*
I'm ____

3 *Mrs Elfin shouted at her children. (angry)*
She was ____

4 *Peter isn't sure if his first business trip will go well. (anxious)*
He's ____

5 *The airline staff felt bad because of the long delay at the airport. (sorry)*
They were ____

6 *Bill decided to turn the radio programme off. (bored)*
He was ____

7 *Old Mrs Price doesn't like going out alone. (nervous)*
She's ____

8 *It was a fantastic surprise to see the huge number of people at the concert. (amazed)*
We were ____

83 Prepositional verbs

She applied for several jobs. *He stole $600 from her.*

Verb + preposition

Some verbs often take one or more prepositions.
These are some of the most common.

غالباً ما تأتي مع بعض الأفعال أداة جر واحدة أو أكثر
وهذه أكثرها شيوعاً.

*Claire **looked for** a job before she left college.*
*She **asked for** details of lots of jobs.*
*She **applied for** several jobs.*
*She **applied to** several companies.*
*She **waited** hopefully **for** the replies, but they were all negative.*

*She **heard about** a good job in New York.*
*She **talked about** it with her friend.*
*She **asked about** the company at the US Embassy.*
*She **thought about** the job a lot.*

*In the end, she **wrote to** the company in New York.*
*They **replied to** her letter immediately.*
*They **talked to** her on the phone.*

look + different prepositions has different meanings.

Look at this photo. It's beautiful. (**Look at**)
*I'm **looking for** my glasses. Can you see them?*
*Could you **look after** the baby for a few minutes?*

think and *dream* + different prepositions have different meanings.

*Claire **thought about** the job carefully.*
*When I **dream about** the crash, I always wake up.*
*I've just **thought of** a great idea!*
*Harry **dreams of** becoming rich one day.*

Verb + object + preposition

Some verbs often take an object and then a preposition.
These are some of the most common.

وتأخذ بعض الأفعال غالباً مفعولاً به متبوعاً بأداة جر،
وهذه أكثرها شيوعاً.

*The company **invited her to** an interview.*
*They **provided her with** air tickets.*
*When she got to New York, she **asked somebody for** directions to the company.*

*At the interview, she **asked them about** the job.*
*They **told her about** the pay and conditions.*
*She accepted the job, and they **congratulated her on** her decision.*

*She also **had a bad experience in** New York. A thief **robbed her of** her money. He **stole $600 from** her.*
*Fortunately, she had **insured herself against** theft.*
*She **blamed herself for** the theft because she had left her purse on a restaurant table.*
*She **described the purse to** the police, but they never found it.*

Exercises

1 Complete the statements with *about*, *for*, and *to*.

Example: *A boy came to the door and asked* for *a glass of water.*

1 *Danny dreams __________ being famous one day.*

2 *I'll wait __________ you outside the cinema.*

3 *Ann is on the phone. Could you talk __________ her, please?*

4 *They're very bad. They take ages to reply __________ letters.*

5 *The family talked __________ their plans every night.*

2 Complete the dialogues with the correct forms of the verbs and prepositions.

Example: ● *There's Mark Blake. He's famous!*
❍ *Mark Blake? I've never* heard of *him! (hear)*

1 ● *Hello, I'm Terry Grant.*
❍ *Hello. I've often ________________ you. It's nice to meet you at last. (hear)*

2 ● *I hear you're looking for a new job.*
❍ *That's right. I've ______________ several companies. (apply)*

3 ● *What sort of job are you ________________ (apply)*
❍ *I'm trying to get a job in sales.*

4 ● *Have you found an answer to the problem yet?*
❍ *No. I've been ____________________ it for ages, but I haven't got any ideas. (think)*

5 ● *Can you see what to do about the problem?*
❍ *Well, yes, I've suddenly ________________ a new idea! (think)*

6 ● *Who waters the plants when you're away?*
❍ *My neighbours ______________ them. (look)*

7 ● *What sort of bike would you like?*
❍ *One like this! Come and ____________ it. (look)*

8 ● *Oh, no! I've lost my wallet.*
❍ *Don't worry. I'll help you ____________ it. (look)*

3 Complete the statements with these verbs. Add prepositions.

ask, congratulate, insure, provide, tell

Example: *Companies need to* insure *themselves* against *injuries to their staff.*

1 *The old man ______________ us ________ some money, so we gave him £1.*

2 *Mrs Brett, we'd all like to ______________ you ________ reaching the fantastic age of 100.*

3 *We ______________ all visitors to the company ________ identity cards.*

4 *There's a reporter here. He wants to ______________ you some questions ________ your plans for a new factory.*

5 *The reporter said, 'Could you please ______________ me ________ your ideas for a new factory in town?'*

4 Complete the statements. Write the words in order and put the verbs in the correct forms. Add prepositions.

Example: *Yesterday a thief* stole my wallet from my pocket. *(my/my/steal/pocket/wallet)*

1 *Tim couldn't understand, so he ________________________________ (the/help/ask/teacher)*

2 *We phoned the doctor, and we ________________________________ (him/the/tell/accident)*

3 *It wasn't Tony's fault, but they still ________________________________ (him/the/crash/blame)*

4 *The police are coming soon, so you can ________________________________ (them/man/describe/the)*

5 *It's my birthday next week, and I'm ________________________________ (my/my/invite/all/party/friends)*

84 Phrasal verbs

come in, sit down, give out, pick up, turn over, etc

FORMS

Subject + verb + adverb

The boys came in and sat down at 10.50.

Subject + verb + adverb + object

The teacher gave out the exam papers.
The boys picked up their pens.
They turned over the papers and began.
Another boy turned up ten minutes late.
At 12.30, the boys put down their pens.
The teacher took in the papers.
He put them away in his bag .

A phrasal verb is a verb + adverb. Some phrasal verbs do not have an object, but most do.

الافعال الظرفية هي التي تتكون من فعل + ظرف، وبعضها لا يتعدى إلى مفعول به، ولكن معظمها يتعدى إلى مفعول به.

Subject	Verb + adverb	Subject	Verb + adverb	Object
The boys	***came in***.	*The teacher*	***gave out***	*the exam papers.*
They	***sat down***.	*The boys*	***picked up***	*their pens.*

An object can usually go before or after the adverb in a phrasal verb. Compare the following.

The boys ***put down their pens***. *The boys* ***put their pens down***.

يمكن ان يأتي المفعول به عادة، قبل الظرف او بعده في الفعل الظرفي. ويتضح الامر من خلال مقارنة المثالين.

But when the object is a pronoun, it must go before the adverb.

The boys put ***them*** *down.* (their pens)
He put ***them*** *away in his bag.* (the exam papers)

ولكن عندما يكون المفعول به ضميراً، يجب وضعه قبل الظرف.

In a phrasal verb, the adverb completes the meaning of the verb. Some phrasal verbs are easy to understand and learn. They mean exactly what you expect, eg *pick up/put down, give out/take in* and *sit down/stand up*.

يكمل الظرف في الفعل الظرفي معنى الفعل. وبعض الافعال الظرفية يسهل فهمها وتعلمها. وهي تعني تماماً ما تتوقعه.

Others are not so easy to understand. Their meaning is not clear from the verb and the adverb together. Compare the following. The first example is clear, but the second is not.

They ***turned over*** *the papers.*
Another boy ***turned up***. (arrived)

ومنها ما يصعب فهمه، فمعانيها ليست واضحة من الفعل والظرف معاً. قارن المثالين، فالاول واضح والثاني غير واضح.

We use phrasal verbs a lot, so you have to learn them as you meet them. Write down the meanings when they are not clear. Here are some more examples.

The car ***broke down***. (stopped working)
He was too tired to do any more and he ***gave up***. (stopped trying to do something)
The man ***made off*** *with my bike.* (ran away)
The weather is ***picking up***. (getting better)

كثيراً ما تستخدم الافعال الظرفية، الامر الذي يوجب تعلمها كل على حدة. ويساعد في تعلمها كتابة المعاني عندما تكون غير واضحة.

Exercises

1 Complete the statements with these phrasal verbs.

come in, give out, pick up, put away, sit down, turn over, turn up

Example: *I can't find my book now, but I know it'll* turn up *later.*

1 *Could you* ______________ *all the rubbish on the floor, please? It looks very untidy.*

2 *I'm going to* ______________ *sets of working clothes to all the new trainees.*

3 *Please* ______________ *on the chairs over there.*

4 *We always have to* ______________ *our papers when we finish work and leave our desks clean.*

5 ______________ *the paper and start the exam, please.*

6 *Don't wait outside the door. Please* ______________

2 Complete the statements with these phrasal verbs without objects.

Moving
come in, come back, go away, go out, move on, turn round

Resting
get up, lie down, wake up

Example: *Please* come in. *The door is open.*

1 *I'm tired. I'm going to* ______________ *and rest.*

2 *If you* ______________ *and live somewhere else, we may we may not see you again.*

3 *Let's* ______________ *and get some fresh air for an hour.*

4 *This place is horrible. Let's* ______________ *and stay in the next town.*

5 *You can go home now, but please* ______________ *to the office by 2.00.*

6 *I don't* ______________ *immediately in the morning. I lie in bed and plan my day.*

7 *That coat looks good on you, but does it look all right from the back?* ______________ *slowly and let me see.*

8 *Pat was so tired that she couldn't* ______________ *She didn't open her eyes for ten minutes.*

3 Complete the statements with these phrasal verbs without objects.

pay in/take out (eg money at the bank)
put on/take off (eg clothes)
put up/bring down (eg shop prices)
switch on/switch off (eg lights)
turn up/turn down (eg radio volume)

Example: *It's getting dark. I'll* switch on *the lights.*

1 *Could you* ______________ *£50 for me? I need some money for the weekend.*

2 *Look. They've* ______________ *the price of these computers. They're only $950 now.*

3 *Could you* ______________ *the TV, please? It's too loud.*

4 *Tom* ______________ *his dirty boots before he went into the house.*

5 *It was raining, so I* ______________ *a coat when I went out.*

6 *Oh, no! The Government is* ______________ *the price of petrol again!*

4 Complete the statements. Change the noun objects into pronoun objects.

Example: *Bob told me to give out the clothes, so I* gave them out.

1 *Ann wanted Tom to pick up the rubbish, so she* ______________

2 *Dad asked us to switch off the TV, so we* ______________

3 *My boss told me to put away my papers, so I* ______________

4 *Sue asked the men to put down the cases, so they* ______________

5 *Steve wanted his brother to turn up the stereo, so he* ______________

6 *Mum told Tina to turn over the chicken legs, so she* ______________

7 *The boss asked us to pay in the money at the bank, so we* ______________

85 Word classes

Verb, adverb, noun, adjective, etc

FUN RIDE TURNS TO DANGER

An enjoyable day out at Britain's biggest fun park, Alton Towers, turned to danger yesterday. It happened when high winds hit the Skyride cable-cars and stopped them in mid-air.

Specially trained firemen safely brought 59 people down from several cable-cars 30 metres above the ground. They successfully used their climbing techniques and equipment to climb along the cables and enter the cars.

Although some passengers needed first aid when they reached the ground, nobody had to go to hospital.

FORMS

There are eight different word classes in English. They are:

Verb:	*hit, stop, use, climb*
Adverb:	*yesterday, successfully, down, safely*
Noun:	*day, Alton Towers, danger*
Adjective:	*enjoyable, high, special*
Pronoun:	*they, them, nobody*
Determiner:	*a/an, the, their, some*
Preposition:	*at, from, above, along*
Linking word:	*and, although, when*

We often use one word in different ways. It may be just a different word class with a similar meaning.

غالباً ما نستخدم كلمة واحدة بطرق مختلفة. فقد تكون فعلاً في الجملة، واسماً من جملة اخرى، ويكون المعنى متشابهاً.

*Did they **climb**?* (verb)
*It's a long **climb**.* (noun)
*Some needed **first aid**.* (part of a noun)
*We climbed along **first**.* (adverb)

Or a word may have different meanings.

ويمكن ان تحمل الكلمة الواحدة معاني مختلفة.

***High** winds hit the cable-cars.* (adjective = strong)
*The tower is 30 metres **high**.* (adjective = off the ground)
*The price of tickets is too **high**.* (adjective = expensive)

CROSSCHECK

There are different kinds of determiners and pronouns.

هناك انواع مختلفة من المحددات والضمائر.

Determiners

Articles: *a/an, the*

Quantifiers: *some, a lot of, no* (+ noun)
Demonstratives: *this, those* (+ noun)
Possessives: *my, your* (+ noun)

Use a determiner before a noun.

يستخدم المحدد قبل الاسم.

***The** car was in the street.*
*They brought down **all** the people.*
*I took **that** photo.*

*Is it **my** newspaper or **your** newspaper?*

Pronouns

Personal: *I, he, she* (subject)
me, him, her (object)

Quantifiers: *some, a lot, nobody* (+ verb)
Demonstratives: *this, those* (+ verb)
Possessives: *mine, yours* (+ verb)

Use a pronoun instead of a determiner + noun.

ويستخدم الضمير بديلاً من المحدد + الاسم.

***It** was in the street.*
***Nobody** had to go to hospital.*
***That** is one of the cable-car passengers.*
*Is it **mine** or **yours**?*

Exercises

1 Label the words in *italics* with these word classes.

Adjective, Adverb, Determiner, Linking word, Noun, Preposition, Pronoun, Verb

Noun An ordinary English *family*

1 *We* are an ordinary 2 *English* family – a mother, 3 *father* and 4 *two* children – 5 *and* we 6 *live* very 7 *ordinarily* in a small town 8 *near* London.

1 ________ 5 ________

2 ________ 6 ________

3 ________ 7 ________

4 ________ 8 ________

2 Complete the paragraph. Use the correct forms of these nouns.

bathroom, bedroom, dining-room, dish, flower, food, garden, house, kitchen, living-room, shop, television, time, vegetable, visitor

An ordinary English home

Upstairs in our house *there are three* 1________ *and a* 2________ *Downstairs there is a* 3________, *where we sometimes watch* 4________ *Then there is a* 5________, *but we only eat there when we have* 6________ *When there are only four of us, we usually eat in the* 7________ *It's easier to serve* 8________ *there and clear away the dirty* 9________ *Outside, there is a large* 10________ *We spend a lot of* 11________ *out there, so we keep it looking nice with lots of* 12________ *We also grow our own* 13________ *They taste better than the ones from the* 14________ *!*

3 Complete the paragraph. Use the correct forms of these verbs in the present simple.

be, cook, drive, drop, get, have, have to, leave, make, take, work

Ordinary weekday mornings

In the morning, I always make *tea for everybody. Then Rosie* 1________ *breakfast while Peter and Lisa* 2________ *ready for school. We all* 3________ *the house at 8.00. Rosie* 4________ *always the driver. First she* 5________ *me at the station because I* 6________ *in London and I* 7________ *catch the 8.20 train. Next she* 8________ *the children to school. Then she* 9________ *back into town, where she* 10________ *a job at a bank.*

4 Complete the conversation with adjectives or adverbs.

Another ordinary morning

Peter: *I* really *don't want to go to school* today. *I'm* ill *! (ill, really, today)*

Lisa: *You're* 1________ *saying that because you've got a* 2________ *exam and you know you're going to do* 3________ *! (badly, big, only)*

Mum: *I think Lisa is* 4________ *You look* 5________, *Peter. So finish your breakfast as* 6________ *as you can, and let's go. It's* 7________ *8.00. (fast, fine, nearly, right)*

Dad: *Yes, come on, everybody. Let's go* 8________ *or I'll be* 9________ *for the train, and I* 10________ *mustn't miss it this morning. (certainly, late, quickly)*

5 Complete the story with pronouns, determiners or prepositions.

Finally … a very unusual day

Last weekend we *took Peter and Lisa* to *Alton Towers.* 1______ *was* 2______ *nice day, but rather windy. (a, it, to, we)*

When 3________ *arrived,* 4________ *decided to take* 5________ *cable-car. Soon after* 6________ *started,* 7________ *wind got worse. Then* 8________ 9________ *cable-car system stopped and* 10________ *cars stopped moving. (a, it, the, the, the, we, we, whole)*

11______ *was over* 12______ *deep valley.* 13______ *people* 14______ *our car waited calmly, but* 15______ *child kept crying. (a, in, most, one, ours)*

16______ *hour later,* 17______ *group* 18______ *rescuers climbed* 19______ 20______ *cable to help* 21______. 22______ *helped* 23______ *climb down* 24______ 25______ *ground. (a, along, an, of, the, the, they, to, us, us)*

86 Sentences: types and structure

Statement, question, etc   Subject, verb, object, etc

FORMS

Sentence types

There are four types of sentence in English. They are:

Statement: *You're driving very fast.*

Question: *How fast are you driving?*

Order: *Don't drive so fast.*

Exclamation: *Help!*

Sentence structure

There are several possible parts of a sentence. They include:

Subject	Verb	Object	Adverbial
The car	*is following*	*us*	*very fast.*

Sentence types

A statement gives information. A question requests information or action. An order requires action. An exclamation expresses an emotion. (See Units 23/24 for more on question forms. See Unit 1 for more on orders.)

تزودنا الجملة الخبرية بمعلومة، في حين تستفسر الجملة الاستفهامية عن معلومة او عمل. ويتطلب الامر القيام بعمل ما في حين يعبر التعجب عن مشاعر معينة. (انظر units 23/24 لمزيد من المعلومات عن صيغة الاستفهام. وانظر unit 1 للمزيد عن صيغة الامر).

In writing, a sentence starts with a capital letter, eg *You, How, Slow, Help*. It ends with a full stop (.), a question mark (?) or an exclamation mark (!).

عند الكتابة، تبدأ الجملة بحرف كبير وتنتهي بنقطة او بعلامة استفهام او بعلامة تعجب.

Sentence structure

Most sentences contain different parts. These parts can include a subject, verb, object, complement and adverbial. A subject is the focus of the sentence. A verb shows an action or a state, eg *brings* and *is*. An object is the thing or person affected by the verb. A complement gives more information about the subject. An adverbial gives more information about the verb. Look at the following statements. The simplest statement contains only two parts. The longer statements contain four. (But a statement or other type of sentence can contain many more parts than this.)

تحوي معظم الجمل اجزاء مختلفة يمكن ان تضم فاعلاً وفعلاً ومفعولاً به وكذلك تكملة واضافة ظرفية. ويشكل الفاعل نقطة التركيز في الجملة، في حين يبين الفعل عملاً ما او حالة. اما المفعول به فهو الشيء او الشخص الذي يتأثر بالفعل، وتعمل التكملة على اضافة معلومات عن الفاعل. اما الإضافة الظرفية فتعطي المزيد من المعلومات عن الفعل. انظر الى الامثلة التالية من الجمل الخبرية. ان ابسطها تحتوي على جزءين، اما الجملة الاطول فتحوي اربعة اجزاء (ولكن الجملة الخبرية، او نوعاً اخر من الجمل يمكن ان تحوي اجزاءاً اكثر من ذلك كثيراً).

1

Subject	Verb
Tom	*is driving.*

2

Subject	Verb	Complement
Tom	*is*	*the driver.*

3

Subject	Verb	Object
Tom	*is driving*	*his new car.*

4

Subject	Verb	Adverbial
Tom	*is driving*	*dangerously.*

5

Subject	Verb	Object	Adverbial
Tom	*is driving*	*his new car*	*dangerously.*

All of these statements have a subject and a verb. They are the most important parts. In statements the subject goes before the verb. (See Unit 23 for word order in questions.) If there is an object or a complement, this goes after the verb.

لكل هذه الجمل الخبرية فاعل وفعل يشكلان اهم جزءي الجملة. ويأتي الفاعل في الجملة الخبرية قبل الفعل (انظر unit 23 لترتيب الكلمات في الجمل الاستفهامية). واذا كان هناك مفعول به او تكملة، فيأتيان بعد الفعل.

In statements 4 and 5 the adverb comes at the end of the sentence, but it can also come in other places. (See Unit 71.)

Unfortunately, he's probably going to stop us ***at the side of the road now.***

يأتي الظرف في الجمل ٤، ٥ في نهاية الجملة، ولكنه يمكن ان يأتي في مواقع اخرى ايضاً. (انظر unit 71).

Exercises

1 Label the sentences with the following.

Exclamation, Order, Question, Statement

Example: *Are you all right?* Question

1 *How much money have you got?* ______

2 *Take these letters to the post office.* ______

3 *Fantastic!* ______

4 *John's birthday is next week.* ______

5 *We all understand what we've got to do, don't we?* ______

6 *I don't like this sort of music.* ______

7 *Absolutely amazing!* ______

8 *Don't spend any more time on this job.* ______

2 Label the sentence parts with the following.

Adverb (A), Adverb phrase (AP), Complement (C), Object (O), Subject (S), Verb (V)

Example: *Is Lucy singing well?* (Lucy = S; Is … singing = V; well = A)

1 *Lucy* / *has become* / *a great singer.*

2 *Don't drop* / *those glasses.*

3 *The boys* / *quickly* / *mended* / *the bike.*

4 *Quickly* / *write down* / *these addresses.*

5 *Has* / *anybody* / *seen* / *my glasses?*

6 *Are* / *the pictures* / *safe?*

7 *When do* / *the boys* / *see* / *their parents?*

8 *Luckily,* / *we* / *reached* / *the airport* / *in time.*

3 Re-order the words to form different types of sentences.

Example: Question *(the/now/we/can/buy/car)*

Can we buy the car now? (we = S; Can … buy = V; the car = O; now = A)

1 Statement *(fast/the/climbed/plane)*

S V A

2 Statement *(seems/brother/tired/very/your)*

S V C

3 Order *(there/the/put/over/don't/boxes)*

V O AP

4 Statement *(as/as/is/Robert/soon/coming/possible*

S V AP

5 Question *(see/you/the/did/yesterday/news)*

S V O A

87 Connecting clauses

and, but, or, so, because, if, when, even though, who, to, for

FORMS

Two main clauses

Ann has got a case, and Jan has got a bag.
They can take a bus, or they can take a taxi. They have to choose.
The taxi is faster, but it is more expensive.
They are late, so they will take a taxi.

Main clause + sub-clause

They need the taxi because they are late.
If they arrive late, they will miss their plane.

Two main clauses

A main clause has a verb and can be a complete sentence.

Ann went by bus. ***Jan went by taxi.***

يضم الجزء الرئيسي (main clause) في الجملة فعلاً، ويمكن ان يكون جملة كاملة.

The words *and*, *but*, *or* and *so* connect two main clauses. *and* adds one thing to another. *but* sets one thing against another. *or* expresses one possibility instead of another. *so* introduces a result.

Main clause		Main clause
Ann went by bus,	***and***	*Jan went by taxi.*
The taxi was faster,	***but***	*it was more expensive.*
You can take a bus,	***or***	*you can take a taxi.*
There are no buses,	***so***	*we'll have to take a taxi.*

تعمل الكلمات and وbut وor وso على ربط جزءين متكاملين في جملة واحدة. وتعمل and على اضافة جزء لآخر في حين تضع but جزءاً ضد الآخر. اما or فتعبر عن وجود احتمال بديل عن آخر. واما so فتقدم النتيجة.

In writing, we usually put a comma (,) between two main clauses, especially long clauses. Compare *and* and *or* in these negative sentences.

*They **didn't take** a taxi, **and** they **didn't take** a bus.*
*They **didn't take** a taxi **or** a bus.*

توضع فاصلة(،) عادة بين الجزءين الرئيسين المكونين للجملة خصوصاً عندما تتكون الجملة من جزءين طويلين. ويوضح المثال الفرق بين استخدام and وor في جملتين منفيتين.

Main clause + sub-clause

We often put a sub-clause with a main clause. A sub-clause has a verb like a main clause. But it is not a complete idea. It adds to a main clause.

Main clause	Sub-clause
They need a taxi	***because they're late.***

We can use a sub-clause by itself in a short answer to a question.

● *Why are they late?* ❍ ***Because Jan's watch was wrong.***

يُوضع عادة جزء رئيسي مع جزء فرعي يحوي فعلاً، مثله في ذلك مثل الجزء الرئيسي، ولكنه لا يعطي فكرة متكاملة بل يضيف معنى للجزء الرئيسي.
ويمكن استخدام الجزء الفرعي بمفرده، في الاجابة المختصرة عن سؤالٍ ما.

Here are some other types of sub-clauses. Most sub-clauses can go before the main clause (but not relative clauses). When we put the sub-clause first, we usually put a comma (,) between the two clauses.

If you ask Alex, *he'll go to the party.* (conditional)
Someone came to the door ***when I was working in the garden.*** (similar to *while* and *as*)
Even though Tom's leg hurt, *he managed to run.* (similar to *although* and *though*)
Bill jumped into the river ***to save the child.*** (similar to *in order to* and *so as to*)
She's the girl ***who won the prize.*** (similar to *that* and *which*)

وهذه مجموعة من انواع اخرى من الاجزاء الفرعية (sub-clauses). وتأتي غالباً قبل الجزء الرئيسي (ولكن ليس في حالة relative clauses) التي تعتمد على الجزء الرئيسي بشكل كلي. وعندما نضع الجزء الفرعي في بداية الجملة نستخدم الفاصلة(،) عادة بين الجزءين.

Note that *because* introduces a reason and *so* introduces a result.

Because they're late, *they need a taxi.*
They're late, ***so they need a taxi.***

تجدر ملاحظة ان because تقدم السبب في حين تقدم so النتيجة التي تترتب على الفعل.

Exercises

1 Connect the clauses with *and*, *but*, *or* or *so*.

Example: *You can buy* or *rent the apartment.*

1 *I'm tired* ______ *I'm hungry too.*

2 *The train was late,* ______ *we couldn't get to the meeting on time.*

3 *The Prince was rich,* ______ *he wasn't happy.*

4 *You can take the money now,* ______ *you can take it later.*

2 Connect clauses 1–4 and a–d with *and*, *but*, *or* or *so*.

Example: *We usually eat at 8.00,*
but we're eating at 7.30 tonight.

a *he can go at 4.00.*

b *he seems very tired at the moment.*

c *he's got to come by taxi instead.*

d *he owns a house in Scotland.*

1 *Ben has an apartment in London,* ____________________

2 *Tom's car is at the garage for repairs,* ____________________

3 *Sam can see the film at 1.45,* ____________________

4 *John is usually very energetic,* ____________________

3 Rewrite the *so* statements using *because/as*.

Example: *It was dark, so we couldn't see much.*
We couldn't see much because/as it was dark.

1 *I was very tired, so I went to bed.*

____

2 *My car is old, so I'm getting a new one.*

____

3 *I have to go out now, so I'll call you later.*

____

4 Rewrite the *but* statements using *even though/although*.

Example: *The engine is new, but it's already going wrong.*
The engine is already going wrong even though/though it's new.

1 *Sally is young, but she does her job well.*

____

2 *The film is old, but it's still very popular.*

____

3 *Their new house was expensive, but it looks terrible.*

____

5 Connect the clauses with *because, if, when, even though* or *who* in the correct position.

Examples: ______ *Mary would lend you £100* if *you asked her.*
When *I got home,* ______ *everybody was eating.*

1 ______ *I'd known about Ann's illness* ______ *I wouldn't have bothered her.*

2 ______ *Mr Hardy is the man* ______ *bought my company.*

3 ______ *I phoned home* ______ *I got to the office.*

4 ______ *Harry worked all day* ______ *he still couldn't finish the job.*

5 ______ *Annie ran home* ______ *she was afraid of the dark.*

6 ______ *Tony gets this note,* ______ *I'll already be in Canada.*

7 ______ *Dr Ross still works very hard* ______ *he's nearly 70.*

8 ______ *Tony has looked after our old car so well,* ______ *I think we should give it to him as a present.*

88 Connecting sentences

and, but, or, so In addition, However, Alternatively, As a result

FORMS

Dear Sir,

Thank you for your order of 13th March for 4,000 K52 Matsuo CD players.

We note your specific colour requirement for black. *In addition*, we note your required delivery date of 30th March. *However*, we are sorry to say we cannot meet that schedule. Demand has been heavy for this popular product. *As a result*, we are now out of stock and are waiting for new supplies from Japan. *Despite this*, we can promise delivery by 10th April. *Alternatively*, we can offer you immediate delivery of the K53 model.

Sentence connectors instead of *and, but, or* and *so*

We use *and, but, or* and *so* to link parts of sentences. (See also Unit 87.)

*The day was warm **and** sunny.*
*Harry found some bread, **but** no butter.*

تستخدم كلمات الربط and وbut وor وso لربط اجزاء الجمل. (انظر unit 87).

We also often want to connect the ideas in two separate sentences. In spoken English, we often use *and, but, or* and *so.*

*He's very good at football. **And** he's a great runner too.*

غالباً ما نريد ان نربط فكرتين في جملتين منفصلتين. وفي الانجليزية المحكية غالباً ما نستخدم and و but و or و so.

In formal and written English, we usually avoid *and, but, or* and *so* at the start of a sentence. Instead, we can use connectors like these. (Note that we put a comma (,) after these sentence connectors.)

***In addition/Furthermore**, we note your required* ... (instead of *and*)
***However**, we cannot meet that schedule.* (instead of *but*)
***Alternatively/Instead**, we can offer you the* ... (instead of *or*)
***As a result/consequence**, we are now out of stock.* (instead of *so*)

ولكن في الامور الرسمية وعند الكتابة، نستبعد عادة استخدام كلمات الربط هذه، ونستعيض عنها باستخدام كلمات ربط اخرى كالكلمات الموضحة في الامثلة، وعندها يصير استخدام الفواصل بعد كلمات الربط.

Sentence connectors with pronouns

Subject pronouns often refer to things outside their own sentence.

*The children are tired. **They**'d better go to bed.*

غالباً ما يشير ضمير الفاعل الى اشياء او الى اشخاص خارج نطاق الجملة ذاتها.

We often use demonstrative pronouns in the same way.

● *Let's have a rest.* ❍ ***That**'s a good idea.*

وغالباً ما تستخدم ضمائر الإشارة بالطريقة نفسها.

Many sentence connectors include demonstrative pronouns or nouns. Some sentence connectors can be with or without demonstrative pronouns or nouns.

***In addition to** this/your colour requirement, we note your* ...
***As a result of** this/the heavy demand, we are now out of stock.*
***Instead of** that/the K52, they will take the K53.*

وتضم كلمات الربط بين الجمل ضمائر إشارة او اسماء. كما ان بعض كلمات الربط يمكن ان تأتي مع ضمائر اشارة او بدون ضمائر اشارة او اسماء.

Some sentence connectors must include a pronoun or noun.

***Because of this**, we are now of out stock.*
***Due to the heavy demand**, we are now out of stock.*
***Despite this**, we can promise delivery by* ...
***In spite of that**, we can promise delivery by* ...
***Except for the K52**, we have stock of all models.*
***Apart from that**, we have stock of all models.*

تتطلب بعض كلمات الربط بين الجمل استخدام ضمائر او اسماء.

Exercises

1 Change the informal spoken statements to formal statements from a business report. Use full verb forms and change *and*, *but*, *or* or *so* to the following.

Alternatively, As a result, However, In addition

Example: *We're unable to meet the schedule, so we won't get the contract.*
We are *unable to meet the schedule.*
As a result, we will not get *the contract.*

1 *It's possible to up-date our present model, or it's possibly the right time for a completely new model.*
________ *possible to up-date our present model.*
________________ *possibly the right time for a completely new model.*

2 *We've reached this year's production target already, and we've managed to cut waste by 8%.*
________________ *this year's production target already.* ________________
________ *to cut waste by 8%.*

3 *We're cutting most costs successfully, but we're failing to hold down the cost of wages.*
________________ *most costs successfully.*
________________ *to hold down the cost of wages.*

4 *We haven't tried selling to America up till now, so we don't yet know if it'll be a good market for us.*
________________ *selling to America up till now.* ________________
________ *if* ________ *a good market for us.*

2 Write nothing (✗) or one of these words to complete the connectors.

for, from, of, to

1 *Apart* from *this*
2 *As a result* ______ *this*
3 *Despite* ______ *this*
4 *Due* ______ *this*
5 *Except* ______ *this*
6 *In addition* ______ *this*
7 *In spite* ______ *this*
8 *Instead* ______ *this*

3 Choose the right connecting statements from a–g to complete the teacher's reports 1–6.

Example: *Susan has not worked hard this year. Despite this,* she has done enough to pass the year.

a *she has behaved badly in class all year.*
b *she could go on to do extra Science.*
c *she has achieved a Grade A.*
d *she has found it difficult to improve.*
e *she has done enough to pass the year.*
f *she has often failed to complete her homework.*
g *she must learn to do some hard work.*

1 *Sally is very intelligent and has worked extremely well. As a result,* ________________

2 *Lisa has worked very well in class. However,* ________________

3 *Tessa has failed to produce any good work. In addition,* ________________

4 *Lucy is clever, but she seems to spend her time thinking about pop music. Instead,* ________________

5 *Kate has tried hard this year. In spite of this,* ________________

6 *Denise is very talented at both Maths and Science. She may decide to take Higher Maths. Alternatively,* ________________

Appendix 1 Irregular verbs

These common irregular verbs have the following forms.

A Verbs with no change

Infinitive	Past tense	Past participle
cost	*cost*	*cost*
cut	*cut*	*cut*
hit	*hit*	*hit*
hurt	*hurt*	*hurt*
let	*let*	*let*
put	*put*	*put*
set	*set*	*set*
shut	*shut*	*shut*
spread	*spread*	*spread*

B Verbs with one change

Infinitive	Past tense	Past participle
beat	*beat*	*beaten*
bring	*brought*	*brought*
build	*built*	*built*
burn	*burnt/burned*	*burnt/burned*
buy	*bought*	*bought*
catch	*caught*	*caught*
deal	*dealt*	*dealt*
dream	*dreamt/dreamed*	*dreamt/dreamed*
feel	*felt*	*felt*
fight	*fought*	*fought*
find	*found*	*found*
get	*got*	*got*
*have** (see below)	*had*	*had*
hear	*heard*	*heard*
hold	*held*	*held*
keep	*kept*	*kept*
lay	*laid*	*laid*
lead	*led*	*led*
learn	*learnt/learned*	*learnt/learned*
leave	*left*	*left*
lend	*lent*	*lent*
lose	*lost*	*lost*
make	*made*	*made*
mean	*meant*	*meant*
meet	*met*	*met*
pay	*paid*	*paid*

*Note that the 3rd person singular of *have* in the present simple is *he/she/it has.*

read (sounds like *need*)	*read* (sounds like r*ed*)	*read* (sounds like r*ed*)
say	*said*	*said*
sell	*sold*	*sold*
send	*sent*	*sent*
sit	*sat*	*sat*
shoot	*shot*	*shot*
sleep	*slept*	*slept*
slide	*slid*	*slid*
smell	*smelt/smelled*	*smelt/smelled*
spell	*spelt/spelled*	*spelt/spelled*
spend	*spent*	*spent*
stand	*stood*	*stood*
swing	*swung*	*swung*
teach	*taught*	*taught*
tell	*told*	*told*
think	*thought*	*thought*
understand	*understood*	*understood*
win	*won*	*won*

C Verbs with two changes

Infinitive	**Past tense**	**Past participle**
*be** (see below)	*was/were*	*been*
become	*became*	*become*
begin	*began*	*begun*
bite	*bit*	*bitten*
blow	*blew*	*blown*
break	*broke*	*broken*
choose	*chose*	*chosen*
come	*came*	*come*
*do** (see below)	*did*	*done*
draw	*drew*	*drawn*
drink	*drank*	*drunk*
drive	*drove*	*driven*
eat	*ate*	*eaten*
fall	*fell*	*fallen*
fly	*flew*	*flown*
forget	*forgot*	*forgotten*
give	*gave*	*given*
go	*went*	*gone*
grow	*grew*	*grown*
hide	*hid*	*hidden*

*Note that *be* in the present simple is *I am, he/she/it is* and *you/we/they are.*
*Note that the 3rd person singular of *do* in the present simple is *he/she/it does.*

know	*knew*	*known*
lie	*lay*	*lain*
ride	*rode*	*ridden*
ring	*rang*	*rung*
rise	*rose*	*risen*
run	*ran*	*run*
see	*saw*	*seen*
shake	*shook*	*shaken*
show	*showed*	*shown*
sing	*sang*	*sung*
sink	*sank*	*sunk*
speak	*spoke*	*spoken*
steal	*stole*	*stolen*
swim	*swam*	*swum*
take	*took*	*taken*
throw	*threw*	*thrown*
wake	*woke*	*woken*
wear	*wore*	*worn*
write	*wrote*	*written*

Appendix 2 Some spelling rules

These spelling rules deal with spelling changes with grammatical word endings.

A Some spelling terms

To study this Appendix you need to know the terms **vowel** and **consonant**.

Vowel letters are *a, e, i, o* and *u*.

Vowel sounds are sounds written with two or more vowel letters, eg *ai, au, ea, ee, ei, ie, oa, oo, ou,* etc.

Consonants are the other letters of the alphabet and their sounds, eg *b, c, d, f, g,* etc.

A **short vowel** is, eg *e* in ***get*** and *o* in ***got***.

A **long vowel** is, eg *ee* in ***keep***, *ea* in ***heat***, *oo* in ***soon*** and *ou* in ***route***.

You also need to know the term **syllable**. This is a unit of sound within a word.
stand (1 syllable) *un•der* (2 syllables) *un•der•stand* (3 syllables)
mis•un•der•stand (4 syllables) *mis•un•der•stand•ing* (5 syllables)

B Word endings

English adds the following grammatical word endings to words.

Noun	Verb	Verb	Verb	Adjective	Adjective	Adjective
+ s + s	***+ ing***	***+ ed***	***+ er***	***+ est***	***+ ly***	
cars	*looks*	*looking*	*looked*	*quicker*	*quickest*	*quickly*
planes	*works*	*working*	*worked*	*slower*	*slowest*	*slowly*
(Plural)	(3rd person present simple)	(Present participle)	(Past simple, past participle)	(Comparative)	(Superlative)	(Adverb)

Sometimes there is a spelling change when we add an ending to a word. There are clear rules for these changes – see sections below.

C Noun and verb endings with *es*

Add *es* when the word ends in *s, ss, sh, ch* and *x*.

bus	*boss*	*dish*	*match*	*box*
buses	*bosses*	*dishes*	*matches*	*boxes*

Many verbs and nouns end in an *e* which we do not say. But if the silent *e* comes after *c, s, x* or *z*, just add *s*. We then sound the *e + s* together.

race	*practise*	*axe*	*organize*
races	*practises*	*axes*	*organizes*

After other consonants, we do not sound the silent *e* – see Section D below.

bikes *scenes* *tapes* *votes* *consumes*

We add *es* after some nouns ending in *o*, but not others. Compare the following.

cargoes	*heroes*	*potatoes*	*tomatoes*	*volcanoes*
discos	*studios*	*photos*	*radios*	*stereos*

Note also the verbs *go* → ***goes*** and *do* → ***does***.

Some nouns which end in *f* or *fe* change their endings to *ves*.

knife	*life*	*loaf*	*shelf*	*wife*
knives	*lives*	*loaves*	*shelves*	*wives*

D Words that end in silent *e*

After final, silent *e* just add *s*.

bikes	*scenes*	*tapes*	*votes*	(Plural nouns)
consumes	*hopes*	*rules*	*types*	(3rd person present simple)

But see Section C for pronunciation of words like these.

races *practises* *axes* *organizes*

Leave out *e* and add *ing* to form the present participle.

dance	*handle*	*hope*	*smile*	*write*
*dan**cing***	*hand**ling***	*ho**ping***	*smi**ling***	*wri**ting***

After *e* just add *d* for regular past tense and past participle forms.

*consume**d*** *hope**d*** *rule**d*** *type**d***

Just add *r* and *st* for comparative and superlative forms.

brave	*large*	*rude*	*wide*
*brave**r***	*large**r***	*rude**r***	*wide**r***
*brave**st***	*large**st***	*rude**st***	*wide**st***

Just add *ly* to most adjectives for adverb forms.

*brave**ly*** *large**ly*** *rude**ly*** *wide**ly***

But if an adjective ends in *le*, leave out *e* and just add *y*.

able	*capable*	*horrible*	*probable*
*ab**ly***	*capab**ly***	*horrib**ly***	*probab**ly***

Note these special *ly* cases.

day	*due*	*true*	*whole*
*da**ily***	*du**ly***	*tru**ly***	*who**lly***

E Words that double the final consonant

Words that end in one short vowel + one consonant often double that consonant before *ing*, *ed*, *er* and *est*.

plan	*chop*	*permit*	(Verb)
*pla**nning***	*cho**pping***	*permi**tting***	(Present participle)
*pla**nned***	*cho**pped***	*permi**tted***	(Past simple, past participle)
fat	*wet*	*thin*	(Adjective)
*fa**tter***	*we**tter***	*thi**nner***	(Comparative)
*fa**ttest***	*we**ttest***	*thi**nnest***	(Superlative)

Most words like *occur*, with two syllables or more, double the last consonant when the last syllable is stressed. Compare the following.

oc<u>cur</u>	*<u>frigh</u>ten*	*per<u>mit</u>*	*<u>ben</u>efit*
*occu**rring***	*frighte**ning***	*permi**tted***	*benefi**ted***

But words which end in one vowel + *l* are different in British English (though not American English). They all double the *l*.

quarrel	*quarre**lling***	(Present participle)
travel	*trave**lled***	(Past simple, past participle)
beautiful	*beautifu**lly***	(Adverb)

F Words that end in *y*

Before *s*, *y* changes to *ie* and becomes *ies*.

body	*copy*	*family*	*sky*	(Noun)
*bod**ies***	*cop**ies***	*famil**ies***	*sk**ies***	(Plural)

apply	*empty*	*study*	*try*	(Verb)
*appl**ies***	*empt**ies***	*stud**ies***	*tr**ies***	(3rd person present simple)

Before *ed*, *y* changes to *ie* and becomes *ied*.

*appl**ied*** *empt**ied*** *stud**ied*** *tr**ied*** (Past simple, past participle)

Before *er* and *est*, *y* changes to *i* and becomes *ier* or *iest*.

happy	*lucky*	*pretty*	*silly*	(Adjective)
*happ**ier***	*luck**ier***	*prett**ier***	*sill**ier***	(Comparative)
*happ**iest***	*luck**iest***	*prett**iest***	*sill**iest***	(Superlative)

But a *y* ending does not change before *ing*.

*appl**ying*** *empt**ying*** *stud**ying*** *tr**ying*** (Present participle)

Most words with a vowel + *y* ending (*ay, ey, oy*) do not change at all.

play	*grey*	*boy*
*play**s***	*grey**er***	*boy**s***
*play**ing***	*grey**est***	
*play**ed***		

But note these special cases.

day	*lay*	*pay*	*say*
*da**ily***	*la**id***	*pa**id***	*sa**id***

G Words that end in *ie*

A few verbs end in *ie*. With these, *ie* changes to *y* and becomes *ying*.

die	*lie*	*tie*
*d**ying***	*l**ying***	*t**ying***

Appendix 3 Punctuation

A Types

Study the punctuation in the following.

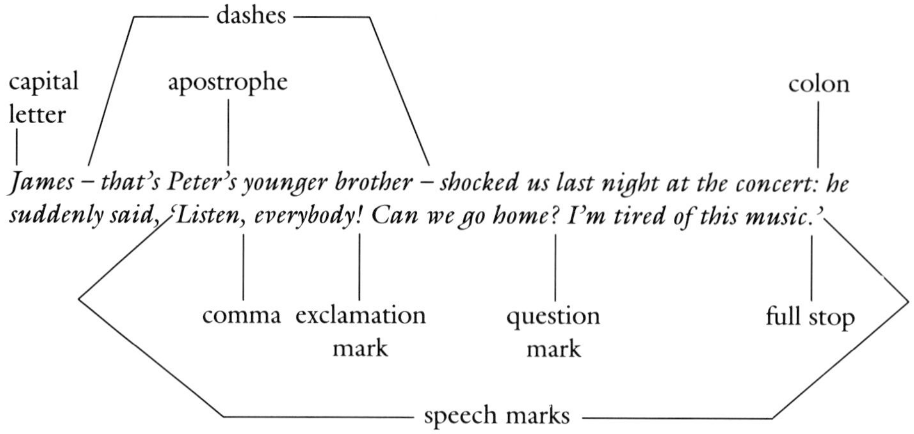

B Apostrophe (...')

Use this:

- in short forms of verbs: ***It's*** *cold.* (***It's*** = *It is*)   ***I don't*** *want to go out.* (***don't*** = *do not*)

Be careful with the different meanings of *'s* and *'d*: ***He's*** *working.* (***He's*** = *He is*)
He's *finished.* (***He's*** = *He has*)   ***We'd*** *finished by 5.00.* (***We'd*** = *We had*)
We'd *like to go home now.* (***We'd*** = *We would*)

- in short forms of other words, mainly years: *I met Joe in June* ***'89***.
- to show possession after nouns: *I'm* ***Peter's*** *younger brother.*

A possessive apostrophe goes after a plural noun with *s*: *We can use my* ***parents'*** *car.*

Possessive adjectives and pronouns do not take apostrophes: *This is my coat, and this is hers.*

Be careful with *its* (possessive adjective) and *it's* (*it is/it has*): *Look at the fish.* ***It's*** *opening and closing* ***its*** *mouth.*

C Capital letter (*I, P, J, L*, etc)

Use this:

- for the 1st person singular: ***I***
- for the name of a person, place, geographical name, country, nationality: ***J****ames,* ***T****he* ***P****alace* ***H****otel,* ***L****ondon, the* ***R****iver* ***N****ile,* ***C****anada,* ***C****anadian*
- for abbreviations: *the* ***UN*** *(the United Nations), the* ***USA*** *(the United States of America)*

D Colon (:)

Use this:

- to introduce a list of things: *Remember to bring the following****:*** *thick jacket, walking boots, leeping bag.*
- to lead from a general heading into a particular example: *Summer camp****:*** *equipment*
- to show a connection between two ideas: *I've got the answer****:*** *2,301.*   *You should take a coat****:*** *it's going to rain.*

E Comma (,)

Use this:

- between separate clauses in one sentence: *We were shocked, but Peter just smiled.*
- to separate other parts of a sentence, eg connectors and sentence adverbs: *We were tired.* ***However,*** *we had to keep running.* ***Surprisingly,*** *it got easier as we continued.*
- between words in lists: *I bought some bread, butter, cheese and tomatoes.* *It was a lovely, warm, sunny day for a picnic.*
- to introduce direct speech in a story: *Bob arrived and said, 'Hello.'*

F Dash (–)

Use this:

- to show an extra idea added to a sentence: *I met Carol –* ***she's the one in a blue dress –*** *when we were both students. She's going to France next month –* ***or at least that's what she told me****.*

G Exclamation mark (!)

Use this:

- to show strong feeling in written form: *'I'm so happy!'* *'That was really stupid!'* *'Listen! I've got an idea!'* *'Help!'*

This takes the place of a full stop – see below.

H Full stop (.)

Use this:

- to show the end of a statement: *The men are not due to go home this week. They will return next week.*
- in abbreviations (optional): *I work for the B.B.C.* *It's 10 a.m.* *Have you seen Mrs. Jones?*

I Question mark (?)

Use this:

- to end a sentence in question form: *Can they do the job?* *They can do it, can't they?*
  This takes the place of a full stop – see above.

J Speech marks (' ... ')

These are also called quotation marks or inverted commas.

Use these:

- to mark direct speech in a story: *Ann turned to Bob and said, 'Hi.'*
  You can also use speech marks in double form: *Ann turned to Bob and said, "Hi."*
- to mark something for special attention: *The letters 'Dr' stand for 'Doctor'.*

Appendix 4 Numbers

A Whole numbers

Write	Say
101	*a hundred and one*
199	*a hundred and ninety-nine*
235	*two hundred and thirty-five*
1,001	*a thousand and one*
1,135	*one thousand, one hundred and thirty-five*
1,000,001	*a million and one*
1,135,199	*one million, one hundred and thirty-five thousand, one hundred and ninety-nine*

Compare the following.

a hundred BUT *exactly one hundred*

about a hundred BUT *exactly one hundred and twelve*

B Telephone numbers

Write	Say
521 301377	*five two one ... three oh one ... three seven seven* OR *five two one ... three zero one ... three double seven*
999 775666	*nine nine nine ... seven seven five ... six six six* OR *treble nine ... double seven five ... treble six*

C Decimals

Write	Say
31.3166	*thirty-one point three one six six*
33.3333	*thirty-three point three recurring*

D Fractions

Write		Say			
$\frac{1}{2}$	$1\frac{1}{2}$	*a half*	OR	*one half*	*one and a half*
$\frac{1}{3}$	$2\frac{2}{3}$	*a third*	OR	*one third*	*two and two-thirds*
$\frac{1}{4}$	$5\frac{3}{4}$	*a quarter*	OR	*one quarter*	*five and three quarters*
$\frac{1}{5}$	$7\frac{4}{5}$	*a fifth*	OR	*one fifth*	*seven and four-fifths*
$\frac{1}{6}$	$9\frac{5}{6}$	*a sixth*	OR	*one sixth*	*nine and five-sixths*
$\frac{1}{10}$	$10\frac{7}{10}$	*a tenth*	OR	*one tenth*	*ten and seven-tenths*

E Mathematical terms

Write	Say
$7 + 2 = 9$	*seven plus/add/and two equals/is nine*
$9 - 3 = 6$	*nine minus/take away three equals/is six*
$6 \times 3 = 18$	*six times/multiplied by three equals/is eighteen*
$18 \div 2 = 9$	*eighteen divided by two equals/is nine*

F Ordinal numbers

Write (eg in dates)	**Write or say**	**Write** (eg in dates)	**Write or say**
1st	*first*	*20th*	*twentieth*
2nd	*second*	*21st*	*twenty-first*
3rd	*third*	*22nd*	*twenty-second*
4th	*fourth*	*23rd*	*twenty-third*
5th	*fifth*	*24th*	*twenty-fourth*
6th	*sixth*	...	
7th	*seventh*	*30th*	*thirtieth*
8th	*eighth*	*40th*	*fortieth*
9th	*ninth*	*50th*	*fiftieth*
10th	*tenth*	*60th*	*sixtieth*
11th	*eleventh*	*70th*	*seventieth*
12th	*twelfth*	*80th*	*eightieth*
13th	*thirteenth*	*90th*	*ninetieth*
14th	*fourteenth*	*100th*	*hundredth*
15th	*fifteenth*	*101st*	*hundred and first*
...			
19th	*nineteenth*	...	

Appendix 5 Days, dates and times

A Days and months – abbreviations

Note that the short forms of days and months may have a full stop, eg *Mon.* and *Oct.*

Days		**Months**			
Full	Short	Full	Short	Full	Short
Monday	*Mon*	*January*	*Jan*	*July*	*Jul*
Tuesday	*Tue/Tues*	*February*	*Feb*	*August*	*Aug*
Wednesday	*Wed*	*March*	*Mar*	*September*	*Sep*
Thursday	*Thu/Thur/Thurs*	*April*	*Apr*	*October*	*Oct*
Friday	*Fri*	*May*	–	*November*	*Nov*
Saturday	*Sat*	*June*	*Jun*	*December*	*Dec*
Sunday	*Sun*				

B Dates – word order

Write	**Say**
1st January *January 1st*	*the first of January* *January the first*

C Dates – abbreviations

Write	**Say**
Monday, 21st January	*Monday, the twenty-first of January*
Mon, 21st Jan	
Mon, 21 Jan	

D Dates in numbers

Write	**Say**
30/6	*the thirtieth of June*
31/12/94	*the thirty-first of December, 1994*

E Times

Write	**Say**
10.00	*ten o'clock*
10 a.m.	*ten a.m./ten o'clock* (in the morning)
3.00 p.m.	*three p.m./three o'clock* (in the afternoon)
10.00 p.m.	*ten p.m./ten o'clock* (at night)
12 a.m./12 p.m.	*midday/midnight*
1.15/1.30/1.45	*a quarter past one/half past one/a quarter to two* OR *one fifteen/one thirty/one forty-five*
2.10/2.20/2.40	*ten past two/twenty past two/twenty to three* OR *two ten/two twenty/two forty*
3.13/3.59	*thirteen minutes past three/one minute to four* OR *three thirteen/three fifty-nine*

Index

(The numbers in the index refer to the units, not the pages.)